Local Matters

Local Matters
Parish, Local Government and Community in Ireland

Finola Kennedy

IPA
AN FORAS RIARACHÁIN
INSTITUTE OF PUBLIC
ADMINISTRATION

Published in 2022
by the
Institute of Public Administration
57–61 Lansdowne Road
Dublin D04 TC62
Ireland
www.ipa.ie

British Library Cataloguing in Publication Data
A catalogue record for this book is available from the British Library.

ISBN: 978-1-910393-42-0

Cover design by Numo, Dublin
Typeset by Computertype, Dublin
Printed by W & G Baird, Antrim

KAK
In memory

Contents

Acknowledgements

The first person to whom I turned when I started on this work was Bishop Eamonn Walsh, who has wide experience of church and community. He opened doors to other members of the hierarchy when I was searching for data. Bishop Walsh also read and commented on a draft. I asked Diarmaid Ferriter to read an early draft, which he did in record time and made valuable suggestions. A friend of many years, with a knack for making me think, Charles Lysaght read a preliminary draft and made many helpful suggestions. Martin Mansergh read a further draft. His views were trebly important as a member of the Church of Ireland, a historian and a former minister of state in the Department of Finance. David Quinn also read a draft and made useful suggestions.

Then I knocked on Philip Hamell's door. He responded with crucial advice and assistance. He helped with the content in substantial ways and corrected my defective punctuation. I first met Philip in 1992 when he was in the Department of Finance and I had been appointed to the Commission on the Status of Women by Taoiseach Charles J. Haughey. Later Philip was assigned the monumental task of overseeing Ireland's changeover to the euro before moving to the Department of the Taoiseach. He has been a long-time member of the Society of St Vincent de Paul. I owe a special debt to Philip. The chief executive officer of Dublin City Council, Owen Keegan, was extremely generous with his time and expertise. He provided unique insights.

As the study concerns both Church and State, I sought help from politicians, including former leaders and members of the main political parties – Fianna Fáil, Fine Gael, the Green Party, Labour, Sinn Féin – and independents: Bertie Ahern, John Bruton, Rev. Trevor Sargent, Eamon Gilmore, Críona Ní Dhálaigh, Éamon Ó Cuív and Maureen O'Sullivan. For many years John Horgan has been a source of encouragement and inspiration. All were unfailingly helpful. It never ceases to amaze me how generous with their time and knowledge are those who serve, or have served, as elected representatives. I am truly grateful to them.

Many others with knowledge of Church and public administration, North and South, helped, including: Frank Allen; Dr Ian d'Alton; Finola Bruton; Margaret Burns; Sandra, Ken and Peter Cardwell; John Costello; Peter

Costello; Msgr John Dolan; Matt Gleeson; Rev. Laurence Graham; Rev. Dr Robert MacCarthy; Deacon Dermot McCarthy; Patsy McGarry; Micheál MacGréil, SJ; Rev. Nick McKnight; Peter Mooney; Msgr Dan O'Connor; Tony O'Grady; Maire O'Higgins; Frank Sammon, SJ; the late Elizabeth Watson; and Betty Watson.

The IPA Book Publishing Committee, chaired by Maurice Manning, are due special thanks, as are Carolyn Gormley and Michael Mulreany, who were very supportive. John O'Neill, Head of Research, Publishing and Corporate Affairs, was extremely helpful, pointing to useful lines of inquiry and improvements in structure. I also benefited greatly from talking to Richard Boyle and Mark Callanan (IPA) and to Gerard Turley (UCG), who have written extensively on local government. I am deeply indebted to John Paul Owens, Managing Editor at the IPA, for his meticulous work in preparing the manuscript for publication. Priceless assistance was given to me on many occasions by librarians in the IPA, including Joanne Grimes, Marie Kilcullen and Trudy Pirkl. The IPA library has been a home of helpfulness and expertise reaching back to its early librarian Mary Prendergast. The late Teresa Whitington in the Central Catholic Library also gave great help.

As always I drew on the support of family. The study resulted from a discussion with Frank regarding his experience on Dublin City Council. Lucy's many telling insights combined with her editorial experience were invaluable. They both, together with Kieran, Ruth, Michael and Susan, know how much I owe to them and how much I love them.

Figures and Tables

Introduction

Change is a sign of life. As old ways falter and fade, new paths open. By the early twenty-first century, the 'old order' of Catholic Ireland had changed, changed utterly, and been replaced by one which embodied a clear separation of Church and State. The Church experienced a loss of influence not just at the centre but also at the local level, where the parish became of less significance in the lives of the people. In the sphere of the State, central government grew stronger while local government became more like local administration, focused on giving effect to central government policy.

Significant social changes in Ireland have been captured in the results of constitutional referendums; for example, the marriage equality referendum which took place in Ireland on 22 May 2015. The celebratory scenes in the courtyard at Dublin Castle, when the result was announced the following day, marked a seismic shift in Irish values and attitudes. While the 'Yes' campaign had been waged over a long period, change was captured in a moment. The vote for same-sex marriage reflected the reality of ongoing social change in Ireland. The same was true with the referendum to remove the Eighth Amendment, or 'right to life' of the unborn, from the Constitution. The vote in this referendum took place on 25 May 2018. The result was two to one in favour of removing the amendment. In an interview with *RTÉ News*, Taoiseach Leo Varadkar described the result as the culmination of a 'quiet revolution' which had been taking place in Ireland over the previous ten to twenty years. Crowds gathered at Dublin Castle to celebrate the result just as they had done three years earlier following the marriage equality referendum. By contrast, a low-key event which captured the reality of another aspect of social change was the passing of the Intoxicating Liquor (Amendment) Act in Dáil Éireann on 25 January 2018 to permit the sale of alcohol on Good Friday – a practice which had been prohibited for over ninety years. The Act was signed into law by President Michael D. Higgins on 31 January 2018. Speaking on national television, one public house proprietor summed up the change in the words 'No longer parish law'. It was a spontaneous observation which summarised a changed reality.

Today, separation between Church and State is welcomed at the highest level in the Catholic Church. In an interview in the French Catholic newspaper *La Croix*, Pope Francis said, 'States must be secular. Confessional states end badly.' Pope Francis is not insisting that the State props up Church law, but that it allows freedom of conscience.[1] Everyone must have the freedom to express his or her own faith. When asked how, in a secular setting, Catholics should defend their concerns on societal issues such as euthanasia or same-sex marriage, Pope Francis said, 'It is up to Parliament to discuss, argue, explain, reason [these issues]. That is how a society grows.'[2]

Social change may happen gradually like a strengthening breeze; at times it happens like a gale with devastating effects – famine, cholera, Covid-19. The first case of Covid-19 in Ireland was announced by the Chief Medical Officer of the Department of Health on 29 February 2020. One month later there were almost 3,500 cases and 85 deaths had resulted from the virus. Within eleven months over 3,000 covid-related deaths had occurred. For the first month of the pandemic the response was centralised, directed by the Taoiseach, the Minister for Health, the Chief Medical Officer at the Department of Health and the Health Service Executive. A local dimension in dealing with the pandemic came on 2 April 2020 with the launching of 'Community Call'. At a press conference to announce Community Call, the Tánaiste said that the initiative would link local and central government with the community and voluntary sectors. The scheme would marshal volunteers throughout the country and would be established in every town and parish. It was clear that the pandemic could not be fought successfully by the central government alone. Response at the local level would be critical. Community Call enlisted the engagement of the thirty-one local authorities in the country to galvanise and coordinate community support at local level. One example in the early stages of the pandemic was the delivery of essential goods by An Post to those who were living in isolated areas. Another example was the establishment of helplines by local authorities, manned by library and community personnel. Yet another example was where local authorities linked with community volunteers to transport people to medical appointments. In February 2021 the National Economic and Social Council published the results of a study of Community Call.[3] One of the lessons learned was that Community Call helped local authorities to be more connected to communities. It was concluded that this could provide a basis for rethinking roles and relationships within local areas.

A further significant change in Irish life which cannot be summarised in any one event, but which has been happening quietly and persistently, is the decline of the Church parish. A not untypical example is St Monica's in Raheny, where the decline of the parish has been described by Derek Scally in his book *The Best Catholics in the World*. Returning to St Monica's after decades abroad, he found greatly reduced, and generally elderly, attendance.[4] The decline of the parish is not an exclusively religious matter as Jesuit sociologist Micheál Mac Gréil has described the parish as 'the only comprehensive community structure which covers the whole of Ireland'.[5] The decline in the parish throughout the country has coincided with the weakening of the support fabric of many local communities as a result of shrinkage in the sphere of local government and the reduction in local amenities, including the closure of small schools, some shops, post offices, bank branches and Garda stations, and the scaling back of some local medical services. This is captured by Donal Harrington,[6] who uses the image of the bypass. With the development of new motorways, many towns and villages in Ireland have been bypassed:

> The parish today is like one of those towns and villages. It has been bypassed. It is no longer part of people's journey, no longer on their itinerary. It may be no more than a memory from their past life. Of course, people still come off the motorway if there is something they need: a petrol station or a bathroom or a snack. It is the same with the parish. People will come for something specific: a funeral, a baptism, Christmas. But it is usually no more than a detour, sometimes only a once off.[7]

Alongside their religious purpose, parishes have overlapped with the wider community in significant ways. This is neatly captured in the Irish language words for the parish church – 'teach an phobail' – house of the people, or house of the community. In the past the parish has been the venue for major elements of the social life of the community. Many parish-based organisations, including the Society of St Vincent de Paul, are rooted in religious belief. Many other organisations and projects, including major social and sporting initiatives, although not springing from a religious source, have also been based on the parish. These include the Rural Electrification Scheme, the GAA in many parts of the country, although not in Dublin, and Muintir na Tíre (Community or People of the Land). The most important group which sprang up in the parish is the primary school: 'the quintessential community institution'.[8] In its original form the primary school in Ireland was not a denominational entity, although denominationalism entered the picture at an early stage.

The Second Vatican Council (Vatican II) brought change in the Catholic Church with consequences for priests and laity. Once more the change is neatly captured by Harrington. He quotes first from a document of Pope Pius X published early in the last century:

> The Church is essentially an unequal society … comprising two categories of persons … the hierarchy and the multitude of the faithful … the one duty of the multitude is to allow themselves to be led, and, like a docile flock, to follow the Pastors.[9]

Harrington contrasts this with the Vatican II view of the Church:

> The church now sees itself as a people, a community, and then, secondary to this, as hierarchically structured. This makes for a corresponding shift of focus from the sacrament of ordination to the sacrament of baptism. Baptism is now central. We are now moving from a clerical institution to a people's church.[10]

Among the visible changes which followed Vatican II were the use of the vernacular in the Mass and the relocation of the celebrant to face the congregation. Lay ministers of the Eucharist and lay readers – women as well as men – were introduced. But despite such changes there has been a drift, even an exodus, from the Catholic Church. Sixty years ago, in 1961, the year before the start of the council, 95 per cent of the population in the Republic of Ireland identified as Roman Catholic in the census. A very small number – 1,107 people, or 0.04 per cent of the population – identified as of 'No Religion'. By the time of the 2016 census the percentage which identified as Roman Catholic had fallen to 78 per cent of the population, numbering 3.7 million. Those with 'No Religion' numbered close to 500,000 and accounted for 10 per cent of the population. There were 126,400 people, or 2.7 per cent of the population in the Republic of Ireland, listed as Church of Ireland in 2016, while there were 26,000 Presbyterians (0.5 per cent) and 6,500 Methodists (0.12 per cent). Membership of the Church of Ireland in Northern Ireland is 260,000, twice the membership in the Republic, and comprises 17 per cent of the population, with 21 per cent Presbyterian and 5 per cent Methodist. In the Republic, immigration has contributed to growth in the Muslim (63,000), Orthodox Christian (62,000) and Hindu (14,000) religions.

The Churches, both Catholic and Protestant, are in decline as measured by census data, church attendance, number of priests and closure of churches. Demand for Catholic literature has fallen sharply, as shown, for example, by a fall in sales of the iconic *Sacred Heart Messenger* magazine from one-quarter of a million copies a few decades ago to just over 50,000 today. The decline in active church participation might be explained in a general way as a result of 'secularisation'. But beyond the secular drift there is also evidence of antagonism towards organised religion. In an extreme form this is manifest in a number of violent attacks on churches and mosques.[11] For example, in October 2017, graffiti was scrawled over Our Lady of the Wayside Church at Broughderg, Northern Ireland, and a few days later a statue of Mary on a nearby hillside was defaced.[12] In summer 2019 St Michael's Church in Longford was vandalised for the second time in two years and a stained glass window of the Sacred Heart was destroyed. Also in 2019 the Maryam Mosque in the city of Galway was vandalised. Attacks have not been confined to Ireland. In France, for example, in 2018 there were 877 incidents of vandalism at Catholic sites.[13]

Sexual abuse by clergy, both diocesan and members of religious orders, which began to come to light in the 1980s, revealed a heart of darkness in the Catholic Church. The abuse was not just handled badly but also covered up, and in many cases abusers were moved around in a way that enabled them to continue to abuse. The impact of the scandals on the Church's credibility was heightened by the fact that the abuse related to sexual matters, an area in which the Church had demanded rigorous conformity from the laity. Scally suggests that the conviction in 1997 of Paul McGennis, who worked for a time in St Monica's Parish, for his abuse of Marie Collins decades earlier 'helped tip Catholic Ireland, already primed for collapse into a tailspin – and St Monica's with it'.[14]

The dissatisfaction of many women with what they perceive as a male Church has led to the disaffection of some. It is the opinion of former President Mary McAleese that the Church's 'clericalised citadel is increasingly of zero interest to many Christian women who grow up in the Catholic tradition'.[15] Her mother's generation of women – married and single – would very likely have been the backbone of the local parish. Is it a case that 'The evil that men do lives after them; the good is oft interred with their bones'? It would falsify reality to focus exclusively on the negative; many priests continue to work hard for Church and community. If an accident, or other tragic event, occurs in a parish, the priest or minister is often the first port of call.

Parish and Community

Milestones from birth to death have been marked in 'a person's parish'. In the course of fieldwork in the west of Ireland in the 1960s, at the time of Vatican

II, sociologist Hugh Brody concluded that 'Religion solemnized and to some extent regulated the family and its institutions.'[16] Sixty years later, sociologist Tom Inglis confirmed the importance of the family in his study *Meanings of Life in Contemporary Ireland*. Inglis says that the results of his study 'indicate that family life is the most important web of meaning for most people.'[17] While many changes have taken place in Irish society:

> the vast majority of people are deeply enmeshed in webs of meaning that are spun within families, neighbourhoods and amongst friends and colleagues. In and through these groups they create strong social bonds that enable them to develop robust identities. [18]

Partly because of changing family patterns, religion is much less likely to feature in solemnising family 'milestones' nowadays. Focusing on the family as married mother and father with children and on life stages marked by sacramental celebration – matrimony, baptism, First Confession, First Communion, Confirmation and requiem Mass – obscures the realities of family change. Increasing numbers are not following traditional patterns prescribed by Church teaching, a fact shown in the increase in cohabitation and the increase in births outside marriage. The latter increased from 2 per cent in 1970 to 3 per cent in 1980, to over 36 per cent in 2017. Pope Francis says that 'There is no stereotype of the ideal family, but rather a challenging mosaic made up of many different realities with all their joys, hopes and problems.'[19] He urges that doors be open to those who fall short of the Christian idea.

The drift away from the parish is reflected in behavioural change which includes a fall in Mass attendance, more civil ceremony marriages and more non-religious funerals. It is also reflected in the long journeys away from home and parish to the workplace, which have become much more common. People may live in one place, work in another and socialise in a third. This fracturing of daily activity leads some to wonder about the relevance of parish in an urbanised, secularised world where 'church-shopping' may occur. Improvements in transport, especially in the number of motor cars, which increased from just under ten thousand one hundred years ago to almost two million today, have provided options to attend churches away from one's local parish. In 2018 the Archbishop of Dublin, Dr Diarmuid Martin, questioned whether the structure of parishes reflected the needs of a society in which there is more mobility. Dr Martin said, for example, that in some circumstances 80 per cent of children in Catholic schools live outside the parish.[20]

A question of relevance, not alone to church members but to the wider community, is whether there are consequences for the community because of the decline in parishes. Is social capital, with its network of social relationships, being lost? If so, how might the loss be stemmed or replaced? Or is the demise of the parish to be welcomed as the inevitable accompaniment of the expansion of secular society? If priests have become a 'vanishing tribe'[21] – the number of diocesan priests in Ireland has halved since 2000 – is it worthwhile for laypeople to strive to keep parishes together for community reasons as well as for religious purposes?

The definition of a community is not simple. A community may be identified with a particular area, or within an area there may be different groups, or local branches of groups, with sufficient common ground to be regarded as a community – for example, the French community or the Polish community in Ireland. Those of one country of origin may be spread throughout Ireland but may still have sufficient in common to form a local community in the area in which they live. Similarly, the Irish-speaking community has a particular identity. Within the European Union the term 'community' is used to refer to geographical communities, communities of interest and communities of shared identity. In the words of the European Union Community Development Network, community 'embraces locality, common interests and shared identity'.[22] A community can be a cross-section of different communities, and often individuals are members of several communities.

There is growing recognition among economists that solid communities are important for economic development. It has been argued by Raghuram Rajan, Professor of Finance at the University of Chicago and former Governor of the Bank of India, that far from hindering economic growth, building up the community is critical to the sustainability of economic and social development.[23] In his book *The Third Pillar,* published in 2019, Rajan examines the relationship between the State, markets and communities, and argues the importance of localism. Rajan opts for a dictionary definition of community:

> According to the dictionary, a *community* 'is a social group of any size whose members reside in a specific locality, share government, and often have a common cultural and historical heritage.'[24]

The parish is no longer identified with the community as it was in the past according to Bishop Eamonn Walsh, Auxiliary Bishop of Dublin. Nowadays, he believes the parish is a community, sometimes small, within the broader community.[25] Nonetheless Maureen O'Sullivan, former TD for the Dublin Central constituency, believes that people in the area which she represented have a close identity with their parish, whether or not they are active participants in church services.[26] The TD, and former Minister for Community, Rural and Gaeltacht Affairs, Éamon Ó Cuív, urges caution when speaking of the fading of the parish. He maintains that the parish has an existence independent of any church. He gives the example of Cornamona in Galway, where he lives. About half the people are fairly disengaged and the other half are more involved than ever in a range of activities associated with the parish, but by no means exclusively church-related. In regard to church-related activities, the decline in the number of priests has led to increased lay involvement via the parish council and a range of parish groups. After the parish, Ó Cuív sees the county[27] as evoking the next level of loyalty; he would regard the diocese as not so relevant, because dioceses are spread over a number of counties.[28] Like politics, religion is first and foremost local.[29]

Local Government

There are historical links between Church parishes and local authority areas. Local authority areas are linked to civil parishes, which in turn were linked to ecclesiastical parishes of old. The decline in Church parishes has coincided with a decline in the sphere of local government. Local authorities account for less than 10 per cent of public expenditure in Ireland compared with more than 20 per cent in many other EU countries. A study by Boyle and O'Riordan (2013)[30] shows how the capacity of local authorities has shrunk in recent years. By comparison with local authorities in the UK, Irish local authorities have fewer functions in regard to education and social services. A later study carried out by Boyle (2016)[31] shows that functions performed by local authorities in Ireland are modest by international standards. This is an assessment with which Owen Keegan, chief executive officer of Dublin City Council, agrees.[32]

The Commission on Taxation (2009) predicted that local authorities would generate 75 per cent of their current income from own resources by 2014; however, by 2020 just 64 per cent of current income was generated from own resources, composed of a combination of commercial rates, property tax, user charges and some miscellaneous revenue. The balance came from central government grants. Boyle considers that the economic crash of 2008 led to cutbacks in employment and expenditure within local authorities and a drive towards increased centralisation. Local government came to be seen as a service deliverer on behalf of central government.[33] Turley and McNena suggest that arguments, including greater democracy, subsidiarity and better reflection of local preferences,[34] support the view that 'functions should be assigned to the level of government whose jurisdiction most closely approximates the geographical area of benefits provided by the function'.[35] In practice this would require that the relevant level of government would have the capacity and resources required to fulfil such functions. But, as Keegan points out, Ireland is a small country where there is a marked difference in capacity to deliver services between, for example, Dublin, which is relatively very large, and some small rural authorities. According to Keegan, this continued difference in capacity depends on the assumption that there is no willingness to depart from the county as the unit of local government in Ireland.[36]

Some areas of responsibility have shifted from the local to the centre, in whole or in part: water services are now in the care of Irish Water (Uisce Éireann) and property tax is collected by the Revenue Commissioners. While local authorities still have significant responsibilities in relation to waste services, domestic refuse collection is undertaken by a range of private companies. One argument used for the establishment of Irish Water was that of economies of scale, which would lead to greater efficiency. However, it is also possible that size can lead to diseconomies of scale with large numbers employed to support large-scale structures. The government believed that planned water charges would provide funding for the new organisation while conceding that there would be no reduction in numbers employed. In the event, the proposed water charges were abandoned following protests. Some dissatisfaction has been expressed regarding Irish Water. For example, Limerick City and County Council passed a motion in 2021 to disband Irish Water and allow local authorities to take over water services.[37]

One of the most valuable tasks undertaken by local authorities with considerable benefit to local communities is the care of public parks. In many areas local authorities support local cultural and sporting activities. The local library service has been beneficial for individuals and communities over the decades and continues to develop, evidenced, for example, by the opening of the Lexicon Library and Cultural Centre in Dún Laoghaire in 2015. An initiative taken by Pearse Street Library in 2019 is a system for lending musical instruments to young people, while Ballyfermot Library facilitates the recording of music and podcasts.

The strength of both parish and county identity was demonstrated by the response to a recommendation of the Waterford Boundary Committee in 2017 that around 5,000 people and 20,000 acres of land should be reallocated from South Kilkenny to Co. Waterford to facilitate the development of Waterford city. Ger Frisby, a member of Kilkenny County Council, said that the people of Slieverue in Kilkenny did not want their *identity* to be changed. Frisby said the parish of Slieverue would be split between Kilkenny and Waterford. Stressing total opposition to the boundary change, Frisby said, 'you are talking about a person's county, a person's parish'.[38] In communities, urban as well as rural, throughout the country, the parish – mainly Catholic, but also for a significant minority, Church of Ireland – provided a sense of identity and belonging which included recognition and support from cradle to grave. The county is also a very strong badge of identity, never more apparent than on an All-Ireland final day in Croke Park.

Coming Together

Does the relative weakening of local government vis-à-vis central government provide a further reason to try to maintain parishes? Is there any scope for cooperation between the two? Many people are as much, or even more, removed from local government as they are from the local parish. In the local elections in 2019 voter turnout fell below 50 per cent for the first time. In some areas barely over one in four persons voted. In two of the four bye-elections held in November 2019, in the constituencies of Dublin Mid-West and Dublin Fingal, turnout was slightly above 25 per cent. Three-quarters of those entitled to vote did not do so. In Bishopstown, part of the Cork North-Central constituency where twenty-one people were registered to vote, not a single person cast a vote.[39] In the 2020 general election voter turnout was less than 63 per cent, compared with well over 70 per cent in the 1970s, 1980s and 1990s. This level of disengagement must be a cause for concern and merits analysis. Questions arise which confront the wider society as well as parish communities. Can a better balance be struck between local communities, local government and the State? Do parishes have a role to play in achieving such a balance while upholding the separation of Church and State?

During the Covid-19 emergency it is probably fair to say that the parish has faded further. One church, although not a parish church, assumed a new role. The Church of St Mary's of the Angels on Church Street in Dublin, in the care of the Capuchins, opened its doors as a venue for homeless people to sit and eat the meals provided for them at Brother Kevin's Day Centre in nearby Bow Street. However, for periods many churches across the island were closed, all priests over seventy were 'cocooned', and sacraments were deferred. Guidelines regarding funerals varied across dioceses. In some dioceses a blessing followed by burial was permitted, while in other dioceses a funeral Mass with a maximum of ten attendees, later increased to twenty-five, was permitted. Speaking on Holy Thursday 2020 in the cathedral in Newry, Co. Down, Archbishop Eamon Martin, Primate of All Ireland, said that 'parishes had taken to cyberspace' for weekly Mass. But he said that the epidemic had struck at the very heart of the ministry of priests, curtailing the sacraments and ministry to the sick and dying. *RTÉ News Now*, as well as many parishes, showed Masses on screen, generally with a lone celebrant. On the other hand, local authorities gained in relevance through the Community Call initiative with a network in each local authority area.

The path followed here begins by examining the origin of the parish and the rise and fall in the number of priests based in parishes, together with a brief examination of the diocesan context. The most important groups and societies associated with the parish are reviewed. Parallel to the decline in the parish, there has been a decline in the sphere of local government, although the Covid-19 emergency necessitated a reliance on local authorities to manage programmes of community support. The diminution in influence of the parish in the wider society is considered in the context of a loss of social capital. How this loss – assuming that it is a loss – may be retrieved is also considered. Some possibilities regarding the regeneration of the Church within the parish framework are considered. For the most part, but not exclusively, 'parish' will refer to the Roman Catholic parish. In many respects the experience of the Church of Ireland parish has been similar to that of the Roman Catholic parish. Together with the decline in the parish, does the decline in the sphere of local government matter? Some possibilities regarding the renewal of both parish and local government are considered. The study examines relevant data and research and draws on interviews with a number of persons from Church and State, including priests and politicians.

1

The Parish Landscape

The word 'parish' comes from the Greek word *paroikia*, which means 'close to the dwelling', implying a local area. The contemporary parish, described in Church terminology as the 'local manifestation of communion of the faithful', [1] refers to a community as well as an area. According to historian Liam Irwin, the diocesan and parochial organisation of the Church essentially goes back to the civil administration of the Roman Empire.[2] Throughout Europe, parishes were formed as early as the eighth and ninth centuries. These parishes had a role in both civil and ecclesiastical administration. Historian Paul MacCotter says there is evidence in England of a clear link between some parochial boundaries and 'secular administrative units'.[3] The secular administrative units refer to Anglo–Norman manors or estates. Compulsory tithe-paying was introduced in the tenth century and 'Payment of tithe necessitated a territorial definition in that parishes had to have fixed boundaries in order to determine payment.'[4] As a result, English parishes have been described as 'the religious expression of the manor'.[5] In France the lowest level of administrative division was the parish, which comprised a church with the surrounding village and land. The parish system endured until communes were introduced after the Revolution. In a sense communes replaced parishes although a number of parishes might be merged into a single commune.

By the nineteenth century civil and religious parishes had formally separated and they are now distinct, although historically they had a common origin. With parishes went church building, so when the election manifesto of the largest political party in the European Parliament, the European People's Party, for the 2019 European Parliament Elections stated, 'While Europe is diverse and nuanced, we have one thing in common: in every town and city there is a Christian church',[6] it was acknowledging history.

Emergence of the Parish System in Ireland

Fr Thomas O'Connor, historian of the Meath Diocese, attributes the origin of the parish system in Ireland to the Normans, who standardised pastoral care by centring it on the manors or estates of the new Anglo–Norman settlers. The parish system, in which the civil and Church parish overlapped, developed as the Normans divided lordships into manors. Church historian Msgr Patrick Corish says, 'A manor implied a church, a parish and a priest, and soon much of Ireland was covered with what have endured under the name of "civil parishes".'[7] Local laymen accepted responsibility for the upkeep of church buildings and the support of the clergy.[8] As the parochial structure evolved, a programme of church building got under way. In 1172 the Synod of Cashel ordered the payment of tithes, which became the financial foundation for the parish system. Also in the twelfth century, a reorganisation took place under Malachy, Archbishop of Armagh. At that time the Catholic Church in Ireland was divided into thirty-eight dioceses, each of which included several parishes. For example, the Diocese of Dublin, which ranked as an archdiocese, contained forty parishes. From the time of the Council of Trent (1545–63), the Catholic Church emphasised that 'religion was to centre on the parish, the parish priest and the parish church'.[9] The main objective in organising the parish network was to facilitate the celebration of Sunday Mass. The parish church would also be the place for the 'parish sacraments', especially baptism and marriage, and for burial of the dead. If, when the parish system was in its early stages, a church was not available – for example, for the celebration of a marriage – the main requirement was that the marriage be performed in the presence of a priest.

After the Reformation two distinct branches of Christianity existed in Ireland – Catholic espoused by a majority, and Protestant espoused by a minority. The Church of Ireland was the biggest component of the latter. The Church of Ireland succeeded to the then existing parish network, while the majority religion became 'an outcast Church' with scant material resources. However, by the end of the eighteenth century the economic circumstances of Catholics had improved with a growth in the number of middle-class Catholics, especially in towns. From around this time a revitalised parish structure developed and became of increasing importance. Parishes could include several townlands (the smallest land units). Corish distinguishes between the 'chapel village', which developed around the Catholic Church, and the 'estate village', built by a landlord with a Protestant church, to which a Catholic church was often added later. Professor Kevin Whelan, in a study of the 'Catholic Parish, the Catholic Chapel and Village Development',[10] has explained the emergence of 'chapel villages'.

By the nineteenth century the civil parish had become in essence an administrative area managed by a parish council, while the Church parish was an area in the charge of a parish priest. Until the introduction in 1838 of poor law unions, comprising a group, or union, of civil parishes, responsibility for the relief of the poor rested with individual parishes, which varied considerably in resources. In 1838 the Irish Poor Law Act, was passed by the Westminster Parliament. It was modelled on the earlier English Poor Law Act of 1834, which provided for a nationwide system for the relief of people who were poor, based on the workhouse and paid for by a local property tax. A poor law union, with a board of guardians, constituted an early local government unit for the administration of relief. In the Irish Free State, workhouses and their boards of guardians were abolished in 1925. The boards of guardians were replaced by boards of health and public assistance, and their work was financed by a county rate. The new boards were empowered to provide outdoor relief (i.e. relief outside the workhouse). Many workhouses were converted into hospitals and county homes.

In his study *Local Government in Ireland*, Desmond Roche concluded, 'The civil parish is now obsolete as a local government area.'[11] Civil parishes were indeed rendered more or less obsolete with the passing of the Local Government (Ireland) Act 1898. This Act provided for administrative counties divided into urban districts and rural districts. Prior to the passing of the Act there were three types of parish in Ireland – civil, Church of Ireland and Catholic. Since 1898 civil parishes have been overtaken by local authority divisions, although they have not been abolished and continue to be used in some legal matters; for example, on occasion, the identification and location of land. The Intoxicating Liquor Act 1988 allows 'any person resident in the parish' in which club premises are situated to object to the granting of an alcohol licence linked to the club.

The Parish Church

The development of the Catholic parish network was linked to the distribution of Catholic wealth, so that the network was best developed in South Leinster and East Munster. Chapel building and the development of new parishes grew with the rapid population growth in the first half of the nineteenth century. In the years between 1800 and 1863, 1,805 churches, 217 convents, and 40 colleges and seminaries were built. During the nineteenth century the Catholic Church embarked on a huge programme of church building 'funded by donations from parishioners and the Irish diaspora'.[12] Following Catholic Emancipation the building of impressive churches was seen as a sign of the growing social and political strength of Catholics, which helped to garner donations from the people. A negative aspect of this enormous volume of church-related building was suggested by Brody, who argued that devoting such a volume of resources, much of which came from the contributions of the ordinary laity, to church building, rather than other purposes, inhibited economic development.[13] A similar criticism was made by Horace Plunkett, who suggested that there was a far greater need for factories and co-operatives than for churches.[14]

Whelan lists different stages in the history of modern chapel building in Ireland:

> It begins with an open-air phase, which has come down to us in folk belief as the 'mass rock in the glen' days … Following the mass rock phase is the mass house or penal chapel phase … Its utter simplicity represents the curtailment imposed by poverty on the Catholic Church throughout much of the eighteenth century … However, increasingly in the late eighteenth and early nineteenth centuries, these penal chapels were replaced by the first modern chapels, which have been called the barn chapel.[15]

Whelan demonstrates that in addition to their significance for religious worship, the chapels provided the nuclei around which small villages developed, with accompanying schools, public houses and forges. The priest 'was the centre of gravity in the parish, a man who led his community and gave it force and cohesion'. Historically, church personnel were 'local'. 'The bishop is local, the clergy are locals and very often the religious men and women [men and women in religious orders] in a diocese are also locals.'[16] In the twenty-first century, bishops in Ireland are less likely to be appointed to their home dioceses.[17] A further significant change is the move away from the appointment of parish priests for an 'indeterminate period of time', usually for life, to the recent system of appointment for specific terms.

As a literate man, the priest was frequently the broker or hinge between the (often non-literate) community and the outside world, especially the outside world represented by central government functions.[18] His role in education was important. Catholic chapels usually had a national school beside them. By 1870 over 70 per cent of national schools were under Catholic control. Commercial establishments often followed chapel and school and, in dairying areas, co-operative creameries began to appear in the early twentieth century. Corish says:

> This 'chapel village' as the rural political, cultural and social centre began with the agitation for Catholic Emancipation in the 1820s, but its real development

came after the Famine, and its full development can be seen about fifty years later, as rural organisations multiplied; one of the most influential in stabilising the parish as a social unit was the Gaelic Athletic Association, founded in 1884. In a phrase made famous by Kickham's novel, published in 1879, all effort should be made 'for the honour of the little village'.[19]

By the mid twentieth century the church building was central to the Catholic community, not only in rural Ireland but in many new housing estates which sprang up in urban Ireland. This is captured by journalist Gene Kerrigan in his description of Cabra West in the 1940s and 1950s:

> If you look at a map of Cabra West you will have no doubt about the location of the Catholic church. The estate, built by Dublin Corporation at the beginning of the 1940s, is laid out in a geometric shape designed around a space allocated for the church. The church is the centre of the web of streets, holding the whole design together … the physical representation of the Church was the central element in the layout of a whole community.[20]

In the past, when Catholic practice was high, the growth in the number of parishes followed population growth and housing growth. For example, in Dublin, following slum clearance by Dublin Corporation from 1926 onwards, new housebuilding led to the creation of working-class suburbs like Crumlin on the south side and Cabra on the north side. Parishes followed. One thousand new homes were built in Marino by Dublin Corporation and it became a model for new development. The Parish of Marino in 1942 followed the building of the new housing estates. The parish has a strong record in producing vocations to the priesthood, as around twenty-five priests have come from there.

In 1974 RTÉ broadcast a documentary made by the Radharc team entitled 'Exploding Diocese, the Churches for our Children'. The director of the film was Fr Des Forristal, who was also an accomplished writer. The documentary was about the building of Catholic churches, schools and community centres in the new communities in Dublin, such as Raheny, Blanchardstown and Darndale. The film showed that in 1965 there were approximately 100 Catholic parishes in Dublin. By 1985 there would be almost 200. Church authorities were faced with the problem of finding £10 million (1974 values, or €108 million in 2019 values) over the next ten years to build churches and schools in the new suburban parishes. The ambitious target was almost achieved. In a lecture delivered in both Lyon and Paris in January 1983, Archbishop Dermot Ryan described the Dublin Archdiocese as a place where new parishes were springing up and, where within a few years, whole areas were transformed from pastures into vibrant parish communities.[21]

The architectural style of church buildings changed in significant ways from the nineteenth century through to the mid twentieth century and post Vatican II. This change in architectural style goes beyond questions of taste, fashion or design. At a deeper level it reflects a change in understanding of the Church. In the 1960s 'more liturgy-conscious designs' began to appear.[22] At a congress held at the Benedictine Monastery, Glenstal, Co. Limerick, in 1962, the main speaker, Urban Rapp, OSB, outlined a meeting point between architecture and liturgy:

> The essence of modern church architecture does not lie in the use of new techniques and materials, but in the constructive realisation, in first-class quality, of the liturgical postulate. The liturgical postulate is: the grouping of the assembly around the altar in such a way that a genuine participation in the sacred sacrifice is possible.[23]

The type of Church architecture which, in Rapp's judgement, placed insufficient emphasis on the connection between architecture and liturgy continued well into the twentieth century. A Gothic-style revival was extensive in Ireland due to the influence of the English architect Augustus Welby Pugin, who judged Gothic to be the more 'religious' style. Irish architect J. J. McCarthy was an influential adherent of the Gothic revival in nineteenth-century church architecture. The massive programme of church building in the nineteenth century reflected both faith and country – self-belief of the Irish Catholic people. A good example of the Gothic revival style is St Patrick's Church in Dundalk, which opened in 1847 in the middle of the Famine. The architect Thomas Duff designed the church in the style of King's College Chapel, Cambridge.[24] Much of the interior, including the high altar, was designed by J. J. McCarthy and completed over a number of years. Church architecture also reflected the general understanding of the meaning of 'Church'. In an earlier era when people spoke of the 'Church', it would have been with reference to bishops and priests. Dominican priest, and expert on the Second Vatican Council, Fr Austin Flannery summed up the situation as follows:

> In popular parlance it was the priest who 'said' Mass, the laity who 'attended' Mass – attended indeed, in the phrase of the Constitution on the Sacred Liturgy, *Sacrosanctum Concilium*, number 47, as 'silent spectators'.[25] … the long Gothic nave and remote sanctuary provided a perfectly appropriate setting for the priest perceived as offering Mass on behalf of the people who knelt, stood and sat in silent ranks at his back.[26]

One of the defining documents of the Second Vatican Council was the Dogmatic Constitution on the Church, *Lumen Gentium* (*Light of the Nations*), published in November 1964, which emphasised not the hierarchical structure of the Church but that its members were 'the People of God'. According to Flannery, the architect need make no distinction between the 'House of God' and the 'House of God's People'. God is present in his people; it is in the assembly that God is encountered. This is why the same word of Greek origin, *ecclesia*, came to be used for the people and for the building, why the same word 'church' is used in both senses.[27] The major shift which took place in the architecture of Catholic churches in the later decades of the twentieth century reflected changed theological emphasis on the nature of the Church. Simplicity, rather than Gothic and Romanesque revival style, became the keynote.

The Irish hierarchy established the Episcopal Liturgical Commission, which in turn established, in 1965, the Advisory Committee on Sacred Art and Architecture. The Advisory Committee published a *Pastoral Directory on the Building and Reorganisation of Churches* in 1966. The Directory emphasised simplicity and spoke of how 'The authentic expression of the Christian virtue of poverty, which does not in any way imply impoverishment, is valuable witness in face of the increasing materialism of modern life'.[28] Whatever about the theological insights, the changes made in church architecture, following Vatican II, were not universally popular. This was especially the case when substantial changes, in some cases involving destruction of architectural elements, were made to older churches by moving altars and tabernacles and removing altar rails.

A graceful example of a post-Vatican II church is the Church of the Holy Spirit in Greenhills, a suburb of Dublin. Planning for the church began in the mid 1960s, following the Second Vatican Council, and the architects who designed the church were Louis Peppard and Hugo Duffy. The side walls are of single-storey height and the roof almost touches the ground. According to Christopher Moriarty, the 'entrance leads to a brilliant interior where immense space and height elicit an immediate feeling of exaltation'.[29] 'So the traditional concept of a slightly distant sanctuary, often with a railing to mark it off from the congregation, was replaced by a minimal separation in which sanctuary and nave merge almost imperceptibly'.[30] Close to the church are the parish offices and coffee shop. According to data supplied by the archdiocese, the capacity of the church is 1,000 (5,000 for the five weekend Masses). In 2008 the combined attendance at all five Vigil/Sunday Masses was 1,115. By 2014 this had fallen to 842, or less than 17 per cent of total capacity.

A remarkable example of ecumenical work is revealed by the history of the oldest Catholic church in Belfast. In the late eighteenth century, when there were fewer than 400 Catholics living in Belfast and no Catholic church, the Presbyterian and Church of Ireland communities took up a special collection at their services and donated it towards building the first Catholic church in Belfast – St Mary's. The pulpit was donated by the Vicar of Belfast, Canon Turner of the Anglican Church in High Street.[31] In the early nineteenth century in various parts of the country, many wealthy Protestants contributed financially, sometimes by donating sites, to the building of Catholic churches and this is usually acknowledged on facades or tablets. The work of cooperation continues in the twenty-first century as the different traditions in Northern Ireland collaborate to keep their fine churches in good repair and to share their heritage.[32]

More than the Building

Perception of what the parish church means can alter over a lifetime. Sinn Féin councillor, and former Lord Mayor of Dublin, Críona Ní Dhálaigh, who grew up in the Dublin suburb of Ballyfermot, said that as a child the Church was to her the actual church building. Later, when she lived for ten years with her young family in Belfast, she said one of the attractions of going to an Irish-language Mass there was meeting and befriending a community. Back in Dublin, although she is no longer a regular churchgoer, the parish with which she would have most connection is Dolphin's Barn. Here, she says, the priests are very active in the community and she now identifies Church more with priests than she did when she was a child.[33]

'As well as containing the rituals for each crucial event in a man's life, its ideology matched traditional social practice as a whole.'[34] The parish has been central to social as well as religious life, not only in Ireland. The Archbishop of Chicago, Cardinal Blase Cupich, sums up the experience of his family and of a multitude of families: 'All of us were churchgoers. We were in the choir, we served Mass … the parish was our second home.'[35] In addition to religious practices, many social customs originated in parishes. For example, 'Mother's Day', a largely secular event nowadays, started as a celebration known as 'Mothering Sunday' in both Catholic and Protestant churches. On that Sunday, people would visit their 'mother church', that is the church where they were baptised, or their local parish church.[36]

Over time the parish has become identified both with a specific area within a diocese and with the community of believers in that area. Micheál Mac Gréil draws a distinction between territorial and personal parishes. He says that parishes of the Travellers are personal while most other parishes are territorial.[37] Fr Tom Naughton, who is chaplain to the Travelling Community, has described how the role has evolved. For many years Travellers were moving from place to place and the chaplain needed to follow in order to celebrate, for example, weddings. Nowadays Travellers tend to be fairly 'settled' and Fr Naughton visits groups of Travellers and organises Masses and other sacraments and pilgrimages.[38] In parts of Latin America and North Africa where some people lead a nomadic, pastoral life, the priest needs to follow the people and bring the sacraments to them. Bringing Mass to the people contains an echo of the Station Masses once held in people's homes and a familiar feature in parts of rural Ireland. By contrast, in big cities people may opt to attend a church of their choice rather than the church in the parish where they reside.[39]

There were 1,359 Catholic parishes on the island of Ireland in 2018. The number had increased steadily throughout the twentieth century, reaching a peak of 1,368 in 2000. The parochial structure of the Church has survived for centuries but according to Emeritus Bishop of Limerick, and former Auxiliary Bishop of Dublin, Donal Murray, its survival is being increasingly challenged. Murray says that the parish is challenged by the facts: priests are no longer readily available even for Masses and funerals; some parishes don't have a resident parish priest.[40] A change in practice by the laity suggests that many laity view their relationship to the parish in a fluid way. Some of those who no longer attend Mass on a regular basis may still regard themselves as belonging to the local parish and will perhaps marry in the local church, bring their children there for First Communion and arrange funerals from there. Some also will 'shop around' different parishes, especially in urban areas. This in itself reflects a more individual-based, rather than community-based, approach to religious practice. Msgr John Dolan is a canon lawyer who has responsibility for support services for members of religious orders as well as for priests coming into the Archdiocese of Dublin from abroad. He was a member of a subcommittee of the Dublin Council of Priests that looked at the planning of parishes for the future. Dolan emphasises the community aspect of parish. He maintains that Christians always exist within a community and that there is an inherent link between Christian communities and the Eucharist.[41]

Rev. Trevor Sargent, former leader of the Green Party, and former TD and minister of state, was ordained a Church of Ireland priest in 2018. He now serves as curate in the Waterford Union of Parishes, which includes the cathedral in Waterford and churches in Dunmore East, Tramore and Annestown. Sargent counts every person within the boundaries of his parish, regardless of religion, and every living creature, as belonging to his parish. This follows from one of the five Anglican marks of mission – to safeguard the integrity of creation.[42] There is a tradition in Sargent's parish of 'Beating the Bounds', an old custom whereby a group of parishioners walk around the parish boundaries periodically. This has the practical purpose of identifying boundaries as well as the social aspect of a shared project. Furthermore it invites the question of what it means to say, 'I live in this parish.' Sargent suggests that in the Catholic Church, church buildings are places where 'Christ is at home' in the sense that Catholics believe in the Real Presence of Christ in the tabernacle, a belief which is symbolised by the red sanctuary lamp in each church and the practice of making the Sign of the Cross when passing a church. According to Sargent, the significance of the church building in the Reformed tradition differs from that in the Roman Catholic Church. For members of the Church of Ireland, there is a sense that the church building is a civic space in which the liturgy is enacted and where a cup of tea may often be provided after a church service.[43]

For Methodists, the basic unit is a society; a group of societies form a circuit. Presbyterians form congregations. Methodists and Presbyterians sometimes refer to their assembly place as 'The Hall', and Quakers to 'The Meeting House'. An example of a thriving Methodist circuit is that in Richhill in Co. Armagh, where at present services are held in the church hall as the church requires renovation. According to Methodist minister Rev. Nick McKnight, services begin with music, continue with words of Scripture and are followed by tea and coffee. Everyone is welcome.[44]

Priests – At the 'Edge of an Actuarial Cliff'

In 2017 a priest of the Archdiocese of Dublin, Fr William King, published a biographical novel, *A Lost Tribe*. King's objective was to depict a vanished way of life; it was not to offer solutions to the dearth of vocations. King has compared his goal in writing the book to that of Tomás Ó Criomhthain in *An tOileánach* (*The Islandman*). Ó Criomhthain, who was writing about the people who lived on the Great Blasket Island off Kerry, said, 'I have done my best to set down the character of the people about me so that some record of us might live on, for the like of us will never be again.'[45]

In 2017 the departing Papal Nuncio, Archbishop Charles Brown, endorsed King's reality when he spoke of the Catholic Church in Ireland as 'at the edge of an actuarial cliff'[46] because of the ageing of priests and the lack of new vocations:

We've a lot of priests in Ireland who are in their 70s, who are working right now. Some are in their 80s. In 10 years they are not going to be working. We're at the edge of an actuarial cliff here, and we're going to start into free fall.[47]

Thirty-five years earlier, in 1983, when there were plenty of priests, the then Archbishop of Dublin, Dermot Ryan, spoke of 'new parishes growing up from the grass'.[48] How did the actuarial cliff edge replace the fertile grass?

At the first census taken in the Irish Free State in 1926, the total number of clergy (priests and ministers) of all denominations in the Twenty-Six Counties was close to 5,000. By mid century, in 1951, the number had risen to almost 6,000. By 2011 the number had halved to just under 3,000. Data given in the *Statistical Yearbook* of the Catholic Church published by the Vatican, which cover the whole island of Ireland, show a similar trend to the census data for the Free State/Republic of Ireland, with an increase in the number of Catholic clergy up to the middle decades of the twentieth century, followed by a subsequent decline.

In 1965 total ordinations for all Ireland peaked when 412 priests, including priests from religious orders, priests destined for overseas missions and approximately ninety diocesan priests, were ordained. The number of diocesan priests ordained in 1965 exceeded the places to be filled in parishes, so that some priests had to emigrate to parishes overseas until places could be found for them at home. Fifty years later, in 2015, the total number of priests ordained had fallen to fourteen. It is noteworthy that ordination of Maynooth students peaked as long ago as 1940, when ninety students were ordained, as shown in Table 1. Coincidentally, this was the first year of the episcopate of Archbishop John Charles McQuaid. Between 1940 and 1969 the number of ordinations of Maynooth students more than halved, falling to forty-one.

Table 1: Ordination of Maynooth Students 1903–69

Year	Inside Maynooth	Outside Maynooth	Total
1903	61	19	80
1910	75	14	89
1920	62	5	67
1930	63	9	72
1940	66	24	90
1950	67	6	73
1960	52	12	64
1969	8	33	41

Source: Hamell (1984).

In 2011 Eoin O'Mahony of the Council for Research and Development of the Irish Catholic Bishops' Conference undertook a survey of the age profile of the 1,965 diocesan priests then assigned to ministry. The survey showed that just 32 priests, or less than 2 per cent, were below the age of 34, while more than 200 were 75 years old and older. A diocese-by-diocese survey carried out by the *Irish Examiner* in 2018 confirmed the ageing profile of the clergy and found that some dioceses were inviting younger priests from overseas to work in Ireland.[49] The relative old age of Catholic priests was brought into sharp relief during the early phase of the Covid-19 pandemic when all those aged over seventy in the population were 'cocooned' on government advice. Those priests 'cocooned' amounted to around 50 per cent of the total.

The number of diocesan priests reached a peak of 4,038 in 1970, as shown in Table 2. Since then the number has fallen steadily (see Figure 1). Between 2000 and 2018 the total number halved. In 1926, according to the census returns, there was one diocesan priest for approximately 800 Catholics. By 2018 the number of Catholics per diocesan priest had increased threefold, to approximately 2,500. The number of Catholics per priest is not uniform across the dioceses, with, for example, a higher number of Catholics per priest in the two Northern Dioceses of Derry and of Down and Connor than in the Southern Archdiocese of Cashel and Emly and the Diocese of Clonfert. In terms of the total number of priests per diocese, Dublin has by far the largest number, followed by Down and Connor. In 2017 the 7 dioceses with the smallest number of priests – Dromore (27), Achonry (30), Killala (30), Clonfert (32), Elphin (43), Galway (44) and Ossory (58) – had a combined total of 268 priests currently assigned to parishes, just 5 more than the total for Dublin.

The decline in the number of priests is set to continue as priests in ministry grow older while the number of candidates entering seminaries has dwindled to a trickle. In autumn 2018 a total of five men started training for the priesthood at Maynooth, the lowest number in its history. The students came from the Dioceses of Dromore, Down and Connor, Elphin, Kerry and Tuam, which sent one student each. Seven seminaries have closed in Ireland in the past twenty-five years: St Patrick's in Carlow closed in 1993; St Kieran's in Kilkenny in 1994; St John's in Waterford and St Peter's in Wexford in 1999; Clonliffe College in 2000; St Patrick's in Thurles in 2002; and All Hallows in Dublin in 2015. By 2012 Maynooth was the only seminary operative in Ireland.

Faced with the decline in the number of priests, the Diocesan Priests' Council in Dublin commissioned the consultancy firm Towers Watson to examine and analyse trends in ministry and personnel numbers for the period 2014–30. According to these trends, Mass attendance is projected to decline by 33 per cent and the number of priests by 70 per cent. However, according to the study, the demand for baptisms, Communions, Confirmations and funerals is not expected to change very much. At best the study predicts a 61 per cent reduction in the numbers of clergy in Dublin, from 369 priests working at full capacity in 2014 to 144 in 2030. If the religious orders were to relinquish parishes, the drop would be 70 per cent, leaving just 111 priests working at full capacity in the Dublin Archdiocese in 2030.

By 2030 almost 80 per cent of available priests will be sixty years old or older. In the face of the changing reality the consultants recommend that the archdiocese should initially reduce the number of Masses within each parish while maintaining the parishes. 'Ultimately, the optimal solution is probably a combination of reduced Masses and combined parishes.'[50] As the number of Masses is reduced, attendance at Mass falls further, and as parishes are combined, clustered or closed, the opportunities for social interaction associated with parishes decline, and social capital, the networks of relationships among people which are necessary for society to function, is almost certainly reduced.

Table 2: Parishes and Diocesan Priests in Ireland (32 Counties) 1900–2018

Year	Parishes	Diocesan Clergy
1900	1,090	2,879
1910	1,113	2,995
1920	1,116	3,082
1930	1,120	3,087
1940	1,120	3,187
1950	1,130	3,552
1960	1,147	3,805
1970	1,192	4,038
1980	1,305	3,801
1990	1,354	3,800
2000	1,368	3,403
2010	1,365	2,536
2018	1,359	1,728

Source: *Irish Catholic Directory*, various years.
The data in the directory for a particular year may sometimes refer to the previous year if the data were not available at the time of submission.

Figure 1: Parishes and Diocesan Priests in Ireland (32 counties) 1900–2018

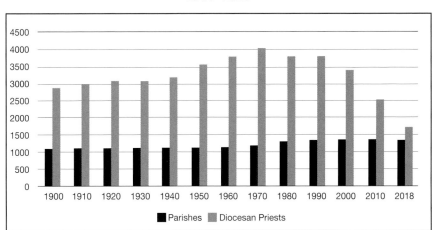

Bishops are keenly aware of the situation and acknowledge the changed reality. For example, the Bishop of Kerry, Raymond Browne, has said that in view of the number of parishes in Kerry – around 15 per cent – without a resident priest, soon a number of churches will be without regular weekend Mass. There are a total of 105 churches in the 54 parishes in the diocese. One parish has four churches, some have two or three churches, and the rest have one church. In the future, many people will have to travel to parishes other than their own in order to attend Mass. One priest in the Galway Diocese, Fr Diarmuid Hogan, believes that the focus should be on too many churches rather than too few priests. He says, 'The churches in Ireland were planned and built long before modern infrastructure and transportation; therefore, in rural areas, they are small and close together.'[51] However, churches were built in order to be close to the people, ensuring intimacy with the local community. Older, less mobile people may experience difficulty in travelling some distance to a church.

In order to understand the current decline in vocations to the priesthood it may be useful to recall the reasons given for the earlier high level of vocations. In a paper on priestly vocations in Ireland, delivered at a Conference on Priestly Vocations in Europe in Vienna in 1958, Dr Jeremiah Newman, then Professor of Sociology at Maynooth, outlined reasons for the 'wealth of priestly vocations'.[52] He listed four main reasons – 'very healthy Catholic family life'; 'general system of education which by and large is permeated by a Catholic outlook'; 'the respected place which the clergy, secular and regular, have occupied in Irish life … where for centuries religion and patriotism went hand in hand'; and 'an appreciation of the Irish priest as a man of culture'. Significantly, Newman spoke of 'the gradually improving economic system, bringing new careers and greater opportunity of suitable employment'. He also spoke of growing urbanisation and the neglect of rural areas. At the time 70 per cent of Maynooth students came from rural areas and 50 per cent were the sons of farmers. Newman's comments were made at a time of economic recession and a full ten years before the landmark introduction of free post-primary education in 1967. The observation regarding the lack of alternative employment opportunities was also made by former Taoiseach John Bruton.[53] This is not to denigrate vocations but to point to the reality of a depressed economy. Furthermore, in the years before the introduction of free post-primary education, a young man or woman who was interested in further education, as well as in religious objectives, might see the possibilities for fulfilment of such objectives through priesthood or religious life.

A further, less worthy, influence on vocations may have been that, in economically poor times, priests had an above-average standard of living. At least until the Second Vatican Council, many priests had housekeepers, while a bishop would have had a number of domestic as well as administrative staff. According to one account given by the Association of Catholic Priests in 2013:

> At the human level, the life-support systems for priests used to be much better. Full-time housekeepers lit fires, put out the ashes, tidied the house, put food on the table and hot-water jars in the bed. Canon William Healy, who was PP of Kilglass in Sligo, had two housekeepers and two men 'in the yard' – tending the needs of his few acres, saving the turf and so on. At the time priests were the equivalent of minor gentry, living in significant houses and in control of everything worth controlling.[54]

Fifty years ago there was a degree of social pressure to have 'a priest in the family', as depicted by Richard Power, a civil servant in the Department of Local Government, in his novel *The Hungry Grass*,[55] published in 1969. The central character is the parish priest, Fr Tom Conroy. As Conroy contemplates death he realises that he has struggled to support parishioners in their lives without any real emotional support himself and without a real vocation. He had entered the seminary because his older brother had quit.

In the 1950s, 'Catholic Ireland' seemed real. However, Frank Duff, pioneer of the lay apostolate, saw things differently. In relation to these years, he wrote, 'Religion has become routine. A terrible conservatism exercises relentless sway, and tells the Irish people they must walk by outmoded ways.'[56] In a letter Duff wrote to Fr Aedan McGrath in 1948, he held that where the laity did not fulfil its role, the Church would fail. He insisted that 'an inert laity is only two generations removed from non-practice. Non-practice is only two generations away from non-belief'.[57] At the time, crowded churches and an abundance of priests seemed to contradict Duff's analysis. In 1987 Inglis could write, 'The priest in Ireland is a spiritual and moral adviser who is consulted on a wide range of social, political and economic issues … informally he is the most respected member of the community.'[58] Although it is not possible to make a precise causal link, an acute decline in vocations followed the emergence and concealment of abuses by priest in the 1980s. Between 1990 and 1998 ordinations of diocesan clergy fell by over 60 per cent.[59]

Permanent Diaconate

Since the end of the Second Vatican Council the Catholic population of the world has almost doubled but the number of priests worldwide has fallen. An increase in the number of priests in Africa, Asia, and Central and South America has been more than offset by a decline in North America, Europe and Oceania. Between 1970 and 2016 the number of priests worldwide fell from 420,000 to 416,000. However, the number of permanent deacons has risen markedly, from 309 in 1970 to 46,000 in 2016.[60] The term 'deacon' comes from the Greek *diakonia*, which is associated with service, especially of the poor. Deacons existed from the earliest days in the Church. However, from the fifth century the diaconate gradually faded and from the Early Middle Ages it was associated with the final stage prior to ordination to the priesthood. There were exceptions to this pattern; for example, Francis of Assisi was ordained a deacon but never a priest. In the sixteenth century the Council of Trent directed the restoration of the permanent diaconate, but this was not given effect until after the Second Vatican Council. In 1967 Pope Paul VI published the Apostolic Letter *Sacrum Diaconatus Ordinem* in which he re-established the permanent diaconate as desired by the council. Referring to the diaconate, the council says, 'Dedicated to the duties of charity and of administration, let deacons be mindful of the admonition of Blessed Polycarp: "Be diligent, walking according to the truth of the Lord, who became the servant of all." ' (*Lumen Gentium* 29). Permanent deacons are growing in number and are beginning to create a pastoral presence in parishes. Deacons may be married men or unmarried men, and candidates are eligible for consideration up to the age of sixty. Deacons may operate a voluntary part-time ministry which they combine with regular employment, or may be full-time and employed by a church agency. Deacons can assist the priest in the celebration of Mass; they can also celebrate baptisms, marriages and funerals, and undertake visitation and bring communion to the sick, but may not celebrate Mass or hear Confession. The first ordination of permanent deacons in the Dublin Archdiocese took place in June 2012 at the Pro-Cathedral, when eight men were ordained to the diaconate. One well-known deacon is Dermot McCarthy, a former secretary general to the government, who is deacon in Westland Row. He has a long association with the Society of St Vincent de Paul attached to St Andrew's Parish, Westland Row.

There were seventy-nine permanent deacons in Ireland in 2017. Slightly less than half were based in Dublin and Armagh, with the others spread over several dioceses. In June 2018 the first permanent deacon in the Diocese of Clogher was ordained. He is father-of-two Martin Donnelly from Enniskillen in Co. Fermanagh. In October 2018 nine men were ordained as deacons in the Down and Connor Diocese. These include two lawyers – Brett Lockhart, QC, and Gregory McGuigan, QC. Lockhart, who was born into a Presbyterian family in Belfast, joined the Catholic Church in 2002. He represented the families bereaved by the Omagh bombing. McGuigan has taken part in many high-profile cases.[61]

Church of Ireland

As with the Catholic Church, the Church of Ireland has experienced a long-run decline in the number of clergy both in the Republic and in Northern Ireland. In 1955 there was a total of 914 active clergy in Ireland, with 531, or 58 per cent, in the Republic and 383, or 42 per cent, in Northern Ireland. The number in ministry dipped until 1990 but since the admission of women to the priesthood, there has been an increase. Sixty-six women have been ordained since 1990 and there are sixty-four women parish priests. In 2017 there were 486 (218, Republic; 268, Northern Ireland) active clergy on the island of Ireland, slightly more than half the number in 1955.[62] In 2019 eight persons were ordained for the priesthood. There are about fifty 'vacant' parishes.[63] Nevertheless, according to Robert MacCarthy, former Dean of St Patrick's Cathedral, the Church of Ireland is finding it extremely difficult to maintain the current system of parishes led by a member of the clergy.[64] A number of parishes have been joined; for example, Donnybrook and Irishtown in Dublin. However, due to falling numbers, St Mary's Church on Anglesea Road, which had been the parish church for Donnybrook, was deconsecrated and closed in July 2020.

There is more lay involvement in the Church of Ireland than in the Catholic Church, as measured, for example, by voting rights. Every lay member of the Church of Ireland who is aged eighteen years or older may be registered as a member of the general vestry of their parish. The general vestry elects the select vestry, which is responsible for parish finances and the care of its property. A select vestry includes church wardens, who are responsible for the control of church services, and glebe wardens, who are responsible for care of church property and land. The General Synod, which legislates for the Church of Ireland, is comprised of a House of Bishops and a House of Representatives. The latter is composed of 216 clerical members with 432 lay members, elected by diocesan synods.

Some rationalisation of Church of Ireland parishes may arise in the future, as attendance at services is low. A census, the first of its kind undertaken on weekly attendance at services, showed that average attendance at Church of Ireland services on the whole island of Ireland, North and South, on three Sundays in November 2013 was 58,000. This represented 15.5 per cent of the Church of Ireland population as defined by Republic of Ireland and UK census results for 2011.[65]

Parish Records

Parish records provide invaluable data, including data on baptisms, marriages and burials, and clerical succession lists. From around the time of Catholic Emancipation in 1829, it became the practice for each Catholic parish to maintain a register of baptisms and marriages. In some towns and cities a number of registers go back into the eighteenth century. The data are used by historians, genealogists, lawyers and many others. The National Library of Ireland (NLI) contains a trove of parish data, including microfilm registers for most Catholic parishes in the Republic and Northern Ireland in the 1950s and 1960s. The work was set in train in the late 1940s when the NLI approached the Catholic hierarchy and offered to microfilm parochial registers. The filming of registers began in the 1950s and took twenty years to complete. The NLI now holds microfilm of over 3,500 registers from 1,086 parishes in the whole island of Ireland. In 2010 the NLI decided to digitise the parish register microfilms, facilitating online accessibility. The Representative Church Body of the Church of Ireland (RCB) has a purpose-built library for parish records in Braemor Park in Dublin. The library holds parish records dating from the late seventeenth century onwards. The RCB placed all lists for the Church of Ireland parishes online in 2016.

Diocesan Framework

The Church of the early medieval period in Ireland was based mainly on monastic settlements; the bishop and the abbot of a monastery could be the same person. One of the earliest monastic foundations was at Glendalough. Well-known monasteries from the later medieval period include Holycross Cistercian Monastery and Fethard Augustinian Monastery in Co. Tipperary. The roots of the system of ecclesiastical administration extend back to the túatha (people or tribes), the basic political and juridical unit of the Gaelic world. An eighth-century tract known as 'The Rule of Patrick' ('Ríagal Phátraic') says, 'Every túath should have a chief bishop to ordain its clergy, to consecrate its churches, to give direction to its chiefs and nobles, and to sanctify and bless their children after baptism.'[66] The rule speaks of 'the small churches of the túath'. Resident priests attached to these 'small churches' came within the responsibility and care of the bishop. The diocesan structure was established in the twelfth century when, at the Synod of Rathbreasail in Co. Tipperary in 1111, a clear distinction was made between monastery and diocese by the establishment of a diocesan episcopate.[67] Many dioceses today trace their origins to decisions taken at Rathbreasail. Further synods, including that at Kells in Co. Meath in 1152, continued the process.

Every Catholic parish belongs to a diocese, which is in the care of a bishop. A diocese includes several parishes and spans a number of counties or parts of counties. For example, while much of Tipperary is in the Diocese of Cashel and Emly, a large part is in the Diocese of Killaloe and a further part is in the Diocese of Lismore. Likewise, parts of Roscommon fall into the three Dioceses of Achonry, Ardagh and Clonmacnoise, and Clonfert. For the people of Tipperary or Roscommon, who have a strong affinity with their county, there can be no comparable affinity with a single diocese.

At present there are twenty-six Catholic dioceses in Ireland, divided into four ecclesiastical provinces: Armagh, Dublin, Cashel and Emly, and Tuam. Each ecclesiastical province has a metropolitan archdiocese which is based around the chief ecclesiastical city where the diocesan cathedral is situated. The sites of the archdiocesan cathedrals are, respectively, Armagh, Dublin, Thurles and Tuam. The other dioceses in a province are known as suffragan dioceses. The ecclesiastical provinces do not coincide exactly with the civil provinces of Ulster, Leinster, Munster and Connacht, but their geographical area is similar to some extent.

The size of dioceses varies greatly in terms of stated Catholic population, parishes, priests and number of churches. The stated Catholic population of dioceses in 2017 ranged from 34,826 in the Diocese of Achonry to 1.16

million in the Archdiocese of Dublin, over thirty times bigger. Down and Connor has a stated Catholic population of 326,000, which is almost ten times bigger than Clonfert, with 36,000, and Killala, with 39,000. Dublin has 200 parishes compared with 23 in Achonry and 24 in Clonfert. Dromore, the fifth-smallest diocese, fell vacant in March 2018, following the resignation of Bishop John McAreavey against a background of controversy which centred on whether the bishop had knowledge of allegations of abuse made against one of the priests (now deceased) in the diocese. In 2019 an auxiliary bishop, Michael Router, was appointed to assist Archbishop Eamon Martin in Armagh while Archbishop Martin was appointed administrator of Dromore.[68]

The future of Ireland's dioceses is on the Vatican agenda. In an interview with *The Irish Catholic*, Papal Nuncio Archbishop Jude Okolo confirmed that the process of amalgamation of dioceses had already started.[69] An indication of the direction of Vatican thinking may be found in the decision not to appoint a bishop to Dromore, at least at the present time. Early in 2022, one bishop, Michael Duignan, was appointed Bishop of Galway as well as continuing as Bishop of Clonfert. Pope John Paul II suppressed 100 dioceses in Italy and Pope Francis has reconfigured dioceses in Brazil. The Congregation for Bishops has expressed the belief that dioceses with less than 100,000 persons are not sustainable; on the other hand the large size of Dublin raises questions. Is it too big for one man? Archbishop Eamon Martin drew a comparison between the Dublin Archdiocese and the Dublin local authorities. From the point of view of the civil authorities, Dublin has been divided into four: Dublin City, Dún Laoghaire–Rathdown, Fingal and South County, but the archdiocese remains intact.

In Appendix 1, aspects of five dioceses (three archdioceses and two dioceses) – Armagh, Dublin, Tuam, Meath and Limerick – are presented in order to provide further context for parishes. Brief notes on the other dioceses are also included. The Archdioceses of Armagh, Dublin and Tuam and the Dioceses of Meath and Limerick have been selected partly to include dioceses in each of the four provinces but also because of availability of data. A unique feature of Limerick is that it convened the first diocesan synod in Ireland in over half a century. Dublin is by far the largest diocese in terms of population and parishes, while Armagh is the Primatial See[70] and spans parts of Northern Ireland and the Republic. Tuam is a more rural archdiocese and includes Gaeltacht parishes. Meath contains both rural and urban areas. Although Meath is in the Armagh province, it is contiguous to Dublin and many Meath residents commute to work in Dublin.

Church of Ireland Dioceses

The Church of Ireland is divided into 12 dioceses with 450 parishes. The twelve dioceses are grouped into two provinces – Armagh and Dublin. The seven dioceses in the Armagh province are Armagh; Clogher; Connor; Derry and Raphoe; Down and Dromore; Kilmore, Elphin and Ardagh; and Tuam, Killala and Achonry. The five dioceses in the Dublin province are Cashel, Ferns and Ossory; Cork, Cloyne and Ross; Dublin and Glendalough; Limerick and Killaloe; and Meath and Kildare. Diocesan synods meet annually and elect members to the General Synod, which acts as the parliament of the Church and decides questions on liturgy, Church teaching and governance.

Between October 2004 and May 2005 Bishop Harold Miller, Bishop of Down and Dromore, carried out seventy-nine parish visitations in his diocese. He came to the conclusion: 'We are losing young people after Confirmation.' He said, 'this is probably the single most common comment spoken out in the same words in a vast number of parishes.' Confirmation comes a little later in the Church of Ireland than in the Catholic Church, usually at age fourteen or fifteen. In the Church of Ireland the reception of Communion follows Confirmation, as was the case in the Roman Catholic Church until the early twentieth century. The decline in numbers was also shown in census data presented in a book by Malcolm Macourt, published in 2008, entitled *Counting the People of God*. In the book's foreword, the Church of Ireland Archbishop of Armagh, Alan Harper, wrote: 'The evidence is stark that the number of Church of Ireland members has declined from the early part of the twentieth century. Church attendance has also steadily declined.'[71]

2

Celebration, Commemoration

The parish church, whether Roman Catholic or Protestant, situated in the Irish landscape is a reminder not just of a physical area or of a certain community; it is also a reminder of the spiritual dimension of people, of the finiteness of material life, a suggestion of transcendence and of communal memory. According to John O'Donohue, when one enters the parish church 'one does not simply enter a building; rather one enters unknowingly into gathered memory.'[1] In an interview, filmmaker and writer Jim Sheridan said that he likes going into churches, 'some place where you stop and think about life'.[2] For many people the parish church will prompt memories of events in a person's life, including funerals which they may have attended. In this way the parish includes the dead as well as the living. According to geographer Kevin Whelan:

> the parish was not just a functional entity: it was a symbolic force of some depth and power. For many people, it was the ultimate world, in that they never spent a night outside its confines. The great rites of passage – birth, marriage, death – had intimate links with the chapel.[3]

The arrival of Covid-19 in Ireland on 29 February 2020 led to the cessation of public Masses, the deferral of most sacraments and strict limitation on the numbers attending weddings and funeral services. As the public vaccination campaign progressed restrictions were gradually eased.

Mass Attendance

The Irish word for Sunday is An Domhnach or Dia Domhnaigh, meaning the Lord's Day, whereas the English word, Sunday, derives from the tradition of sun worship or worshipping the god of the sun. Easter Sunday is known in Irish as An Domhnach Mór or the Great Day of the Lord. Since the nineteenth century, when possible, attendance at Sunday Mass in the local parish church was a central feature of individual and community life in Ireland. After Mass, news could be exchanged and stories shared. For many decades newsvendors would have stands outside the church where Sunday newspapers were on sale.

Historically, people from every sphere of life recognised the commitment of the Irish to the Mass. Famously, Augustine Birrell, Chief Secretary for Ireland, 1907–16, expressed that sentiment when leaving in 1916:

> It is the Mass that matters. It is the Mass that makes the difference: so hard to define; so subtle it is yet so perceptible between a Catholic country and a Protestant one; between Dublin and Edinburgh.[4]

Decades later, champion jockey Kieren Fallon captured the centrality of Mass-going in his childhood in Co. Clare in the early 1970s:

> We just had one family ritual, which was going to Mass every Sunday, either in Crusheen or up in Ballinruan.

> Religion was a big thing back then. Not like today. It's all changed now. You had to go but you enjoyed going. If you missed it, it was like something bad was going to happen. But it was a social occasion as much as anything else. It was something that bound the community together.[5]

Non-attendance at Mass was visible: 'the black sheep is very conspicuous in the country.'[6] Much had changed by the late twentieth century when the Benedictine priest Fr Vincent Ryan said that the 'culture of Sunday' associated with going to Mass, wearing one's 'Sunday best', abstaining from 'servile work' and spending time with family had vanished.[7] The Saturday Vigil Mass, partly to facilitate workers, together with the widespread increase in Sunday trading, changed the rhythm of Sunday, which for many people is now like any other day. An example of the secularisation of Sunday was illustrated by the 2020 general election – the first time in the history of the State that a general election was held on Saturday followed by the work of counting the votes taking place on Sunday.

In a study of Irish Catholicism, published in 2002,[8] Louise Fuller quotes data from two surveys of religious practice carried out in 1973–74 and in 1988–89 in the Republic. Both surveys show that the percentage who said that they went to Mass once a week was surprisingly stable at 67 per cent. However, data on Mass attendance for Sunday (including Saturday Vigil) obtained from six dioceses in 2016 generally showed a marked fall in attendance compared with 1988–89.[9] The six were the Archdioceses of

Cashel and Emly and of Dublin together with the Dioceses of Clonfert, Kerry, Killala and Killaloe. All six dioceses recorded fairly modest attendance levels, although there was high attendance in some individual parishes. For example, in the Diocese of Cashel and Emly, based on average attendance in all parishes over a three-week period in 2013, Mass attendance represented 31 per cent of the Catholic population, but in individual parishes within the diocese attendance ranged from a low of 13 per cent to a high of 62 per cent. In the Kerry Diocese in 2014 Mass attendance in parishes ranged from 20 to 70 per cent. Sunday Mass attendance (including Saturday Vigil Mass) in Dublin between 2008 and 2014 showed a marked decline. In 2008 total attendance was 186,212. Six years later, in 2014, total attendance was 151,257, a decline of 35,000, or close to 20 per cent. Speaking in Würzburg in July 2017, Archbishop Diarmuid Martin gave a picture of further decline. He said that 'there are parishes in Dublin where the presence at Sunday Mass is some 5 percent of the Catholic population and in some cases, even below 2 percent.'[10] The archbishop said that on any particular Sunday about 18 per cent of the Catholic population of the archdiocese attends Mass. A small number of parishes in Dublin bucked the trend and showed increases, including Laurel Lodge and University Church. Among other parishes which registered increases were Gardiner Street, where there is a vibrant African community and a Gospel choir, and Harrington Street, which celebrates the Latin Mass.

It is difficult to reconcile the decline in Mass attendance with the substantial, although declining, proportion of the population which defines itself as Catholic in the census. One interpretation was suggested by Bishop Eamonn Walsh, who drew a distinction between attendance and membership. Many who regard themselves as members of the Church show poor rates of attendance – rather as one might be a member of a sports club and identify with the club yet have a poor attendance record at matches.[11] One occasion when many churches are relatively full for Mass is at Christmas, a time when family and community bonds are affirmed in the shared celebration.

As the number attending Mass declines, excess capacity in church buildings becomes very apparent. Parochial churches in Dublin and other urban areas were mostly built to accommodate much larger numbers than those currently in attendance. To take some examples from information provided by the Archdiocese of Dublin: the capacity of the church in Athy, Co. Kildare, is 1,000. At the four Masses which were celebrated weekly for Sunday/Vigil Mass in 2014, total attendance was 826 while total capacity for four Masses was 4,000, giving a ratio of utilisation to capacity of 21 per cent.

Finglas West and Mourne Road in Dublin both have a capacity of 2,000. The utilisation ratio for Finglas West in 2014 was 10 per cent and slightly less for Mourne Road. The Church of Our Lady of Victories, Ballymun, has a capacity of 1,900. The potential capacity for five Masses is therefore 9,500. The total attendance was 1,412 in 2014, or just 15 per cent of total capacity. The figure is even starker for Westland Row, with a capacity of 1,700, or 8,500 for five Masses. The ratio there was 7 per cent.

The practice of having Mass celebrated in people's homes goes back to penal times. According to Fr Vincent Ryan, towards the end of the penal days and throughout the nineteenth century, the custom took on the form of the Station Mass, a peculiarly Irish phenomenon.[12] In each parish or townland houses were designated for the Stations, which usually took place twice a year, before Christmas and before Easter. Neighbours were invited to join in the Mass and to receive Confession. John Scally, who remembers Station Masses from his childhood, says that it was also a social event. 'This sharing of gossip and humour helped to keep the community alive, but also revealed the heartache and quiet desperation that underlined so many lives in the parish.'[13] At the Synod of Thurles in 1850 Cardinal Cullen, then in Armagh and due to become Archbishop of Dublin in 1852, objected to Station Masses on grounds of alleged abuses, possibly related to the consumption of alcohol. Even in remote areas of the Dublin Diocese the policy was to remove Station Masses to the local parish church. In dioceses apart from Dublin, Station Masses continued. However, where Dublin led, other dioceses eventually followed, and Station Masses became more or less extinct – although not entirely. In a letter sent to friends in 2016, some months before his death, Mr Justice Dermot Kinlen, who owned a home in Sneem in Co. Kerry, wrote about his Station: 'I get the honour every seven years when I must give a party for all my neighbours. Cardinal Cullen the Papal Legate tried to abolish it but the feisty bishops of Kerry and Tuam ignored it. All neighbours were welcome. A sense of community flowered.'[14] Former TD, senator and MEP John Horgan has suggested that Station Masses 'could recharge Christian batteries in extraordinary ways'.[15] And, in the words of Dermot Kinlen, a sense of community could flower.

One of the perhaps unforeseen outcomes of the concentration on the Mass as the central liturgy since Vatican II has been the decline in popular devotions. Since Vatican II 'the Mass has become the only form of public worship for many, if not most, believers.' Among the well-practised popular devotions before Vatican II were the Rosary, the Stations of the Cross, the Holy Hour and Benediction.[16] Micheál Mac Gréil found in the Tuam Diocese that the practice of Benediction was vanishing.

The Sacraments

The Synod of Thurles, which took place during the pontificate of Pius IX (1846–78), was held from 22 August to 9 September 1850. The synod included among its aims the standardisation of administrative and sacramental practices in Ireland. An example of administrative standardisation was that each parish was mandated to provide a parochial house for the parish priest. The expansion of church building which took place during the pontificate of Pius IX facilitated the celebration of sacraments in a church. Msgr Ciarán O'Carroll, former rector of the Irish College in Rome and now administrator of Donnybrook Parish in Dublin, said, 'During the era of the penal laws the sacraments of baptism, marriage and reconciliation were celebrated mostly in private homes, and these practices continued into the mid-nineteenth century.'[17] From the latter part of the nineteenth century, sacraments, traditionally celebrated in the home, made their way to the church. The Synod of Thurles laid down that baptism should normally take place in a church and the hierarchy allowed few exceptions. 'The practice of marriage in a church with Mass and the nuptial blessing, spread more unevenly, but it too became the rule.'[18] The traditional funeral Mass in the house also drifted slowly towards the church. Removals to the church were introduced in Ireland in 1896 because the bishops wished to curb the 'disrespectful carry on', presumably alcohol-related, that was occurring in homes. In 1917 the new *Code of Canon Law* laid down that 'all funeral rites must take place in the church'.[19] Now, in the twenty-first century, the trend is once more shifting away from a removal to the church on the evening prior to the funeral Mass: frequently the deceased will be taken from his or her home, or from a funeral home, directly to the church for the funeral Mass.[20]

Irish literature abounds with priests and sacraments. A number of short stories by Irish writers focus on one or other of the sacraments and illustrate the extent to which the sacraments permeated everyday life. In Frank O'Connor's story 'First Confession' he vividly describes preparation for the sacrament – the threats of hell, the threats of his sister, then the event itself when he unburdened the 'sins of a lifetime' to the priest. The story tells how the young boy Jackie is frightened to make his First Confession because he had plans of killing his grandmother and his sister Nora, who were both a source of grief to him. He meets a priest, who sees Nora hitting him and instantly grasps the situation. The priest advises Jackie that it's never worth killing grandmothers because hanging is a 'horrible death'. The priest spends a full ten minutes with him, 'and then walked out the chapel yard with me. I was genuinely sorry to part with him, because he was the most entertaining character I'd ever met in the religious line.'

Bryan MacMahon's story of First Communion is called 'The Holy Kiss'. It concerns the first kiss a child gives after receiving First Communion. In his story MacMahon conveys the deep awe felt by the people for Holy Communion. He describes how a child is brought from his Communion in the church to his mother who is ill at home:

> And the kiss is snatched with a passion far outmatching the marriage kiss which it exceeds by the same measure as the spirit transcends the body. It is as if the mother were to say: 'Here, Glory be to God, I have reaped the first of conscious purity. I am greedy to snatch the lips that have held the Lord. Here is the reward of travail.'

Similarly with Confirmation, Brendan Behan, in his story 'The Confirmation Suit', shows how Confirmation was a central event in his childhood:

> The big fellows, who were thirteen and veterans of last year's Confirmation, frightened us, and said the Bishop would fire us out of the chapel if we didn't answer his questions.

Not long afterwards Behan tells how he wore his Confirmation suit to the funeral of the woman who made it:

> At the funeral, I left my topcoat in the carriage and got out and walked in the spills of rain after her coffin. People said I would get my end, but I went on till we reached the graveside, and I stood in my Confirmation suit drenched to the skin. I thought it was the least I could do.

Baptism

Baptism is the portal into the Christian community and is also the 'naming' ceremony for the child. In the past when a child was presented for baptism in a Catholic church it was assumed that the child was coming from a Catholic home and would be brought up as a Catholic. In many contemporary cases the reality of that assumption is less certain. It is possible that some children may be baptised in order to improve their chances of a place in a Catholic primary school.

Mac Gréil considers that the sacraments of baptism, penance, Communion and Confirmation continue to be important 'rites of passage' for children and for their parents. While Deputy Maureen O'Sullivan says that there is solid evidence in the north inner-city area of Dublin that the sacraments of baptism and marriage continue as important markers on life's journey. In the case of baptism there is a sense in which the child becomes part of the community. Funerals are of great importance, as are First Holy Communions, although in the years of the Celtic Tiger emphasis on First Communion as a social event undoubtedly increased.[21] Deputy O'Sullivan says that the parishes within her constituency have been lucky in their priests, who have had a focus on social justice and have always supported families regardless of parental status. In turn, the people, regardless of whether they attend church, have been supportive of the priests. She cites the example of North Wall Parish (Sheriff Street), where the weekly collection made at Masses for the support of the priests is three times the second collection, much of which goes on diocesan administration.

Table 3: Baptisms in Twelve Dioceses 2000 and 2014

Diocese	2000	2014
Armagh	3,163	3,856
Elphin	510 (2005)	819
Clogher	1,262	1,567
Cloyne	1,708	2,361 (2013)
Kildare and Leighlin	4,446 (2007)	4,684 (2012)
Dublin	16,235	16,548 (2013)
Ferns	1,774 (2002)	1,974 (2012)
Down and Connor	4,724 (2006)	4,963
Killala	441	549
Killaloe	1,762	2,219 (2010)
Kilmore	871	1,145
Raphoe	1,311	1,422

Source: Diocesan data. When data do not refer to 2000 or 2014, the year is given in brackets.

The principal records of the Catholic Church in Ireland relate to baptisms and marriages.[22] Data were sought directly from all twenty-six dioceses of Ireland, North and South.[23] At least some information was received from twenty-two dioceses. Table 3 shows that, in the twelve dioceses listed, the number of baptisms increased in the early years of the twenty-first century. This may be assumed to be related to the increase in births, including those of children born to Catholic immigrants.

Confession (the Sacrament of Penance and Reconciliation)

The *Catechism of the Catholic Church* refers to the Sacrament of Penance and Reconciliation while the *Code of Canon Law* uses the older term Confession. No statistics are available on Confession but a huge fall in numbers has been observed. It seems that in the decades since Vatican II the sacrament of Confession has all but disappeared. The long lines outside Confession boxes on Saturday evenings in parish churches have vanished. However, in some churches, including Clarendon Street and Merrion Road in Dublin, the frequent availability of Confession may act as an encouragement to partake of the sacrament. According to Mac Gréil's study, monthly Confession was the norm for 60 per cent of adult Catholics in the early 1970s. Today the norm might be once or twice a year, with a growing percentage going rarely, if ever. At one time it was unusual to receive Communion without first going to Confession. Now the reverse is the case.

It is difficult to determine precisely why Confession in any form has gone so much out of fashion. Some blame the abuse scandals for a general disillusion with the Church and with Confession in particular. Others speculate that in the past huge stress was placed on sin associated with sexual behaviour – 'living together/living in sin', giving birth out of wedlock/illegitimacy, using contraceptives, obtaining a divorce. The encyclical *Humanae Vitae* (1968), which repeated the ban on artificial contraception, became for many a litmus test of 'relevancy'. Fr Enda McDonagh, Professor of Moral Theology at Maynooth University, suggested that the encyclical was the main reason that the Catholic Church lost its dominance in Irish life.[24] It seems that the encyclical has been largely ignored by the generations born after *Humanae Vitae*. A Church which bans artificial contraception and regards cohabitation as mortally sinful and homosexual acts as intrinsically evil seems alien to the realities of life of many people. The suggestion by Pope Francis that unions between same-sex couples could be recognised in civil partnerships signalled a move to draw a line between Church and State. Campaigners for both marriage equality and the repeal of the Eighth Amendment of the Constitution came from all age groups. The marriage equality referendum was carried by 62.07 per cent and the repeal of the Eight Amendment referendum was carried by 66.4 per cent. While the biggest percentages of 'Yes' voters were among the younger voters, the proportion of older voters in favour of marriage equality was striking and demonstrates a continuum of disaffection from the teaching of the Catholic Church on these matters.

Augustinian priest Fr Iggy O'Donovan, based in Fethard, Co. Tipperary, claims that when the people rejected sexual sin they also rejected Confession.

O'Donovan says that, following independence, 'throne and altar conspired to create an atmosphere of anti-sexual terrorism. … The day the Irish people threw off those shackles was the day Confession collapsed.'[25] Not everyone agrees with O'Donovan. A Redemptorist priest in Galway, Fr Clement Mac Mánuis, said that he was struck by the number of people who said they were going to Confession more regularly. To some degree Confession provides an alternative to counsellors.[26] Novel approaches are being adopted by some priests; for example, on the afternoon of Holy Saturday 2017 seven priests from the Maynooth Deanery[27] were available for Confession in the Liffey Valley Shopping Centre.

Parish missions, retreats and novenas, which often carried warnings of hellfire, were once a regular feature of parish life. An intrinsic component of the parish mission, or retreat, was reception of the sacrament of Confession. One of the most memorable episodes in modern Irish literature is the school retreat conducted by a priest in the Jesuit Belvedere College in *A Portrait of the Artist as a Young Man* with its depiction of hell where fires rage eternally and there is a stench of rotting bodies. But missions have dwindled, if not disappeared, in many parishes, together with school retreats. The Redemptorists in Limerick were once renowned as retreat-givers. They tended to warn of fire and brimstone if the laws of God were contravened. By the 1970s, following Vatican II, the tone had changed.[28] Novenas, when special prayers are recited over nine days, have continued over the years; for example, the Novena of Grace in St Francis Xavier Church in Gardiner Street in Dublin, the Galway Novena to Our Lady of Perpetual Succour held in Galway Cathedral and the National Novena at Knock Shrine. These novenas, during which Confession would generally be available, continue to attract large numbers.

First Communion

Preparation for the sacraments of Confession, First Communion and Confirmation is usually undertaken in school and reception of these sacraments is closely linked with attendance at Catholic schools. One aspect of First Communion which had grown markedly in recent years until the Covid-19 pandemic is the aspect of social celebration. It was common to find hotels offering First Communion and Confirmation lunches while outfits, especially dresses for girls, have become increasingly elaborate. According to long-standing practice, First Communicants visit friends and relatives from whom they generally receive gifts of money. What is remarkable for the communicants of today is the quantity of money collected. *The Irish*

Times writer Patsy McGarry refers to an Ulster Bank Communion survey of 189 parents in 2017 which showed the average amount collected by children receiving First Communion was €570, an increase from €546 in 2016. According to the survey, almost one in four children in 2017 received over €800 and one in eight received over €1,000.[29] In an interview in the *Sunday Business Post* in 2017, Minister for Social Protection Regina Doherty spoke about going from her First Communion ceremony to the Fine Gael Ard Fheis with her parents and getting 'a good few bob' on the occasion.[30] Also in the *Sunday Business Post*, an events planner is quoted as saying that the 'average' sum spent on a First Communion is €1,500.[31] Celebration in the wake of church events is not new. Corish says that as long ago as the sixteenth century, Church authorities 'expressed concern at the lavish feasting which took place at baptisms and funerals'.[32]

The increasingly material aspects associated with First Communion, at least until the onset of Covid-19, have been subject to criticism by a number of priests, including Fr Paddy O'Kane, parish priest of Ballymagroarty in the Derry Diocese,[33] and Fr Tom Little, parish priest in the Parish of Askea and Bennekerry in Co. Carlow.[34] Collecting money at a landmark religious event is not exclusive to Catholicism. In the Jewish faith, bar mitzvah comes at a later age than First Communion or Confirmation, around fourteen, and is also associated with the receipt of money gifts. For example, former Minister for Justice Alan Shatter, who describes himself as a cultural Jew, records that he received cheques from family friends at his bar mitzvah and that the money was deposited in the Bank of Ireland.[35]

Confirmation

The sacrament of Confirmation is traditionally administered to children between the ages of eleven and twelve, at the end of primary school. The sacrament is conferred by the bishop and is therefore a diocesan, rather than a parish, event. Frequently, however, the bishop delegates the function to a priest as he may be unable to carry out all Confirmations himself. Confirmation is intended to mark a point of maturity in the young Christian but often it can mark the point at which disengagement from the Church begins. For decades 'taking the pledge', whereby young people would pledge to abstain from alcoholic drink until the age of eighteen years (the minimum legal age at which alcohol may be bought or consumed in Ireland), occurred at the time of the Confirmation ceremony. In 2015 the Irish bishops proposed the introduction of a Confirmation 'commitment' as an alternative to the pledge. The commitment was to a healthy lifestyle and the Confirmation sponsor, who presents the child to the bishop for Confirmation, was to engage with the process and undertake to be a role model.

Archbishop Diarmuid Martin believes that the sacrament of Confirmation is being eclipsed by social celebration and has described Confirmation as 'becoming like a school party':

> In primary school every child in the class makes their communion and their confirmation, with few exceptions. Confirmation is becoming like a school party, where everyone participates and feels left out if they don't. I had a letter from the HSE asking me why a Muslim child wasn't allowed to do her confirmation.[36]

According to Church teaching, Confirmation is the sacrament which enables the confirmed to fulfil their role in the Church and to help spread the message of the Gospel. Instead it has become something of a step on the road to a terminus when religious practice ends. This is borne out by a study of young people under the age of twenty-five years, undertaken at the Jesuit Georgetown University in the US and entitled 'Going, Going, Gone', which shows that the median age for 'disaffiliation' from the Church is thirteen.[37]

What's Happening to Marriage?

The population of the Republic of Ireland has risen substantially since 2000, when it was below 4 million; it is now close to 5 million. Since 2000 the total number of marriages has increased but the total number of Catholic Church marriages has fallen. Falls in the number of Catholic Church marriages have been recorded in about half the dioceses, with sharp falls in Dublin city and Limerick city. At one time marriage was the almost universal precursor of giving birth but that has changed; by 2017, 23,340 births, or 37.6 per cent of total births, were outside marriage.

Over the period of nearly 100 years between 1920 and 2017 the annual total number of marriages increased by almost 3,500, from 26,826 to 30,321. Marriages in the Republic of Ireland were responsible for the overall increase; in Northern Ireland the number of marriages fell. In 2017, the year following the marriage equality referendum, there were 22,021 marriages in the Republic, including 759 same-sex marriages. Although the number of marriages has risen in the Republic, the marriage rate, that is, marriages per 1,000 of population, at 4.8, is the same as it was 150 years ago in 1864 when records began. The rate peaked at 7.4 per 1,000 in 1973 but has dropped back since then.

In both Northern Ireland and the Republic there have been marked increases in the number of civil marriages (see Figures 2 and 3). In Northern Ireland the share of civil marriages rose from 5.4 per cent in 1920 to 35.5 per cent in 2017. In the Republic the share of civil ceremony marriages rose from less than 1 per cent in 1920 to 29 per cent (over 6,000 marriages) in 2017. Rates for civil marriages varied across the country, from about 10 per cent of marriages in Donegal to over 50 per cent in Dublin. In over 2,000 marriages, or 10 per cent of total marriages, in the Republic in 2017, at least one member of the couple was a divorced person.

Tables 4 and 5 show Catholic and civil marriages as a proportion of total marriages in Northern Ireland and the Republic of Ireland over the period 1920–2017. A feature to emerge from the long-term data is the increase in the share of Catholic marriages in the Northern total, from 30 per cent in 1920 to 45 per cent in 1980, followed by a steady fall back to 32 per cent in 2017, just slightly higher than the share in 1920. This compares with the very

Table 4: Marriages, Catholic and Civil, in Irish Free State/Republic of Ireland 1920–2017

Year	FS/ROI Total	FS/ROI % Catholic	FS/ROI % Civil Ceremony
1920	17,276	91	< 1
1940	15,212	94	< 1
1960	15,465	96	< 1
1980	22,180	94	3
2000	19,667	80	16
2010	20,594	67	29
2017	22,021	51	29

Table 5: Marriages, Catholic and Civil, in Northern Ireland 1920–2017

Year	NI Total	NI % Catholic	NI % Civil Ceremony
1920	9,550	30	5.4
1940	9,795	31	6.9
1960	9,881	33	4.8
1980	11,034	45	11.2
2000	7,584	38	25.2
2010	8,156	36	30.1
2017	8,300	32	35.5

Source: 1920–1980: *Irish Catholic Directory*, various years; 2000–16: Northern Ireland Statistics and Research Agency (Northern Ireland); Central Statistics Office (Republic of Ireland).

Figure 2: Marriages, Catholic and Civil, in Irish Free State/Republic of Ireland 1920–2017

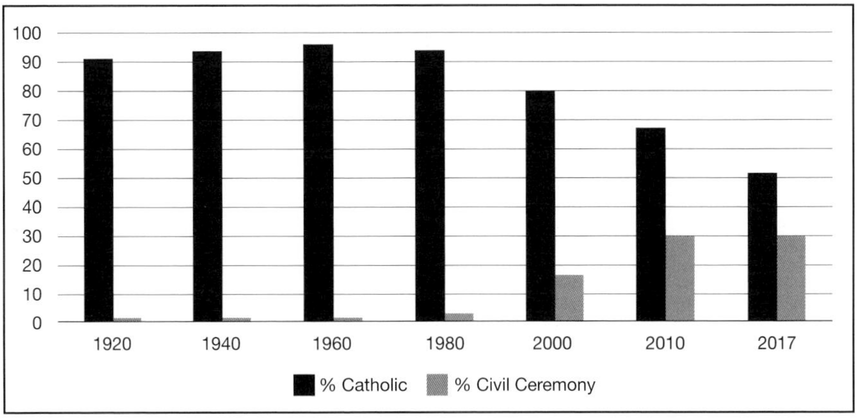

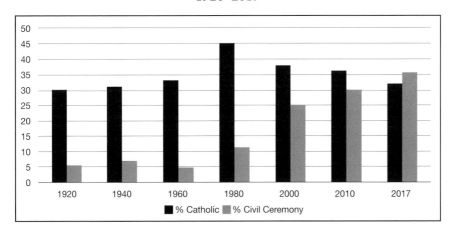

Figure 3: Marriages, Catholic and Civil, in Northern Ireland 1920–2017

steep decline in the share of Catholic marriages in the Republic, from 91 per cent in 1920 and 96 per cent in 1960 to slightly over 50 per cent in 2017. The rate fell further, to below 50 per cent, in 2018.

Table 6 shows marriages in the Republic of Ireland in 2017 by form of ceremony. Roman Catholic ceremonies accounted for just half of total marriages while civil ceremonies accounted for almost 30 per cent. The growth in civil ceremonies has been marked in the past fifty years. When Ireland joined the EEC in 1973, civil ceremonies comprised less than 1 per cent of the total.[38] Other forms of ceremony, including humanist and spiritualist, have been growing in popularity. Spiritualist ceremonies may appeal to those who believe in a spiritual dimension to life but do not follow any particular religion. Many marriages are now taking place in hotels with a licensed wedding minister. The facility to have the wedding reception in the same premises as the wedding ceremony appeals to some. More exotic ceremonies are to be found also.[39]

In the context of the numbers classified as Catholic in the census data, and given the steady increase in those opting for civil marriage ceremonies, it is not surprising that attendance at the parish church is dwindling. At a time when many options are available, church marriages should be a reasonably good barometer of church participation. It is a free choice by two adults to marry in church, which implies a degree of commitment to the Church.

Table 6: Marriage by Form of Ceremony in Republic of Ireland 2017

Form of Ceremony	Number	Per cent of Total
Roman Catholic	11,219	51.0
Civil Ceremonies	6,417	29.1
Humanist Association	1,727	7.8
Spiritualist Union of Ireland	1,159	5.3
Church of Ireland	379	1.6
Other Religious Ceremony	1,120	5.2
Total	22,021	100.0

Source: Central Statistics Office.

Table 7 shows marriages in certain parish churches in the Dublin Archdiocese in 1992 and 2012. The data show a marked decline in the number of church marriages in those parishes, although care must be taken with interpreting the data. A certain church, because of size or location, may be the preferred venue for a wedding even if it is not the parish church of either party to the marriage. University Church in Dublin is one such example. A very large church may be regarded as unattractive as guests might occupy only a small portion of the building, although this could become an asset in the future with mandatory social distancing for health purposes. There is also the practice of selecting churches outside Dublin which are adjacent to desirable venues for the wedding reception. For example, one Dublin priest reported completing nearly forty prenuptial enquiry forms which stated that the prospective bride/groom had been baptised and confirmed, but he had solemnised just two marriages in his parish.

Cratloe Parish in the Diocese of Limerick illustrates how difficult it is to establish meaningful marriage trends on a single-parish basis. This is due to

Table 7: Marriages in Certain Parishes in Dublin Archdiocese 1992 and 2012

	1992	*2012*	*% change*
Total Archdiocese	4,735	2,476	−47.7
	Ranked by highest in 1992		
University Church	151	74	
Swords	123	17	
Sandyford	120	83	
Mount Argus	85	16	
Ballybrack	80	20	
Finglas West (Annunciation)	77	14	
Crumlin	75	26	
Finglas (St Margaret's)	71	26	
Larkhill/Whitehall	71	15	
Greenhills	68	14	
Total – 10 Parishes	**921**	**305**	**−66.9**
	Ranked by lowest in 2012		
Merrion Road	7	0	
Ardlea	39	2	
Artane	15	3	
Dundrum	40	7	
Ballyroan	27	7	
Blackrock	26	11	
Ballyfermot Assumption	51	12	
Ballymun Road	56	13	
Ballyfermot Upper	55	14	
Greenhills	68	14	
Total – 10 Parishes	**384**	**83**	**−78**

Source: Data supplied by the Archdiocese.

the unique history of each individual parish. In Cratloe in 1976 twenty-one marriages were recorded. For the next ten years marriages remained stable, until the number plummeted to four in 1988. But within a couple of years the number increased, jumping to 41 in 1991, and soaring to 134 in 2006. Then the number dropped to 95 in 2009. Behind these merry-go-round figures is the fact that in the late 1980s there were plans to demolish the church. This generated a great deal of controversy as the building was judged to be of architectural importance. According to Limerick Diocesan archivist David Bracken, the church in Cratloe, originally an old 'barn' church, was restored and became a popular venue for weddings, with couples travelling from all over Ireland to be married there. Adare is another parish in Limerick with a relatively high level of marriages. It is a picturesque location with a number of quality hotels and therefore an attractive wedding venue both for those who live nearby and for those who come from a distance. A striking consequence of the Covid-19 pandemic is that it has led to 'simpler sacraments'. Under mid-level restrictions (level 3), attendance at weddings was limited to twenty-five, with consequences for those who had planned bigger weddings. Other sacraments were affected also: attendance at Confirmation was limited to eleven children, with a total of fifty persons in the church. Often the sacrament of Confirmation was conferred in the evening time, which restricted the time for post-Confirmation celebration. Many First Communions were rescheduled for later in the year.

A comparable trend of decline in Catholic marriages is found in England and Wales, where the number of Catholic marriages has fallen by more than two-thirds in the last twenty-five years. According to data published by the Office of National Statistics, there were just over 7,000 Catholic marriages in 2015, compared with more than three times that number in 1990. These statistics do not take account of church marriages known as convalidations for those who have already had a civil wedding, but the trend is clear. Over the same period of 1990–2015 Anglican weddings in England and Wales fell by 60 per cent, from 115,000 to 46,000. The same pattern of decline in church weddings is found in the United States, where the number of marriages celebrated in Catholic churches fell by 60 per cent between 1972 and 2011, from 415,500 to 165,500.[40]

Funerals

The presence of a priest at a person's deathbed was part of Irish Catholic tradition for generations. This is captured in Yeats's poem 'The Ballad of Father Gilligan', which tells how an old priest, exhausted from tending to dying parishioners during the Great Famine, fell asleep, although requested to the deathbed of another man. When he awoke he went immediately to the man's house. The dead man's widow greets him with the words 'Father! You come again!' and says that the man had died 'as merry as a bird' following the priest's earlier visit, which it transpires had been a miraculous one.

The coincidence of priest and deathbed is also captured by Seamus Heaney in his poem commemorating his mother's death, 'When All the Others Were Away at Mass':

So while the parish priest at her bedside
Went hammer and tongs at the prayers for the dying
And some were responding and some crying
I remembered her head bent towards my head,
Her breath in mine, our fluent dipping knives –
Never closer the whole rest of our lives.

The poem, from which the above quotation is one verse, was voted Ireland's best-loved poem of the last 100 years in 2015. At the poet's own funeral in Donnybrook Church in Dublin in August 2013, the church was overflowing for both the removal service and funeral Mass. Heaney's wife, Marie, said afterwards that Heaney had asked for a traditional requiem Mass. 'For him it gave to people a sense of transcendence, a sense of something beyond us even though you may not believe in it.'[41] Likewise the writer and non-believer John McGahern, whose short story 'The Country Funeral' counts among his finest writing, had a traditional Church funeral in Leitrim in 2006. Another writer, Maeve Binchy, who said that she had lost her faith, died in 2012. She also had a church funeral in Dalkey, where she lived. The phenomenon of non-believers having church funerals is not just an Irish one. For example, the funeral of the professed atheist and renowned scientist Stephen Hawking was held in Great St Mary's, the University Church of the Church of England in Cambridge.

Seán Ó Ríordáin's most famous poem, 'Adhlacadh Mo Mháthar' ('The Burial of My Mother'), moves from a sunlit orchard in June to a snow-covered graveyard where his mother was buried six months earlier. For the poet a robin brings 'the air of Paradise'. The funerals of well-known men and women – for example, Parnell, O'Donovan Rossa, Collins and Hyde – have become landmarks in history. The funerals of hunger strikers Terence MacSwiney and Bobby Sands and of Republican Martin McGuinness were exceptional events with enormous attendances. The funeral Mass of Seamus Mallon, which took place in his parish church close to Markethill in Co. Armagh, drew attendance across the religious and political spectrum in recognition of his role as a peacemaker.

Humanist weddings are more common than humanist funerals. In 2015 the Humanist Association of Ireland conducted 1,280 weddings, compared with 97 funeral services. Former government minister and Honorary President of the Humanist Association of Ireland Justin Keating had a humanist funeral in 2010. In October 2015, when playwright Brian Friel died, there was no church service, although Fr Pat Prendergast, parish priest in the Glenties in Donegal, where Friel was buried, had helped to select the burial place. When the actress Anita Reeves died in July 2016 a humanist ceremony was held in Dublin's Mansion House, led by celebrant Susie Kennedy.[42] In May 2018, when playwright Tom Murphy died, a humanist service was conducted in the Mansion House in Dublin prior to cremation.

According to one funeral director around 15 per cent of funerals in Ireland are taking place outside of a Church setting.[43] Although there is a move towards non-religious funerals, churches are generally attractive locations in which to hold funeral services and it can happen that non-believers select a church location with the agreement of the local priest. In October 2016 the Dublin Archdiocese published a document on funeral ministry policy. The document 'looks to the future when the lay faithful will be more centrally involved in carrying out this ministry in our parishes. It also acknowledges the relative distance of many people from parish life and religious practice in recent times.'[44] Bishop Laurence Duffy, who was installed as Bishop of Clogher in early 2019, has announced his intention to invite laypeople to fulfil parts of funeral liturgies because of a lack of priests. Already three parishes in his diocese are without a priest.[45]

Cemetery Sunday and Pattern Days

During the summer months all over rural Ireland and in some urban areas, Cemetery Sunday is celebrated. In the words of journalist Rosita Boland:

> This is the day of the year when long-scattered families come together with those who have remained in the area, and for one significant day, they briefly form a community again, as they honour their dead relatives. A special Mass is followed by blessing of the graves, which will have been cleaned and tidied in the preceding days.[46]

In the days preceding the designated Sunday relatives visit the cemetery and tidy the graves of their relatives and of those who have no relatives on hand to do the job. On the day itself Mass is celebrated and the graves blessed, and prayers are said for the dead. All generations, from the youngest to the oldest, are present, as well as some who have returned from overseas for the occasion. One of those who spoke to Boland said, 'Cemetery Sunday brings the whole parish together in one day.'[47] A pattern day is a day when special prayers and devotions take place in a parish in honour of the patron saint (in Irish, patrún) of the parish. The event takes place either on the feast day of the patron saint or on the nearest Sunday, which is called 'Pattern Sunday'. In addition to prayers and devotions, a pattern would include music and dancing, resulting in a type of parish festival bringing the people together.

Pilgrimages and Processions

The tradition of pilgrimage remains strong in Ireland, with many parishes organising, or promoting, pilgrimages to Knock, Lough Derg, Croagh Patrick, Lourdes, Fatima, the Holy Land and other destinations. Groups within parishes – for example, the Scouts – have organised numerous pilgrimages to Lourdes. Also, pupils from a number of schools go to Lourdes as helpers for the sick. The annual pilgrimage to climb Croagh Patrick has taken place for centuries. To some extent charity cycles and walks for good causes such as suicide prevention are the new pilgrimages. The best-known pilgrim path in Europe is the Camino de Santiago de Compostela, attracting very large numbers each year. St James's Gate[48] in Dublin, the site of the Guinness Brewery, was a historical starting point for Irish pilgrims.

Following a meeting in Nenagh in Co. Tipperary in 2013, a group called Pilgrim Paths Ireland (PPI) was founded. PPI represents community groups associated with the main pilgrim paths in Ireland. 'In 2016, a PPI initiative linked five medieval routes under a national pilgrim passport which must be completed to obtain the Teastas Oilithreachta (Pilgrim Certificate).'[49] There are currently a dozen routes, including Tóchar Phádraig (Patrick's Well) at Ballintubber Abbey in Co. Mayo, Cosáin na Naomh (Saints' Path) in Co. Kerry and St Kevin's Way in Co. Wicklow. Pilgrim Paths Week is an Easter-time festival aimed at giving thanks for the wonders of nature.

A survey of young people undertaken in the Dublin Archdiocese in preparation for the Synod of Bishops on 'Young People, the Faith and Vocational Discernment', held in Rome in October 2018, found that activities which mobilised groups of young people were a valuable means to engage them in faith-related activities.[50] As the phenomena of 'believing without belonging' and 'belonging without believing'[51] begin to take root, pilgrimages and related activities are gaining in popularity. Until the 1960s Corpus Christi processions and May processions took place in most parishes. For example, 'The ritual of the Corpus Christi Procession began in the church (St Nicholas of Myra) and brought a great sense of community to the streets in the Liberties.'[52] Often, elderly or sick parishioners, unable to attend Mass, would be brought out on to the streets by family and friends for a blessing during the procession.

Church of Ireland

In 2013 the Church of Ireland undertook the first census of its worshipping population.[53] The census was taken over three Sundays in November 2013. Average attendance at services on the three Sundays was 58,000, or 15.5 per cent of Church of Ireland membership as defined in the national census carried out by the Central Statistics Office. The Church of Ireland census also contained information on baptisms, Confirmations, weddings and funerals. In 2013 there were 3,700 baptisms. Ninety per cent of these were infant baptisms (0–3 years), 7 per cent were of children and young people (4–17), and the remaining 3 per cent were of adults. Also in 2013 there were 2,300 Confirmations in Church of Ireland churches. Ninety-two per cent of these were of children and young people and 8 per cent related to adults. In the same year there were 1,300 weddings and 3,500 funerals in Church of Ireland churches. The census report points out that 'Contrary to popular perception, the Church of Ireland conducts slightly more baptisms in an average year than funerals (3,700 baptisms to 3,500 funerals).'

3

Parish Groups

At least three types of group or society, predominantly composed of laity, originated in parishes.[1] The first group is directly related to the functioning of the parish and church services. This category includes pastoral councils, finance committees, sacristans, parish secretaries, ministers of the word, ministers of the Eucharist, choirs and organists, altar servers and church collectors. A second type of society has a religious motivation but the scope of these societies extends beyond the administrative functioning of the parish and a support role for the liturgy. These include the Society of St Vincent de Paul, the Legion of Mary and the Pioneer Total Abstinence Association (PTAA). A third group, originally parish-based, has over time adopted a broader designation than a specifically Catholic one; for example, Muintir na Tíre. The GAA officially welcomes those of all faiths and none, but historically has had a close association with the parish network of the Catholic Church, especially in rural areas. The parish school falls within the third category, which is dealt with in the next chapter. In practice the demarcation between the three categories is not entirely rigid. Sometimes a group, for example, a choir, may start as a specifically church-related activity and then develop a broader identity beyond the confines of the parish and church.

Parish Pastoral Councils

Parish pastoral councils were developed in the Catholic Church as a consequence of the Second Vatican Council, which sparked the desire to involve the laity more fully in the mission of the Church. A 'Parish Pastoral Council is a leadership group through which priests and people work together as partners in fulfilling the mission of Christ in their own place.'[2] The parish pastoral council envisions and plans for the spiritual and social needs of a particular parish. Membership of the council comprises the parish priest, curates, members selected by the parish in general and others co-opted for their expertise, as well as representatives of schools and other organisations.[3] In the Church of Ireland, where there has been a stronger tradition of lay participation in the administration of parish affairs, select vestries are groups chosen to manage and organise parish life. Until the mid to late nineteenth century, the vestries also had extensive roles in local government.

The usual model of pastoral council is based on a single parish. However, according to Bishop Eamonn Walsh, the decline in the number of priests has led to increased interest in parish community councils which may bridge a number of parishes.[4] For example, a parish community council exists in Hollywood in part of Co. Wicklow under Bishop Walsh's care. Among its activities the council organises the annual Hollywood Fair. For the past few years the fair has celebrated the rural heritage of pre-1950s life in Ireland. In 2016 there was a dramatic re-enactment of some of the events of 1916. An ecumenical service also took place in celebration of community harmony.

In many parishes a weekly parish newsletter is produced, often by the parish secretary. In addition to providing information about church services and information regarding recent baptisms, marriages and deaths, the newsletter may provide information relating to wider community activities. Such activities might include concerts with religious music or details regarding the planning work for entry into the Tidy Towns competition. Parishes throughout the country have websites with information on various activities within the parish. Some parishes produce an annual newsletter, or magazine, with articles about the life of the parish, past and present. A striking example of such a magazine is the *Tuosist Annual Newsletter*, which has been published for over twenty years and is the work of a voluntary committee. The parish of Tuosist is located near to Kenmare in Co. Kerry. Some parishes have video and radio links so that parishioners who are unwell or are housebound are able to follow church services from their homes. Video links may also enable people who have emigrated from the parish to watch services in the parish church from abroad, especially funerals and weddings.

Finance Committees: Parishes as Source of Church Income

Parishes play a critical role in the financial system of the Church. A major part of Church financing comes via parishes which collect funds and send a certain portion to the diocese, which in turn forwards funds to the Vatican. At parish Masses on Sundays and at the Saturday Vigil Masses there are generally two collections. The first or 'Common Fund' collection is for the maintenance of priests in ministry and for the support of retired priests. The second goes towards administrative and other costs of the diocese in which the parish is located. In Dublin in the 1970s Archbishop Dermot Ryan introduced the 'Share' collection as the second collection. For many years it was used to transfer funds to less well-off and developing parishes, mainly to help to build churches, but now a good proportion is spent on administration and diocesan running costs. Today falling attendance at Mass in the archdiocese is reflected in a marked decline in the collections. Total income in the Dublin Archdiocese fell by nearly 40 per cent between 2007 and 2014, from €86.2 million to €52.6 million. According to a report in *The Irish Catholic* in May 2017, 'Most Dublin parishes are struggling to stay afloat and many are not sustainable in the long term.'[5] The fall in income has been exacerbated by the effects of Covid-19, which led to church closures and/or suspension of services.

Parish churches are also an important venue for the annual collections of organisations such as Trócaire, which supports projects in developing countries, or Accord, which provides a marriage advisory service. One parish which has combined fundraising with community bonding in an original way is Barntown in Co. Wexford. A charity election for 'Mayor of Barntown', which aims to bring the community together at the same time as fundraising for the parish, is the brainchild of parish priest Fr John Carroll. The mayor acts as a 'first citizen' who both listens to and articulates the needs of parishioners. A number of people have volunteered to run for the role of mayor. Voting is on the basis of 'one euro, one vote'. A number of events are organised by the candidates and their supporters and all have a social dimension which brings the people of the parish together. Events include a treasure hunt in the national heritage park in the parish. Fr Carroll says that the contest for mayor is building community spirit:

> Anything that pulls people together and gives them a sense of who their neighbour is, where their community is, what their parish looks like … if you start to get that movement going, even if it never made money, it would start to reinforce local social capital, local Christian capital, local Catholic capital.[6]

Liturgy Groups, Choirs

Lay ministers of the word and lay ministers of the Eucharist exist in every parish. Sacristans and altar servers are less visible than lay ministers for a variety of reasons, partly economic in the case of sacristans and partly as a consequence of the child abuse scandals in the case of altar servers. Some parishes have excellent choirs and organists, the fruits of which have extended into the broader community. For example the foundation for Siamsa Tíre (Entertainment of the Land) was laid in 1957 when Fr (now Msgr) Pat Ahern founded a Gregorian choir in St John's Church in Tralee. In 2017 the choir celebrated its sixtieth anniversary. Some years after founding the choir, Ahern produced two major religious pageants – *Massabielle*, the story of Lourdes, and *Golgotha*, a Passion play. Following the success of the pageants, Ahern, together with some others, formed a group known as Siamsóirí na Ríochta (Entertainers of the Kingdom). Among its aims was the preservation of North Kerry traditions in music and dance, including those which accompanied traditional rural tasks; for example, threshing, churning and cobbling.

When Siamsa Tíre was established in 1974, Ahern became artistic director. He remained in the position until his retirement in 1998. At the heart of Ahern's plan was 'the fostering of traditional Irish folk culture in a series of Tithe Siamsa or Folk Academies located in strategic, tradition-rich parts of rural Ireland.'[7] Until 1991 Siamsa Tíre's principal locations included the Ashe Memorial Hall and the old Theatre Royal, both in Tralee. In 1991 a new theatre and arts centre was opened. A few years later another cultural initiative was taken by Msgr Pádraig Ó Fiannachta, a noted scholar, who became parish priest in Dingle, Co. Kerry, in 1992, following over three decades as professor in Maynooth. In 1996 he founded An Díseart, a centre for Irish spirituality and culture in Dingle.[8]

Another example of the growth of a choral society from a church choir is St Mary's Choral Society in Clonmel. RTÉ broadcaster Andy O'Mahony describes how in his family of 'grocers and spirit dealers', there was 'a special room reserved mainly for male members of the St Mary's Choral Society, a musical organisation founded in 1940 as an outgrowth of St Mary's parish church choir.'[9] They sang operatic choruses and assorted church music as well as popular songs of the period like 'On Moonlight Bay'. Among the tenors in the group 'was a teenage Frank Patterson, destined to become the most acclaimed Irish tenor since John McCormack'.[10] O'Mahony judged that the political arena was secondary to their lives; 'the real action was in the parish church and its environs.'[11] The Tallaght Choral Society (TCS), founded by Fr Dónal Sweeney in 1967 as a small church choir in the Dominican Priory in Tallaght, has grown into a major choir, giving performances in the National Concert Hall and at venues around Ireland and overseas. In 2017 the TCS celebrated its first fifty years with a performance of Mozart's *Requiem* in the National Concert Hall.

A successful music and drama Group in Meath Street in Dublin was founded by two local women, Joyce Reid and Madge Clabby, mother of singer Imelda May, in the 1980s in The Little Flower Hall in Meath Street Parish. The Little Flower Hall was well known for 'The Little Flower Penny Dinners' associated with the hall since 1912, and so named because the dinners which were provided for the needy were funded by weekly contributions of one penny from local families. In 1904 the Jesuits built a hall in Gardiner Street named the Francis Xavier Hall. The purpose of the hall was to provide a venue for lectures, concerts and drama which would be available to the less well-off. It was an objective supported by Labour leader Jim Larkin, who wanted to improve opportunities for Dublin workers and their families. In Dolphin's Barn Parish Church, adjacent to Francis Street in Dublin, a fifty-minute reading of Charles Dickens' *A Christmas Carol* was launched in 2013. The reading was the brainchild of the actor Michael Judd. It has become an annual event in which professional actors volunteer their time. The event takes place one Sunday in December and a collection is taken up for the Peter McVerry Trust for the Homeless.

The writer Peter Sheridan points to the school choir as a nursery for musical talent. In his introduction to *Dublin: The Heart of the City* he refers to St Laurence O'Toole's School, where Luke Kelly of The Dubliners learned to sing in the school choir.[12] Another example of the link between school music, this time in the case of a band, and the community is given by journalist Patsy McGarry. He described how, when he attended Ballaghaderreen primary school in Roscommon, the De La Salle Brothers held a bazaar before Christmas every year in the local parochial hall. Funds were raised for the primary school and also for the award-winning fife and drum band.[13]

A contemporary example of the use of street drama to interpret the Gospel as social drama is *The Passion Project* in Ballyfermot/Cherry Orchard in Dublin. *The Passion Project* was the idea of Joyce Jackson, the creative arts producer of the Ballyfermot Civic Centre.[14] The theme revolves around housing and homelessness.[15] The project drew on participants from local schools as well as some professional actors. The Men's Sheds[16] were involved with carpentry work for the show. While not a church event, the project was supported by the local parish. The Church of the Assumption in Ballyfermot was used as part of the venue, together with the surrounding grounds. Others involved included Dublin City Council and especially the Brokentalkers Theatre Company. Hundreds participated in a mixture of drama and music. *The Passion Project* journeyed through the streets of Ballyfermot Parish on Saturday 8 April and Sunday 9 April, the beginning of Holy Week, 2017.

Society of Saint Vincent de Paul

The Society of St Vincent de Paul was founded in Paris in 1833 by a student with a special interest in literary history, Frédéric Ozanam.[17] His observation then remains true today:

> The question which is agitating the world today is a social one. It is a struggle between those who have nothing and those who have too much. It is a violent clash of opulence and poverty which is shaking the ground under our feet. Our duty as Christians is to throw ourselves between these two camps in order to accomplish by love what justice alone cannot do.

In 1844, eleven years after its foundation in Paris, the society came to Ireland on the eve of the Great Famine. It arrived six years after the passing of the Poor Law (Ireland) Act 1838, which allowed for relief only within a workhouse (indoor relief). Frederick Lucas, editor of the English Catholic weekly *The Tablet*, wrote about the wretched conditions of the poor, while the *Freeman's Journal* wrote that the Poor Law would excite outrage.[18] Lucas, who had been at the initial meeting of the Society of St Vincent de Paul in London in January 1844, became an MP a few years later. He saw the society as a means of awakening in young men the care of those who were not well off:

> The Society of St Vincent de Paul habituates us early in life to the practice of Charity. It thus prepares a generation of men who will have learned, at the age of generous dispositions to see in the world other things besides themselves.[19]

Those who attended the first meeting in Ireland included John O'Hagan, first professor of political economy in Newman's Catholic University, and Bartholomew Woodlock, the priest who succeeded Newman as rector of the Catholic University and later became Bishop of Ardagh and Clonmacnoise. From its beginnings the society emphasised giving material aid but also sought to improve living conditions. One hundred and seventy years after its arrival in Ireland, Gerry Martin, who has written about the history of the society, said:

> In the Ireland of today, poverty may have changed its name to 'exclusion', but the role of the Society would still be recognised by those men whose names are contained in the first minute book.[20]

Membership of the society was at first for Catholic men but membership is no longer limited either to Catholics or to men. In 1968 provision was made for the acceptance of women and of other Christians as full members.[21] In describing its basic principles, the society says that it is:

> Catholic in character, it is open to all who wish to live their faith by loving and serving their neighbour. In some countries circumstances may lead to the acceptance of Christians of other beliefs, or other creeds who sincerely accept its principles.[22]

Rev. Trevor Sargent, a Church of Ireland clergyman who has participated in the St Vincent de Paul Society, says that the society looks at need without checking denomination and does not rest on denominational identity.[23]

There are now over 1,000 conferences (local units) of the St Vincent de Paul Society on the island of Ireland. There are approximately 11,000 volunteer members and 500 employees, including employees in the St Vincent de Paul charity shops.[24] Local volunteer members are complemented by professional staff who take care of general administration, run the 199 St Vincent de Paul charity shops and undertake other work, including hostels for the homeless. In 2015 the turnover of the charity shops was €25 million, with costs of €18.2 million and profit of €6.8 million.[25]

A conference remains the primary building block of the organisation. It is comprised of a group of volunteers who generally meet in a parish.[26] The society is a lay organisation, independent of ecclesiastical jurisdiction, but operates in parishes with the permission of the parish priest. The core work of the society is the visitation of homes by pairs of volunteers with the purpose of bringing practical help. The visitation of prisons and hospitals is also undertaken. The society supplies financial support, advice, counselling and a budget service.[27] Liam Fitzpatrick, who joined the society over fifty years ago in Cork, says that back then the emphasis was on material need but that today the need is for much more than material aid:

> Many of the people we visit in their homes or who live in our hostels have other complications in their lives, including broken relationships, addiction problems and counselling/psychiatric needs … The role of advocacy has become an important part of SVP activities in recent decades.[28]

The society receives subventions from State and local authorities to support its work. One member, Kieran Murphy, sees the voluntary work of the society as a necessary complement to the work of the government. Referring to the service for the homeless provided by the society in Ennis, Co. Clare, Murphy says that the vision and commitment of the volunteers showed that:

> Communities have a role and a responsibility to respond to the needs of people within their community who are homeless, and that if we hand over this role exclusively to the government we will never succeed in providing sufficient services.[29]

An initiative taken by student members of the Society of St Vincent de Paul in Trinity College Dublin contributed to the development of a resource centre located in the former St Andrew's National School on Pearse Street, close to Trinity College. St Andrew's National School opened at the end of the nineteenth century and closed in 1976 due to a significant fall in population in the area. Members of Trinity's St Vincent de Paul Conference began to offer voluntary tuition on a weekly basis to primary and secondary school students in the area. Elizabeth Watson, who lives in St Andrew's Parish, was a founding member of the Voluntary Tuition Programme. The eldest in a large family, she left school early to take a job but always retained an appetite for education. The Voluntary Tuition Programme has worked closely with the Trinity Access Programme (TAP), which aims to help those who are educationally disadvantaged to enter third-level education. In 1996, when Goldsmith Hall opened in Trinity, TAP relocated there. In 2003 when TAP was twenty years old, Elizabeth Watson was awarded an honorary degree from Trinity in recognition of her pioneering work.

Gradually, a community centre providing multiple services covering the Parishes of St Andrew's, Westland Row, and Immaculate Heart of Mary, City Quay, evolved. These include a kindergarten, a homework club, a day centre for older people and an adult education group. St Andrew's Resource Centre publishes a magazine called *The New Link*, which is filled with local information and stories about members of the community.[30] Dermot McCarthy, who is chairman of St Andrew's Resource Centre, says that the resource centre:

> aims to address the needs of the local community in an integrated way, offering literally under one roof a wide range of services catering for individuals and families at all stages of the life cycle … Eleven major programmes and services are delivered with funding received from eight statutory agencies … All are tailored to local circumstances.[31]

Funding also comes from local businesses, philanthropic donors and community fundraising. The services provided range from childcare to youth services to family support services. There is an adult education programme and an employment service. The employment service endeavours to connect the local community with opportunities arising from the major investment in the neighbouring docklands area of Dublin.

Legion of Mary

The Legion of Mary is a voluntary organisation without any paid employees. It was founded 100 years ago in Dublin in 1921 by a civil servant, Frank Duff. The legion is an organisation of Catholics, men and women, 'at the disposal of the bishop of the diocese and the parish priest for any and every form of social service and Catholic action which these authorities may deem suitable to the legionaries and useful for the welfare of the Church'.[32] Today the legion exists in close to 200 countries worldwide. The basic unit of the legion is the praesidium, a name derived from a detachment of the old Roman Legion. A praesidium is usually parish-based, although some praesidia exist in colleges, hostels and other institutions, including prisons. Legionaries undertake a range of works, including home visitation and visitation of hospitals and prisons. As in the Society of St Vincent de Paul all visitation is done in pairs. Legionaries do not give material aid but rather engage in works of service. The legion has a number of hostels for the homeless where residents make a small contribution towards their accommodation costs, frequently from social welfare payments, so that legionaries are placed in the position of providing the residents with a service rather than with charity. As long ago as 1930 the legion pioneered care of unmarried mothers and their children and sought to give mothers the option to keep their children rather than being forced to give the children up for adoption, as most unmarried mothers at the time had no means of support. Staff in the legion hostels work on a voluntary basis and are provided with food and lodgings.

The most recent census for the Legion of Mary in the Dublin Archdiocese was undertaken in March 2015. It showed that there were 914 legionaries in 146 praesidia. Eleven of these praesidia are hostel-based, which means that 135 praesidia are based in parishes. Some parishes have a legion praesidium which is not strictly a 'parish' praesidium. For example, there are two praesidia which meet in Berkeley Road Parish in Dublin, whose members visit Mountjoy and Dóchas Prisons but have no direct involvement with Berkeley Road Parish. Outside the Dublin Archdiocese the latest Legion of Mary membership census was for 2011, when active adult membership was 2,005. Since then membership is estimated to have declined by 10 per cent. In 2011 the legion was active in 338 parishes outside Dublin, but it is estimated that the number had declined to around 312 parishes by 2015. Total membership in Ireland at the present time is probably around 2,500 in over 400 parishes. In contrast with the situation in Ireland, the legion is growing strongly in many parts of the world, so that worldwide membership is estimated at over 3 million. It is noteworthy that of fifteen ordinations (diocesan and religious orders) which took place in Ireland in 2017, five made a connection between their vocation and their earlier experience of legion membership. Among them was Philip Mulryne, OP, a former Manchester United player, who belonged to the Legion of Mary in Belfast.[33]

In the 1950s, when conditions were bleak in rural Ireland, Duff coined the term 'True Devotion to the Nation' to describe a particular form of legionary community work. The earliest example of a practical 'True Devotion' project was in the parish of Inchigeela, Co. Cork. It came about as the result of a suggestion to Duff in the late 1950s by a young doctor and legionary, Michael McGuinness, who proposed that something might be done about improving the tourist facilities in that locality. In a letter to a German legionary in 1961 Duff described the work:

> I do not know if you have heard of the Inchigeela project in Co. Cork which was run by the Legion. They took that place which is also a beauty spot and they turned it into a tourist resort. It was simply done by stirring up all the people and getting them to work together. They tidied up and beautified it. When this preliminary process was gone through, the place was advertised, and in the first season, 135 visitors were brought in, and subsequently declared that it represented the best holiday they had ever had.[34]

Following the success of the Inchigeela project, attention moved to Tuosist in Co. Kerry. Tuosist is located on the southern side of Kenmare Bay. The population of the parish had fallen from 9,000 in the nineteenth century to 873 in the mid 1950s, with no marriages and just two children born over a period of five years. Faced with the extinction of his parish, the parish priest approached the local Legion of Mary and asked for their help. The legion mobilised the local community and undertook remedial work of every sort, which included cleaning and painting and persuading a Cork legionary, Marie Caulfield, to provide B&B accommodation.[35] In a relatively short time the community had been energised and Tuosist was transformed into a viable tourist attraction, which it remains to the present day. The work in Tuosist was the subject of a documentary in the early 1960s made by the television production company Radharc.

Conscious of the environment and opposed to every form of waste, in 1959 Duff wrote an article in the *Irish Independent* entitled 'The Key to National and Spiritual Welfare: Waste Not, Want Not!'[36] He went so far as to say that there should be no waste, that everything should be put to economic use, to vital purposes. He called this 'the great unrecognised truth of the day'. Today there is much greater awareness of the damage done to the environment through waste, and recycling is practised widely. Throughout his long life, Duff's mode of transport was his bicycle. In this regard and in regard to the avoidance of waste, Duff, a former Department of Finance official, was a prescient environmentalist.

When Fr [later Bishop] Joseph Duffy, a young priest based in Iniskeen, Co. Monaghan, wrote to Duff enquiring whether work in the Young Farmers' Club and the Irish Countrywomen's Association provided suitable work for legionaries, Duff replied in the affirmative. He stressed that, with the exception of activities which involved the giving of material relief, 'It is intensely desirable that as many activities as possible would be gathered in under the Legion umbrella. It would mark a very unhappy condition if all these efforts to ameliorate the social conditions were to be abstracted from religious auspices and only undertaken under secular ones.'[37] Duff went on to say that he had long been advocating for 'societising', by which he meant the creation of societies of different kinds into which would come people who were not prepared to take the step of legion membership, but who would engage in societies of various sorts which could be run by legionaries and fulfil the work obligation for some legionaries. An early example in legion history of societising was the Marian Arts Society, which promoted interest in art and was open to Protestants and Catholics alike. Other examples included choral societies, drama groups and football clubs. The Overseas Club for foreign students; the Mercier Society [later named the Pauline Circle], a society for dialogue with those of other Christian faiths; the Pillar of Fire Society for dialogue with Jews; and the Common Ground, a discussion group for writers, all fell into this category. A society organised by legionaries to build up Irish language and culture is An Réalt. The idea for An Réalt originated with Nuala Moran, daughter of D. P. Moran, founder and editor of *The Leader*. Nuala, who also edited *The Leader*, was a member of the Legion of Mary. In a talk to members of An Réalt in 1971, Duff gave an intriguing analysis in which he cast the Irish language in a wider context. He said that the fact that a language was ancient, was full of treasure, had shaped history and even religion, was no passport to survival. He observed that Mary, the mother of God, has a special name, Muire, while other women named Mary are called Máire in Irish. He questioned if that was the case in any other language.[38]

The Pioneer Total Abstinence Association

The PTAA was founded in Dublin over 120 years ago in December 1898 by Fr James Cullen, SJ, and four women, Mary Bury, Ann Egan, Lizzie Power and Frances Sullivan. Frances Sullivan (Donovan) was born in the United

States and married A. M. Sullivan, editor of *The Nation* newspaper and future Nationalist MP. At the start the organisation was intended for women and girls, as they were thought to be more likely apostles of temperance than men. Cullen based the association on the parish unit. Each parish centre would have a spiritual director and be affiliated to the Central Council in Dublin.[39] Micheál Mac Gréil, former President of the Pioneers, maintains that Cullen's vision for members of the association extended beyond abstention from alcohol to work in their communities.[40]

The PTTA followed in the wake of Fr Mathew's temperance crusade in the earlier part of the nineteenth century. However, according to Elizabeth Malcolm, author of '*Ireland Sober, Ireland Free*', 'despite Father Mathew's crusade, to many Catholics, temperance remained a Protestant-inspired movement'.[41]

At the time of its golden jubilee in 1948 the PTAA had a membership of 350,000, with 1,200 affiliated centres. The Jubilee Mass and Benediction in Croke Park on 26 June 1949 was attended by close to 100,000 people. The main address at the rally was delivered by the founder of the rural-based community organisation Muintir na Tíre, Canon John Hayes. In the general election of 1948, the jubilee year, two high-profile Pioneer TDs were elected: Oliver J. Flanagan for Laois–Offaly and Joseph Blowick for Mayo South. Blowick, who was leader of the Clann na Talmhan (Family of the Land) Party, also known as the National Agricultural Party until it disbanded in 1965, was appointed Minister for Lands in 1948. Twenty years after he was first elected to the Dáil, Deputy Flanagan, father of Minister for Justice Charlie Flanagan, stated in *The Irish Times* on 6 December 1968 that it was his personal opinion that:

> the hallmark of every Irish man and woman should be the Pioneer emblem and the Fáinne, because in the grand tradition of our faith and fatherland, temperance, good citizenship, love for our country, its language and culture should and must be our aim.[42]

In time the Pioneers spread overseas to other countries in Europe as well as to Australia, America, Africa and Asia. According to historian and author of a history of the Pioneers, Diarmaid Ferriter, Pioneer groups in America contrasted with parish-based groups at home: 'emigrant communities did not remotely resemble the small homogeneous parishes which formed the backbone of the Association in Ireland'.[43] In 1950 Seamus O'Boyle, a Pioneer in New Jersey, wrote to Fr Seán McCarron, SJ, Central Director of the Pioneers in Dublin: 'We are like no parish centre in Ireland. We are drawn from the 32 Counties and have different ideas from all the different areas.'[44]

Dr Cornelius Lucey, Bishop of Cork and Ross, suggested that the Pioneer body could legitimately be termed a parish movement.[45] The intimate link in Ireland between the Pioneers and the parish was made clear by Mac Gréil, when he set out in 2006 to visit every Pioneer centre in the country. He started with the Meath Diocese and it was his intention 'to visit every active and lapsed centre and make contact with local Pioneer leaders and the parish priest'.[46] By June 2008, when Mac Gréil's term as Pioneer chairman ended, he had succeeded in visiting 994 centres from a total of 1,077, in practically every Catholic parish in Ireland. This was exactly half the number of centres which existed forty years earlier, in 1967, when there were 2,152 centres.[47]

Alcohol abuse can cause personal damage but there are social consequences also. Official awareness of the costs of alcohol abuse includes recognition of health costs as well as loss of life and injuries due to drink driving and alcohol-fuelled violence. As with tobacco, awareness of the health hazards associated with alcohol has grown. Excessive drinking has a big impact on the health services, where alcohol-related illnesses absorb significant resources. In 1959 the Department of Justice queried the Department of Health as to the scale of the problem of alcoholism in Ireland. According to Ferriter:

> The reply was a staggering indictment of the ignorance that existed at the highest levels of Irish society concerning drink abuse, and again characterises the ambivalent attitudes to the Irish drinking culture which existed, despite the attempts of the Pioneers: 'Off hand they [The Department of Health] have said that it is not a problem in this country: that fewer than 400 persons are received into institutions (public or private) for treatment in any year.' [48]

In 2015/16, according to *National Income and Expenditure*, published by the Central Statistics Office (CSO), annual spending on alcohol in Ireland was €6.36 billion. According to the *Household Budget Survey*, also published by the CSO, the average Irish household spends close to €1,500 on alcohol and tobacco annually. This compares with annual expenditure of €1,760 on clothing and footwear.

Alcoholics Anonymous (AA), a worldwide organisation which encourages sobriety 'one day at a time' with a twelve-step programme for recovering alcoholics, has a strong presence in Ireland. At first the growth of AA in Ireland was slow but today there are AA groups nationwide. Meetings are frequently held in parish centres and are attended by members of all faiths and none. Likewise Narcotics Anonymous offers a programme similar to AA for those suffering from drug addiction.

Youth Clubs and Youth Conferences

In his book *Youth Ministry in Ireland*, Gerard Gallagher points to Belfast as a city which has a strong history of parish involvement in youth clubs.[49] As long ago as 1935 the Down and Connor Youth Committee was set up. In the wake of the Troubles in Northern Ireland Fr Colm Campbell began to develop services in the 1970s, especially for unemployed young people, as those who were caught up in the Troubles were often young. In 1985 a youth conference called 'World Watch 85' was held in the diocese. Gallagher maintains that since the ceasefire and the Good Friday Agreement in 1998 there has been a decline in Mass attendance by young people in Northern Ireland.[50] It is hard to interpret, but perhaps prayer was seen as one response to the horrors and dangers of the conflict.

In Northern Ireland the story of parish and community was made more complex by the Troubles. Church authorities were cool towards the Republicans but, according to Gerry Adams, following Bloody Sunday in Derry in 1972, Church people reacted.[51] Fr Des Wilson, who had come to Ballymurphy as a curate in 1966, and Fr Alex Reid, originally from Tipperary and a member of Clonard Redemptorist Monastery, began to play a role in trying to end the conflict. According to Adams, the general lack of involvement by clergy was felt by its absence:

> Father Alex Reid and Father Des Wilson not only helped to resolve feuds, they also played leading roles in various efforts to end the conflict. They were two of only a very small number of clergy who engaged in such work, and in many ways the inability or unwillingness of any of the churches to develop a coherent strategy for justice and peace has been one of the great failures of our time. Father Des, a radical community priest, and Father Reid, a Redemptorist priest based at Clonard, were both dissatisfied with the absence of any real strategy by the church establishment or the wider political establishment.[52]

Down and Connor has a strong tradition of folk music for young people and has inspired many parish liturgies and larger diocesan events over past decades. In the millennium year 2000 a number of youth missions were held. An annual youth pilgrimage to Lourdes has been held since 1985. The Bishop of Derry, Edward Daly, set up the Derry Diocesan Youth Council and in 1980 an open-air Mass for young people was held in the Brandywell, a football and greyhound stadium near the Bogside area in Derry.[53] The Mass was attended by young people from every parish in the diocese.

The visit of Pope John Paul II to the Republic of Ireland in 1979 was the catalyst for a new emphasis on youth Masses and youth events and in 1981 young people from all over Ireland participated in a National Return Visit to Rome. Some parishes encourage the use of Alpha courses. These courses were started in the 1977 by Charles Marnham, a curate in a Church of England parish in London. The course, which involves study of the faith over a number of weeks, has been adopted by Catholics in all age groups. An Alpha session begins with a meal and continues with discussion. The course is also used by other Churches, including Methodists, for example, in Richhill in Co. Armagh.[54]

Church of Ireland

Martin Maguire, who has written extensively on the history of Irish Protestantism, suggests that for most people 'religious identity is less a matter of precise beliefs than one of different social practices.'[55] He says that the Church of Ireland parishes in Dublin generated 'an array of political, social and religious organisations, societies and clubs'. In the 1930s the inner-city parish of St George's had sixteen different societies, including the Parish Guild of Youth, the Missionary Union and the YMCA. In the Parish of Clontarf there was even a bigger number, including a lawn tennis club, a badminton club and a hockey club. Maguire concludes that the community of the Church of Ireland relied on a network of voluntary organisations to 'sustain a sense of community'.

The Church of Ireland has many caring organisations which, although not necessarily parish-based due to the smaller number of parishes than that of the Catholic Church, are often accessible via parishes. These include adoption and fertility counselling (NI); adoption and unplanned pregnancy services (ROI); Changing Attitude Ireland, which works for full affirmation of lesbian, gay, bisexual and transgender persons; and the Choice Housing association. Probably the best known organisation is the Mothers' Union, which operates on an all-Ireland basis to support families. The union has about 7,000 members and is present in all twelve Church of Ireland dioceses. One of its objectives is to overcome domestic violence in all its forms.

4

Branching Out

Schools

Archbishop Donald Caird, former Church of Ireland Archbishop of Dublin, once remarked that the school is 'the heartbeat of the parish'. This may no longer be the case, as the traditional connection between the religion of the parish and of the school has altered. Furthermore, in cities, especially in Dublin, a high proportion of children travel outside their parish to school, so it may be asked whether the social relevance of the school to the parish is now only of historical interest. Following changes in government policy contained in the Education (Admissions to Schools) Act 2018, a national school located in a Catholic parish will no longer be entitled to prioritise Catholic children in the enrolment process. The government policy to remove any 'baptism barrier' on grounds of religious affiliation would cause problems for Church of Ireland schools, where members of their Church could become a minority in schools under Church of Ireland patronage, so exceptions are made for the minority Church. This requires the determination of which children are Catholic and which are not. A legal perspective on the implications of the 2018 Act for schools has been given by Feichín McDonagh, SC, who suggests that the State involving itself in deciding whether somebody is a member of one religion or another is a surprising development.[1]

The parish school has a long history from the time when, under a Tudor statute following the Reformation, land was granted in each parish for a resident Protestant schoolmaster, thus establishing an early link between Protestant parish and school. Oliver Goldsmith, in his poem 'The Deserted Village',[2] immortalised the village schoolmaster:

> There, in his noisy mansion, skill'd to rule,
> The village master taught his little school …
> And still they gazed, and still their wonder grew,
> That one small head could carry all he knew.

The decline of rural villages in the twenty-first century finds an echo in Goldsmith, who, in the eighteenth century, was expressing regret for rural decline. Over 200 years after Goldsmith wrote of a Westmeath village, sociologist Tom Inglis, in a study of a Meath village, concluded that it is the local school which keeps the community alive:

> The backbone of Ballivor, what keeps it alive as a community, is the local school and the way people come together for sports, special events and meetings of the parents' association.[3]

How did the Churches – Catholic and Protestant – get to play such a central role in national schools in Ireland? According to the Irish National Teachers' Organisation (INTO), the Irish national school has two antecedents, one official and one unofficial. The official or legal ancestor was the State-recognised parish school, originating in the sixteenth century and licensed by the local Anglican bishop. This arrangement was unacceptable to the majority Catholic population, who instead sent their children to the other antecedent of the national schools, the 'hedge schools'.[4] These small schools were established on a secret basis to provide some basic education for Catholic children. There were also some schools for Presbyterian children.

Catholic schools were proscribed under the Penal Laws for much of the eighteenth century but, despite the law, Catholics, mainly women, began to open schools. Nano Nagle set up her first school for poor pupils in Cove Lane in Cork in 1754. Within three years she had opened seven schools – five for girls and two for boys. Nagle went on to found the Presentation Sisters in 1775. In 1766 Teresa Mulally, a milliner who would join the Presentation Sisters, had a similar plan to Nagle for the education of the poor. She approached Fr Mulcaile in the Parish of St Michan's, Mary's Lane, the oldest parish in Dublin. The school which opened in May 1766 was located in a house beside the church.

Nagle was one of a group of women and one man who contributed in a unique way to the education services in Ireland, education services which were predominantly parish-based. In addition to Nagle and Mulally, the others were Elizabeth Coppinger, Mary Aikenhead, Frances Ball, Catherine McAuley and Edmund Ignatius Rice.[5] Later, in the nineteenth century, they would be followed by Margaret Aylward. In the wake of the Great Famine, Aylward opened St Brigid's Orphanage for destitute children at Eccles Street in Dublin. She favoured fosterage rather than institutional care for orphans and accordingly she made payments to foster mothers. She opened schools at a number of locations in Dublin, all of which had links to the local parish.

By 1869 the Sisters of the Holy Faith, the religious order founded by Aylward, had an attendance in all their schools of 1,000 children. Edmund Ignatius Rice founded two orders – the Presentation Brothers and the Christian Brothers. In 1802 he opened a school for poor boys in Waterford. Rice came to Dublin and founded a school in Hanover Street in 1814, which later developed into CBS Westland Row. He also founded O'Connell School, named after Daniel O'Connell, in 1828 in North Richmond Street.

A defining moment occurred in 1831, two years after Catholic Emancipation, with the publication of what is known as the 'Stanley Letter'. Chief Secretary Stanley wrote to the Duke of Leinster asking him to agree to be president of the proposed new Board of Education and setting out the government's proposals for education in Ireland. The nub of the proposal was that the new system should provide, 'if possible, a combined literary, and a separate religious education, and should be capable of being so far adapted to the views of the religious persuasions which prevail in Ireland as to render it, in truth, a system of national education for the poorer classes of the community'.[6] If the schools followed the rules, they could apply for grant aid. Because much of the success of the scheme would depend on the cooperation of the resident clergy, 'the Board will probably look with peculiar favour upon applications proceeding either from: the Protestant and Roman Catholic clergy of the Parish, one of the clergymen, and a certain number of parishioners professing the opposite creed, or parishioners of both denominations.' The grant aid would be combined with a local contribution which comprised the site, at least one-third of the cost of building, funds to maintain the school, a salary for one master and other items. According to the Stanley Letter, the hours for teaching secular and religious subjects were prescribed.

The response to the letter, in which, according to Séamas Ó Buachalla, the emphasis was on 'integrated schools and community commitment',[7] was mixed. In the words of Donal Akenson, 'The basic principle that underlay each of the national system's original religious regulations was that the schools were to be undenominational in character.'[8] Archbishop Murray of Dublin accepted a seat on the Education Board while some bishops, in particular Archbishop Mac Hale of Tuam, opposed the proposals. Overall the hierarchy accepted the proposals at first but then vigorously sought concessions. The schools remained multi-denominational for just nine years. In 1840, at the General Assembly of Presbyterians, the moderator, Dr Henry Cooke, applied, on behalf of the Presbyterian Church, for funds to establish Presbyterian schools. Henceforth funding was provided on a denominational basis.

By the middle of the nineteenth century over 90 per cent of national schools in Ireland were under denominational management. 'Attempts at a non-sectarian official school structure had failed.'[9] In 1900 the Catholic bishops, at their national synod held at Maynooth, stated, 'the system of national education … in a great part of Ireland is now in fact, whatever it is in name, as denominational almost as we could desire.'[10] Following independence in 1922, the Catholic Church, through the Association of Catholic Managers, asserted that, as their fundamental principle, the 'only satisfactory system of education for Catholics is one wherein Catholic children are taught in Catholic schools by Catholic teachers, under Catholic control'.[11] In 1924 the Department of Education was established and took over the work of the Education Board.

While the initiative for national schools came from the State and the State has contributed financially over the years, there has been a substantial voluntary input, including the provision of sites. The national scheme envisaged that the local patron (generally the bishop in whose diocese the school was located) would provide the site and be responsible for the hiring of teachers. Throughout the twentieth century Catholic primary schools were managed by the local priest/parish priest and were mostly 'parish schools', while some schools were managed by religious orders of nuns, priests and monks. A strong link between primary school and parish was forged and schools became an integral part of parish life.

In his examination of the Church of Ireland community in Dublin, Martin Maguire concludes:

> The survival of its own denominational parish schools, more than any other factor, served to preserve the sense of a Dublin Church of Ireland community as the daily routine of delivering and collecting children at the school gates created social networks, revived old friendships, and laid the basis of new ones.[12]

In 2016 the Catholic Church in Ireland, in the person of the bishop in his diocese, was patron to approximately 90 per cent of the State's 3,200 primary schools – over 2,800 schools – while the Church of Ireland was patron to nearly 200 schools. Other patrons include An Foras Pátrúnachta na Scoileanna Lán-Ghaeilge Teo, Educate Together, Presbyterian, Methodist, Jewish, Islamic and other religions.[13]

Since 1975 management of Catholic schools is carried out by a board of management. According to the Catholic Primary Schools' Management Association's *Board of Management Handbook 2016*, 'The Board of Management ensures a spirit of partnership with the patron and trustees, parents and children, school staff and the parish community.'[14] The board comprises the principal teacher, an elected teacher, elected representatives of the parents and nominees of the bishop. All 18,000 board members throughout the country give their time on a voluntary basis. The board manages the school on behalf of the patron and is accountable to the patron and the minister.[15]

While there have been modifications to the boards of management over the years, with the result that Church influence has been reduced, the connection between the primary school and the parish remains strong. For example, Msgr Dan O'Connor, head of the Education Secretariat at Archbishop's House in Dublin (Episcopal Vicar for Education), was formerly parish priest in Dún Laoghaire, where he was chaplain to all three junior schools in the parish. The schools are St Nicholas Montessori, which is multi-denominational, the Dominican school on Convent Road and St Joseph's. All three schools are co-educational and the children's choir for the parish is supplied by the schools. The principal of the Dominican primary school in Dún Laoghaire, Peter Mooney, has a very positive experience of the links between parish and school, which go back to his boyhood. He grew up in Marino on Dublin's north side and continues to live in Marino, such is his bond with that parish and community.[16] In addition to the Christian Brothers' boys' school in Marino, there was also a school for girls organised by the Cross and Passion Sisters, as well as a school run by the Daughters of Charity of St Vincent de Paul. Also in Marino parish are two secondary schools, Ardscoil Rís and the Dominican school which has relocated from Eccles Street. Furthermore, the Carmelites, the Rosminians (who were responsible for the school for the visually impaired) and All Hallows College (now closed) were all in the parish. In his role as principal in Dún Laoghaire, Mooney has considerable contact with parents, especially in regard to preparation for First Holy Communion.

Former Ministers for Education Richard Bruton and Ruairí Quinn and the Catholic Archbishop of Dublin, Diarmuid Martin, are in agreement that change in patronage of schools is required. Minister Quinn set up a Forum on Patronage and Pluralism, chaired by the late Emeritus Professor of Education at Maynooth John Coolahan. The forum recommended the handing over of some schools to the State where the parents so wished. As Irish society has become more diverse and more multicultural, with a growing spectrum of nationalities and of belief and non-belief, the demand for this diversity to be reflected in the ethos of schools has increased. It is forty years since the first multi-denominational school opened in Dalkey in Co. Dublin, yet there were fewer than 100 multi-denominational schools in the Republic in 2017 (84 Educate Together primary schools and 13 at second level). Discussions are taking place about divesting some Catholic schools, that is, about the process of removing schools from Catholic Church patronage. When he was Minister for Education and Skills, Richard Bruton, set a target for transferring the patronage of 200 schools from the Catholic Church to the education and training boards which run community national schools, a new form of State school. To date, a relatively small number of schools have been divested. These include a handful in Dublin where the school had closed or was amalgamated; for example, the De La Salle primary school in Finglas and St Peter's boys' national school in Greenhills. The position is complex and some, perhaps surprising, reactions have occurred. For example, in Ballyfermot, the plan to amalgamate four local schools prior to the handover of the schools was opposed by local parents on the grounds that enrolments were being curtailed in one school and classes were being amalgamated in another, leading to increased class size.[17]

High levels of immigration have helped to maintain the viability of some small schools. In general, in rural Ireland Catholic national schools enrol pupils who are not Catholic without difficulty. In August 2019 three small national schools transferred from Catholic to multi-denominational patronage: the fourteen-pupil Scoil an Ghleanna on the Iveragh peninsula, Co. Kerry, which is a Gaeltacht school; Tahilla national school, also in Kerry, which has eight pupils; and Lecarrow school in Co. Roscommon, which also has eight pupils. The three schools will be brought within the orbit of the local education and training board and will be able to avail themselves of administrative support.

When schools are divested it seems likely that more State funds will be required in order to replace such church funds as are provided at present. Msgr Dan O'Connor cites cases where parish funds were needed to keep schools viable. Speaking in 2018, O'Connor said, 'There are three schools in our diocese [Dublin] that had to get loans from their parishes last year' and 'there are 40 schools in our diocese in serious financial trouble.'[18] The financial problems for schools have resulted from a reduction in the capitation grant from which the schools provide for maintenance and running costs, including insurance. Declan Lawlor, a member of the Dublin Archdiocese Education Secretariat, says that when funds are needed by the schools, 'their first port of call is the parish'.[19]

The Northern Ireland education system shares some historical similarities with the Republic of Ireland but also exhibits marked differences, as shown by historian Neil C. Fleming.[20] In pre-Partition Ireland most primary schools had come under clerical management of different religious denominations.

In 1921 the Marquess of Londonderry, who was responsible for education in Northern Ireland, believed that integrated schools were a bulwark against sectarianism. Bonaparte Wyse, permanent secretary at the Education Ministry, who advised Londonderry, was a Catholic. Londonderry attempted to transfer Church schools to the State and established a committee to explore ways of achieving this goal. Cardinal Logue of Armagh declined to participate and forbade other Catholic clergy from participating. It was feared that a secular mantle would cloak non-Catholic dominance. In 1923 the Education Act (Northern Ireland), commonly known as the 'Londonderry Act', was passed. The appointment of teachers became a battleground between the Protestant churches and the Education Ministry, as Protestant schools which had been transferred to the State were precluded from hiring or firing teachers on the basis of religion. On the Catholic side there was strong opposition to Catholics attending Stranmillis Teacher Training College. Instead Catholics opted to train at the Catholic Strawberry Hill College in London, now St Mary's Twickenham. In recent decades integrated education has been growing in Northern Ireland but the system remains largely segregated.

Some argue that denominational schools are divisive and that children should be educated together regardless of religious belief. This reflects the thinking behind the Educate Together movement. While perhaps not a perfect analogy, the very successful Gaelscoileanna have grown up on the foundation of parents who are keen on developing the Irish language. Gaelscoileanna include schools which are denominational, inter-denominational, multi-denominational and non-denominational. There is a fine balance between inclusion and exclusion and it is not always possible to achieve a perfect balance.

The GAA

'Patriotism begins and ends for most of us with the parish.' This was the belief of Fr Doyle expressed in an address to the Annual Convention of the Leitrim GAA on 27 January 1967.[21] From the beginning the GAA was closely linked with the parish, especially outside the cities:

> In 1887 the GAA ruled that the dividing lines between clubs were to be the boundaries of a parish. This rule was not slavishly adhered to – it was not applied, for example, to Dublin and in the countryside various clubs were also allowed (on request) to represent areas both smaller and larger than parishes, should a certain community make a compelling case. Nonetheless the idea of one parish, one club became the hallmark of the GAA and immediately Gaelic games were defined by a passion for place.[22]

In a report in the *Meath Chronicle* early in 2018, Dermot Farrell, the newly appointed Bishop of Ossory, and native of Co. Westmeath, spoke of how hurling was linked in his mind with many Kilkenny parishes. 'The names of many places were emblazoned in my mind by the commentaries of Mícheál O'Hehir, Mícheál Ó Muircheartaigh – places like Ballyhale, Clara, Dunamaggan, Freshford, Glenmore, Tullaroan – linked the names of the great Kilkenny hurlers down the years to their clubs most of which coincide with the names of parishes.'[23] On 29 December 2020 it was announced that Bishop Farrell had been appointed by the Vatican as the new Archbishop of Dublin, to succeed Archbishop Diarmuid Martin. Farrell will continue as administrator of Ossory pending an appointment to the Diocese of Ossory.

The GAA was founded in 1884 by Michael Cusack, a teacher from Co. Clare; the first patron of the GAA, together with Parnell and Davitt, was Archbishop Croke. Croke's resounding acceptance of the invitation to become patron gave an important signal of clerical support for the organisation. According to Fr Vincent Twomey:

> The Church's parish system provided, and still provides, the basic structure of the Gaelic Athletic Association (GAA) so that, whatever reservations the clergy might initially have had about Fenian nationalist influence on the incipient athletic movement, it evidently did not adversely affect the close identity that grew up between the GAA and the Catholic Church … It is thus not surprising that from its ranks came its finest priests, to such an extent that, in rural areas at least, the Irish Catholic Church was the GAA at prayer. One of its greatest trophies is, significantly, a replica of the Ardagh chalice.[24]

Over the years many Catholic laymen, as well as bishops and countless priests, have played a significant part in developing the GAA. The tradition of the Archbishop of Cashel throwing in the ball at the All-Ireland hurling final symbolised the close relationship between the GAA and the Catholic Church.[25] The practice continued until the mid 1960s. An example of a Catholic layman with deep religious belief is the former manager of the Tyrone team, Mickey Harte. Former captain Sean Cavanagh has described how Harte asked the team to pray the Rosary together before games.[26] Fr Harry Bohan, who trained the Clare hurling team in the 1970s, also achieved important work in community development as founder of the Rural Housing Organisation in Co. Clare. Msgr Tommy Maher, who died in 2015 at the age of ninety-two, was one of the most significant figures ever in the history of hurling.[27] Hailing from Gowran in Co. Kilkenny, he was Kilkenny coach/manager for over twenty years, from 1957 to 1978. Kilkenny won seven All-Ireland titles under Maher's management, which was carried out in his spare time. Fr Tom Scully, OMI, trained Offaly to reach the All-Ireland football final in 1969. Fr Peter Quinn, who died aged ninety-one in 2016, was a member of the Mayo All-Ireland back-to-back winning football teams of 1950 and 1951, the last year that Mayo won the Sam Maguire Cup. Ordained in 1950, he was a member of the Columban Missionary Order and served in the Philippines and the US. Fr Quinn played under the name Peter Quinlan because of an episcopal ban on clerics playing inter-county football at the time.[28]

In rural Ireland the GAA and the local parish priest often operated as close partners:

> Times of matches and fund raising events were given from the pulpit. The priest was usually chairman of the local GAA club, sometimes its trainer or manager, and a great man to organise the raising of money for the improvements of the pitch. If he was blessed with a generous parish (and when it came to the GAA he usually was), a great effort would be made to build a community centre. This would become the heartland for most communities as the venue for the Christmas play, 25 Drives, a weekly disco, talent shows and the numerous ingenious ways to raise money for the local teams.[29]

From its foundation the GAA aimed to be in every corner of Ireland. It would do this by building its organisation around parishes and local community networks; in turn creating networks all of its own. GAA Lotto, used to finance clubs, is organised in many parishes, and church-gate collections for clubs also occur. John Scally, sportswriter and theologian, describes the power of Gaelic games to harness communal values 'for the glory of the parish'.[30] He talks of the respect for place that is at the heart of the GAA. The 'Parish Rule' of one parish, one club, whereby players played for their parishes and did not switch to a different or stronger parish, was vital throughout rural Ireland. Historian, and member of the Church of Ireland, Ida Milne, researched attitudes of Southern Protestants to the GAA in rural Ireland. Milne undertook a number of interviews to assess these attitudes. While there are some well-known names among Protestant GAA members, for the most part Protestants participated in 'an unassuming way'.[31] Milne says that, for Protestants, 'Playing or following GAA was a mode of identifying with their local community, a way of making bonds with neighbours they could not meet in church.'[32]

In Northern Ireland the situation was different for certain groups comprised overwhelmingly of Protestants. Rule 21 of the GAA, in force for over 100 years, from 1897 to 2001, banned members of the British armed forces and the police from membership of the GAA. Furthermore, members of the GAA who participated 'in dances, or similar entertainment promoted by or under the patronage of such bodies, shall incur suspension of at least three months' (from Rule 21). The rule was abolished as part of the peace process and following the establishment of the Police Service of Northern Ireland.

A divisive aspect of the GAA was the 'Ban' introduced in 1901 which prohibited members from playing 'foreign' games like soccer and rugby.[33] The GAA lobbied to have the ban included as a condition of county council and corporation scholarships so that pupils in schools in which, for example, rugby was played would not have the option to obtain such scholarships. The Ban was removed by unanimous agreement at a congress in Belfast in 1971. In the summer of 2018 controversy flared regarding the location of a benefit football game for the family of Liam Miller. Miller, who was born in Cork, had been a Manchester United and Irish international soccer player. He died at a young age from cancer early in 2018. Páirc Uí Chaoimh, the home of Cork GAA, was sought as the venue for the game but refused by the GAA on grounds that it had no authority to host games other than those under its control. However, following public debate which was largely critical of the GAA, the association agreed to the use of Páirc Uí Chaoimh. The reaction of Fianna Fáil leader, and Corkman, Micheál Martin to the initial refusal was unequivocal. He tweeted, 'The GAA is rooted in community. Liam Miller and family are of our community. … The unique event organised to reflect that community ethos and to honour Liam Miller should be held in Páirc Uí Chaoimh.'[34]

The second-level schools which dominated hurling and Gaelic football throughout the twentieth century were schools run by the Catholic Church: St Flannan's in Ennis (now co-educational), St Jarlath's in Tuam, St Kieran's in Kilkenny, St Mel's in Longford, North Mon in Cork, the Carmelites in Moate (now closed) and St Brendan's (the Sem) in Killarney. Christian Brothers' schools at both primary and secondary level, for example, Marino in Dublin, have produced a huge number of players who have gone on to play at inter-county level. The growth in the number of GAA clubs has been striking. Between 1924 and 1945 the number of GAA clubs on the island of Ireland more than doubled to 2,000. Since then the number has grown further to over 3,600.

Michael Cusack was anxious that social activity related to the GAA should not revolve around pubs. He was wary of a historical association of drink with sporting endeavour. Diarmaid Ferriter quotes a pre-GAA seventeenth century observer who wrote of hurling matches in which parishes would challenge each other: 'The prize is generally a barrel or two of ale, which is brought into the field and drunk off by the victors on the spot, though the vanquished are not without a share of it too.'[35] According to Ferriter, the Pioneer Total Abstinence Association (PTAA) felt that they had a 'benevolent partner' in the GAA.[36] The relationship between the GAA and the PTAA was helped by the fact that the general secretary of the GAA for thirty-five years, from 1929 until his death in 1964, Paddy O'Keeffe (Pádraig Ó Caoimh, after whom Páirc Uí Chaoimh in Cork is named), was a committed Pioneer. Ferriter says that GAA publications 'included temperance as one of the key components in the make-up of the true Gael'. In a spirit of mutual support the *Pioneer* magazine and the long-running Pioneer column in *The Irish Catholic* often referred to, and commended, the GAA. For example, the column in *The Irish Catholic* on 1 October 1959 recorded:

> The All-Ireland Hurling final between Waterford and Kilkenny which ended in a draw on September 6 was a brilliant and exciting game. The players deserve high praise for the skill they displayed, but much more for their sportsmanship. We are glad to say that quite a number of the hurlers on both sides are Pioneers. Many compliments have been paid to referee Gerry Fitzgerald for the adept manner in which he controlled the game. He is a Pioneer from Rathkeale in County Limerick. [37]

For over a century the GAA declined sponsorship from the drinks industry. Then in 1995 the association accepted Guinness as sponsors of the hurling championships. This action was regarded as a sell-out by some. Fr Gerard Moloney, editor of the Redemptorist magazine *Reality*, described it as 'a scandal'.[38] The sponsorship of the hurling championship by Guinness ceased in May 2013. Former chairman of the Pioneers Micheál Mac Gréil said:

> In my experience, the impact of advertising and sport-sponsorship by the drinks industry was crucial in promoting the acceptability of alcohol among young people. ... The association of drinking and group sport in Ireland is notorious. ... The growing commercialism of group sport in Ireland has been part of the problem.[39]

Joe Brolly, a barrister, a member of the Derry team which won the All-Ireland Senior Football Championship in 1993 and an RTÉ pundit on *The Sunday Game*, says that commercial factors are becoming too dominant in the GAA. He wants to 'return the GAA to being a community-based organisation with community-based ideals based on voluntary effort'.[40]Among the GAA sponsors are Eir and AIB. A critical voice was raised regarding the sponsorship by AIB of the All-Ireland senior club football championship by the chief sports writer with *The Irish Times*, Keith Duggan, who says that AIB has been 'aligning itself to the root values of Irish communities' via a brilliant advertising campaign. He maintains that AIB and other banks once held a pivotal role in communities where local branches were led by managers who knew a great deal about those communities. Then local branches were downgraded and 'headquarters' dictated what happened at local level with, according to Duggan, disastrous consequences. He thinks it is inappropriate to see one of those banks 'buying its way into a spiritual and commercial partnership with the GAA'.[41]

Former Kerry footballer Dara O Cinnéide has expressed the view that 'The identity of the parish is becoming less relevant in parts of Ireland and that's sad to see',[42] while Dublin GAA chief executive John Costello says that Dublin GAA is not built on the parish community in the manner in which it tended to be in rural Ireland; rather the GAA in Dublin is itself building communities.[43] The GAA employs full-time development officers who go into schools and help to forge links between blocs of classes and local GAA clubs. This is the sort of work that traditionally Christian Brothers would have done in their schools. Today lay teachers are often not in a position to build the school-club links, as many teachers live at a distance from the schools in which they teach. For example, in Tyrrelstown, a North Dublin suburb, the GAA employs a full-time officer. An interesting feature of the Le Chéile secondary school in Tyrrelstown is that it was among the first schools where parents were allowed to choose the patron. It was widely expected in an increasingly pluralist era that parents would opt for non-denominational but they chose Catholic.[44] Tyrrelstown is located within the Parish of St Luke the Evangelist, Mulhuddart. Other churches active in the area include Blanchardstown Methodist Church, which is located right in the heart of Tyrrelstown.

As the strength of the churches has decreased, some organisations, including the GAA, have continued to grow even stronger. Physical therapist Gerard Hartmann maintains that sport and faith are intertwined to the extent that they are the 'matrix' for strong parish communities. 'Where you see strong communities you typically see faith and sport being prominent.'[45] However, in many cases the GAA is no longer able to contribute to strong communities in rural areas because of the population shift from rural to urban areas and associated rural decline. Author and sports writer John Harrington sums up the situation: 'Rural GAA clubs are struggling to field teams because they just don't have the numbers, while urban GAA clubs are struggling to cater for the surging population in their catchment areas.'[46] As with parishes, the possible way forward may be for clubs to combine resources. That will not be without difficulty given club or parish loyalties, but could be fruitful in the longer run.

Muintir na Tíre

On 7 May 1931, exactly one week before the publication of the papal encyclical *Quadragesimo Anno*, which would stress the importance of small groups in society, Fr John Hayes, who had been born in a Land League hut in Ballyvoreen, Murroe, Co. Limerick, in 1887, founded Muintir na Tíre (People of the Land) Ltd (MNTL). MNTL was a co-operative marketing society which aimed to improve the economic conditions of farming and, as a result, to unite farmers and labourers. The capital of the society was to consist of ordinary 10/– (10 shilling) shares and no member was allowed to hold more than twenty shares. The majority of those who became shareholders were middle-class professionals, including clergy, with no great direct experience of farming. MNTL did not achieve its objective of uniting farmers and labourers and was wound up in 1937.

MNTL was replaced by Muintir na Tíre, an inclusive rural organisation based on the parish.[47] Muintir na Tíre inherited from MNTL its voluntary basis and its system of parochial guilds or councils, but it changed from being a co-operative organisation into a social movement with an emphasis on neighbourliness or 'muintearas'. It sought to bring all social groups in a parish into a single unit rather than focusing on economic benefits for farmers alone.[48] The first parish guild was founded in Tipperary town in February 1937. Within a few years Muintir na Tíre had guilds or branches in sixteen of the Twenty-Six Counties. The aim of the guilds was to improve the living conditions of people in rural Ireland, including conditions for women working in rural homes. Muintir na Tíre had three stages in its development. The years 1931–37 represent an experimental phase. During the twenty years from 1937 to 1957, the year when Hayes died, Muintir na Tíre was consolidated as a community parish-based movement. In the sixty years since then Muintir na Tíre has continued as a community development organisation.

Hayes drew inspiration from the Belgian community organisation known as the Boerenbond, in which the central unit was the parish.[49] Fr Mark Tierney, a Benedictine monk from Glenstal Abbey in Murroe, the place where Hayes was born, and author of *The Story of Muintir na Tíre*, argues that in choosing the parish as the basic unit for his organisation, Hayes owed much to the GAA, which for over fifty years had helped to generate a 'local 'patriotism' within the parish.[50] Hayes had a vision of rural Ireland based on a vocational order rather than one of social class. A vocational order implied that various groups, for example, all those involved in farming, would manage their own farming activities independent of the State. To overcome class stratification ranging from the big farmers to the landless labourers, 'We then searched for a unit for co-operation and found that one already existed, having a religious, social, economic and traditional basis – the parish.'[51] Nor did Hayes's organisation confine itself to the agricultural community. If confined to the agricultural sector, 'parish unity could not be attained. So we decided to take the whole parish and include all classes, neglecting none.'[52]

The inspiration for Muintir na Tíre may have sprung in part from papal encyclicals but Muintir was stated to be Christian rather than Catholic; non-Catholics were welcomed into its ranks. Writing in 1943, Hayes summed up his policy:

> Our policy is a very simple one – to create a spirit of citizenship in every little parish in Ireland, to drive out bitterness and class-work, to get people to co-operate with their neighbours and thus, through the age-old Christian principles of our social life, to build up a truly Christian and Irish nation.[53]

Hayes made the claim, remarkable at the time, 'that Ireland was becoming so Catholic that it was forgetting to be Christian'.[54] The use of the term 'Christian' closed some doors as Muintir na Tíre was refused access to the Dublin Archdiocese on account of using the word 'Christian' rather than 'Catholic'. 'Dr. John Charles McQuaid refused to allow the movement to be started in his diocese unless the word "Catholic" was substituted for "Christian" in the constitution. But Muintir na Tíre held firm.'[55]

As a young priest, Hayes had worked at the sectarian interface in Liverpool, which probably gave him a more tolerant attitude.

A very successful initiative undertaken by Muintir na Tíre was the annual Rural Week held from 1937 onwards. The attendance at the first Rural Week in Ardmore in Co. Waterford exceeded all expectations. Women played a prominent role and won newspaper headlines, including 'Women, the Important Factor in Rural Ireland' and 'Overwork and Drudgery Driving Women from the Land'.[56] As in the case of the Belgian Boerenbond, a European influence was discernible in the Rural Weeks. [57] Hayes maintained that his organisation, while Irish in practice, was European in inspiration. During the Second World War, or the Emergency as it was known in Ireland, turf-cutting schemes were organised in parishes by Muintir to provide fuel.

In one area a thousand tons of turf were saved and offered to poor people at a very cheap rate. There were also potato schemes and in some towns women members operated 'penny dinners' – an idea which had originated with work by Quakers at the time of the Famine.[58]

From 1944 onwards Muintir na Tíre produced a popular monthly publication entitled *The Landmark*. In 1959 Muintir launched an annual publication called *Rural Ireland*. It contained a section entitled 'Among the Parishes', which summarised work done by parish guilds in the previous year. Typical examples would be Kilballyowen in Co. Clare and Doneraile in Co. Cork. The Kilballyowen report included: 'Many successful projects in the Guild's first year of existence. Formation of dramatic club; plays produced at home and in neighbouring parish. Lectures in agriculture resulted in large quantities of lime etc. being purchased … Successful arts and crafts class being run in two centres'.[59] The Doneraile Guild reported:

> Renovations to the parish hall. Representations to Co. Council for improvements to roads. Rural leadership courses. Two dances and fortnightly Whist Drives held during winter months … Public lighting procured for 3 side streets off Main Street.[60]

Through the lens of 2022 these may seem modest achievements, but in the context of the times the work of the guilds added up to a substantial achievement.

The building of parish halls in close proximity to churches and chapels was started by the Catholic Church in the 1930s. The halls added a valuable social venue for dances (following the Public Dance Halls Act 1935, which regulated dances), drama and concerts, as well as providing a meeting place for parish events and organisations. In the 1930s communities were still recovering from the Civil War, so anything that brought people together was important. Muintir na Tíre also built halls. The first hall built by Muintir was in Murroe in Co. Limerick. Completed in 1941, the hall remains a feature of the village to the present day. During the Second World War the hall in Murroe was used as a meeting place for the Local Defence Force and the Red Cross. In the 1940s and 1950s there were a number of travelling drama groups which visited rural parishes and put on plays in the halls. Muintir na Tíre also organised film shows with their own mobile film unit. This initiative was made possible by the advance of rural electrification, which was launched in the 1940s.

Muintir na Tíre was closely involved with the promotion of rural electrification. W. F. Roe, the man in charge of the Rural Electrification

Scheme, became a member of the National Executive of Muintir na Tíre in 1948. Many towns in Ireland had electricity before the launch of the ESB (Electricity Supply Board) but only 2 per cent of those living outside towns and larger villages were within the electricity network by 1947. Historians of the ESB, Maurice Manning and Moore McDowell, draw attention to the fact that the rural electrification scheme in Ireland was based on the Catholic parish.[61] In 1944 the board of the ESB arranged for the preparation of an internal report on the scheme. Following is a summary of the first two provisions of the report:

> 1. The territorial unit which was to be adopted was the Roman Catholic parish, of which there were at the time around nine hundred in country areas. Existing parish councils, emergency committees and the like would be used to excite local interest in the scheme.
> 2. Each existing Board district would contain, on average, four parishes, with an office in each one, supervised by a small rural electrification division in each district office, which in turn was answerable to the district engineer.[62]

Many Irish country people tended to be cautious about innovation and viewed 'modernisation' with a degree of suspicion.[63] However, Hayes saw rural electrification as part of the community development process central to Muintir na Tíre, and Muintir na Tíre guilds were important in promoting the scheme. Bansha, where Hayes had been parish priest since 1946, was the first rural parish to be electrified in 1948, despite stiff competition from Cahir. The rivalry between the two – Bansha, a Muintir stronghold, and Cahir, a Macra na Feirme (Sons of the Soil) stronghold – was intense. According to one writer, 'Bansha was selected on the basis of a better economic return (for the ESB), although Cahir had a better sign-up, and a deputation from Cahir called to W. F. Roe to protest against alleged favouritism.'[64]

Towards Increased Professionalism

Quarrels succeeded in bringing to an end an initiative for agriculture known as the Parish Plan, which was launched by Muintir na Tíre in 1947. The object of the Parish Plan was to achieve increased agricultural production by the voluntary improvement of farming methods. Organising each parish for the purpose of the plan would be done by Muintir na Tíre and progress would be monitored and overseen by an elected parish council. In 1948 the Minister for Agriculture, James Dillon, lauded the scheme in the Dáil:

> I want to say to Muintir na Tíre that I think they can do an immense service to this State. I think that one of their prime services would be the organisation of the parish and to make our people see and understand that the natural unit for co-operative work in rural Ireland for men and women, and for children too, is the parish.[65]

It was envisaged that the plan would avail of services provided by the Department of Agriculture and that there would be a special agricultural advisor for each parish or group of parishes. A rift developed between the government, which was offering professional help, and Muintir, which was based on cooperation and self-help at a local level but which also wanted to retain control. In the words of Mark Tierney, 'Muintir na Tíre hoped that the Parish Plan would remain in the hands of the parish council.'[66] Following the general election in 1951 the incoming government abandoned the plan. However, when Dillon returned as Minister for Agriculture in 1954, the plan was revived. An unsuccessful effort was made to work on a three-parish plan with a departmental advisor for groups of three parishes. The final nail in the coffin of the Parish Plan came with the government's *Programme for Economic Expansion* in 1958, which stated, 'The Parish Plan will not be developed further.'[67] In *Economic Development*, a document drawn up in the Department of Finance, which had a critical influence on the *Programme for Economic Expansion*, it was stated that the Parish Plan 'is more or less moribund'.[68] Coincidentally, there is no mention of local government in *Economic Development*; presumably, it was not seen as having any role in economic development at that time.

One of the conclusions that Muintir drew from its experience with the Parish Plan was the need to shift in a more professional direction. An important organisational change took place in 1949, when Muintir decided to appoint a full-time paid organiser. In due course further employees were appointed. From 1958 onwards a major shift of emphasis occurred in Muintir's approach to the role of the State. The government and Muintir were sometimes at odds as the government prioritised centralised decision-making while Muintir continued to emphasise the local. But now Muintir accepted the United Nations model of community development,[69] which argued for both the State and the voluntary sector to promote development together:

> This was a significant change of heart, and led to the creation of a partnership between the State and Muintir. Following on this partnership agreement, there was the need for a high level of professionalism on the part of Muintir if it was to co-operate to the fullest extent with the state.[70]

A further significant change in the organisation of Muintir was the replacement in 1971 of the term 'parish guild' or 'parish council' by 'community council' and the establishment of a Central/National Council. Muintir also decided to have a professional development unit, with paid employees, to provide services to the community councils and proposed National Council. Muintir would also seek funds from both central government and local authorities for community development in urban as well as rural areas.

In 1974, following Ireland's entry into the EEC, Muintir received a grant from the European Social Fund to establish a development unit and to begin training people for community development work. Over the next four years Muintir was involved in a number of projects throughout the country known as 'communities at work' projects. In June 1978 Muintir na Tíre published a report by its national director titled *The Training Programme for Community Development Officers*. A pilot training project was offered to 200 community councils throughout Ireland and was financed by the European Social Fund.

One initiative in this phase was participation in the 'Community Alert', and later the 'Community Text Alert', programme established by An Garda Síochána to counteract crime and vandalism in rural areas. Community Alert is a very successful initiative of Muintir 'based on co-operation with government'. The idea of Community Alert was Muintir's response to a number of vicious attacks which took place on elderly people in Co. Cork in the autumn of 1984, and elsewhere the following year.[71] In 2013 the Garda Síochána launched Community Text Alert with the cooperation of Muintir, the Irish Farmers' Association and other rural groups. Using Community Text Alert, the Garda Síochána can provide information by text or email to each registered community contact, who in turn forwards the information by text or email to all members of their community group. An example of the work of Community Text Alert is illustrated by the response to a violent attack on a farmer who lived alone in Coolderry, Co. Offaly, in autumn 2017. Following this attack the Coolderry–Kilcoman text alert committee called a meeting to show solidarity and to discuss plans for security in the area.

Political Parties

Prior to independence, many priests were active in politics. One in ten of the delegates to the first Sinn Féin convention after the Rising were priests. They included Fr Michael O'Flanagan from Roscommon, who was elected joint vice-president, and Fr Pat Gaynor from Tipperary, who was elected a member of the executive. Following independence, and the Civil War, priests withdrew from politics. In his classic study *The Government and Politics of Ireland*, published in 1970, Basil Chubb summarised the historical background to political organisation in Ireland, quoting from a study by Warner Moss:

> The old Parliamentary party having had a committee in each parish it was natural that Sinn Féin should do likewise in its struggle with the party and that the two daughter parties, Fianna Fáil and Cumann na nGaedheal, carried on the practice.[72]

Chubb explains that 'the local branch or cumann [of Fine Gael or Fianna Fáil] tends therefore to be based on the ecclesiastical divisions'. In fact the boundaries of parishes and local government areas were often identical and, as Moss pointed out, 'the chapel door is one of the most suitable places for speeches and the collection of funds'.[73] Canvassing outside churches after Masses was undertaken by all political parties. Former Labour Party TD and MEP John Horgan recalls canvassing for the party outside churches.[74]

Parishes played a fundamental role in the organisation of the two main political parties, Fianna Fáil and Fine Gael. Describing its organisation on its website, Fine Gael says, 'At its core level, Fine Gael is made up of units of the organisation called branches which are organised at parish or community level'.[75] However, on the day of his election as leader of Fine Gael in June 2017, Leo Varadkar was quoted as saying that younger people do not engage in the traditional structure based around the parish or branch. He said that there are new structures to be explored around the workplace or around social media groups.[76] This is an acknowledgement of the weakening of the parish as a community focus and search for an alternative community. On its Galway East home page, Fianna Fáil says that in general a cumann (branch) represents a parish or polling station area. Traditionally, branches of Fianna Fáil and Fine Gael were based on the church area or the polling station area in the countryside and on the local government unit (urban area or ward) in the towns and cities. It is recorded in the archives of Fianna Fáil that 'The basic unit of the organisation was the Cumann, usually contiguous with parishes in rural areas, and with groups of streets in urban areas'.[77] The Labour Party constitution provides for the setting up of branches in 'districts', which are defined by the Central Administrative Council. The link between Fianna Fáil and the parish goes back to the earliest days of the party when, according to Conor Lenihan, 'It was left to Seán Lemass to visit every parish and town in the countryside to mobilise the hard-headed IRA men to join the new party led by de Valera'.[78] And in an interview in

The Irish Times on 15 August 2015, Sinn Féin TD Pearse Doherty described how he received a phone call which changed his life. The call was from Pat Doherty, Sinn Féin activist and abstentionist MP. Out of that call came a commitment by Pearse Doherty to help build Sinn Féin 'parish by parish' in his locality.

As well as seeking votes at church gates, church-gate collections for political purposes, generally only outside Catholic churches, were common for a century. Following the Military Services (No. 2) Act 1918, which provided for conscription, 'church gate collections were organised [by those opposed to conscription] to raise what was called a National Defence Fund, while, in theory, a Local Defence Fund was established in every parish.'[79] The object of the fund was to finance resistance to the imposition of compulsory military service. The clergy were authorised by the bishops to hold church-gate collections with this objective. Thirty years later, in 1949, a countrywide collection outside churches took place in support of the anti-partition candidates in the Northern Ireland elections.[80] In 1956 when Seán Lemass was a TD and Director of Organisation for Fianna Fáil, he advised Frank Loughman, a candidate in Tipperary, to deal with parish priests before bishops in relation to church-gate collections. If any priests objected to fundraising outside Mass, Lemass promised then to go over the head of the priest to the relevant bishop.[81] Following Fianna Fáil's success in the 1957 general election, Lemass returned as Minister for Industry and Commerce. He wrote to every cumann (branch) of Fianna Fáil in the country telling them of the need to raise funds through collections after Mass in order to maintain 'a live and effective organisation'.[82] By 2018 canvassing at churches, although still practised, had become less frequent, a development which presumably reflects the decline in church attendance. Fianna Fáil continues to hold church-gate collections in some areas and Fianna Fáil and Fine Gael continue to canvass at some churches. Councillor Críona Ní Dhálaigh does not recall any collections or canvassing for Sinn Féin at churches in Dublin, but says they occur in some rural areas.[83]

The term 'parish-pump politics' is often used in a derogatory sense, to imply that a politician is more interested in local issues and garnering the local vote than in the wider issues of governing in the interests of the people and country as a whole. Somewhat harshly, political scientist R. K. Carty expressed the opinion nearly forty years ago that 'As a result of the parties' inability to control the recruitment processes, the Dáil is filled by self-starting political entrepreneurs whose primary skills are those of the parish-pump machine boss, or by their inheritors.'[84] In criticism of the Catholic Church, and of political parties, in particular of Fianna Fáil, Carty states:

Certainly the dominant authority structure in Ireland is the church. It is in a word omnipresent: to be Irish is to be Catholic. The church's values permeate the political culture and constitutional order; its teachings and teachers dominate the socialization system; its formal structures set a standard for social and political organization. The Irish church is an anti-intellectual, male-dominated, hierarchical organization which rewards loyalty and faithful service. So are Irish political parties. Indeed Fianna Fáil's predominance, in the nineteenth century tradition of there being but one Irish party, constitutes a secular caricature of the church's unchallenged position in the society.[85]

Carty goes on to suggest that in their relationships with their local constituents and with their party, TDs occupy much the same structural position as priests in the Catholic Church. Carty maintains that priests acted as the Irish peasant's primary contact with external authority.[86] Much has changed in the forty years since 1981, when Carty published *Party and Parish Pump*, but it is clear that the closeness between TDs and their constituents has remained strong over the years. The closeness appears particularly marked with some independent TDs; for example, the Healy-Rae brothers and cousins from Kerry. For those TDs, links with the local community or parish never seemed stronger. It is easy for some in academe or who live in parts of Dublin close to decision-makers of all kinds to decry clientelism, but in remote parishes, far away from the centre, people feel the need for local advocates. The results of the 2016 general election, when nineteen independents and four 'Independents for Change' were elected, and of the European election in 2019, when independents obtained almost one-quarter of the votes and won four out of thirteen seats, contrast sharply with Carty's quotation from a 1973 report, to the effect that the 'days of Independent deputies are fast fading into memory'.[87]

5

Local Government

Local Government and Subsidiarity

According to historian and former senator Joe Lee:

> Ireland has almost no serious local self-government, in marked contrast to
> many Western European countries. 'Local issues decided locally' are relatively
> rare in Ireland. Local issues are largely decided nationally, in so far as they are
> decided at all. National decisions have fundamental implications for local
> welfare in areas like policing, education, health and conservation, which often
> come under local control elsewhere.[1]

There was no reference to local government in the Constitution as adopted
in 1937. However, the Constitution has been amended on several occasions,
including in 2001 when the Twentieth Amendment of the Constitution Act
was passed by the Oireachtas following a referendum in June 1997. This Act,
which provided for constitutional recognition of local government for the
first time, followed from a recommendation in the first report of the All-
Party Committee on the Constitution, which had been established in 1996.

Ten years after Lee passed judgement, a new Article 28A provided for
constitutional recognition of local government in Ireland.

Article 28A 1 says:

> The State recognises the role of local government in providing a forum for the
> democratic representation of local communities, in exercising and performing
> at local level powers and functions conferred by law and in promoting by
> initiatives the interests of such communities.

Article 28A 2, 3, 4 and 5 deal with the powers and functions of local
authorities, the election of members of local authorities, the electorate in
those elections and the procedure for the filling of casual vacancies which
may occur.

Both historian Diarmaid Ferriter and senator and former Attorney General Michael McDowell have expressed strong criticism of the current state of local government. Ferriter speaks of the 'thirst for centralisation' which stretches back for decades,[2] while McDowell says, 'The real question is one of power and control.'[3] Gerard Howlin, a *Sunday Times* columnist and former advisor to Taoiseach Bertie Ahern, has suggested that among the areas encompassed by the Department of Housing, Local Government and Heritage, the area of local government has been sidelined. He refers to a plan by former minister Phil Hogan to finance local government with a property tax and water charges, but the water charges never became a reality.

Councillors are elected to local authorities every five years and decisions are made by councillors at their regular meetings; for example, passing the annual budget. The chief executive and team assist the councillors as well as having responsibility for certain areas, including the implementation of the corporate plan and the allocation of grants. The chief executive is appointed for a seven-year term with optional extension of a further three years. Tensions may sometimes occur between a chief executive and a council although more often there are disagreements between the different political parties on the council itself. Councils are divided according to the political affiliation of the councillors and decisions are taken by majority vote. Owen Keegan, chief executive officer of Dublin City Council, expresses a view that, from his experience, additional tensions can arise when the political composition of the controlling group on the council differs from the political composition of the government of the day.[4]

The stated areas of responsibility of local authorities are impressive: housing, roads, recreation and amenities, planning, libraries, environmental protection, fire services and keeping the register of electors. But on closer examination it appears that local government autonomy is constrained in key areas. For example, in relation to housing, a central government body, the Housing Agency, was set up in 2010 to work with the Department of Housing, Local Government and Heritage, the local authorities and approved housing bodies. In regard to roads, Transport Infrastructure Ireland (TII), which was set up in 2015 by merging the National Roads Authority and the Railway Procurement Agency, has responsibility for all national primary roads while local authorities deal with regional and local roads. The Environmental Protection Agency was established in 1992 and waste management is among its responsibilities. Councils which previously managed domestic refuse collections have been replaced by private companies such as Panda and Greyhound.

However, it is probably fair to say that the Housing Agency and TII largely exercise functions that were previously exercised by central government departments or utilities such as Iarnród Éireann. It is not a simple question of removing functions from local authorities. Keegan explains:

> The real problem is not just that local authorities have lost functions (e.g. overall responsibility for water supply and waste water services) but even where they have retained functions they are increasingly dependent on Government funding with the inevitable result that they have become implementing agencies for Government policy – a system of local government has gradually been replaced by a system of local administration.[5]

Attempts to quantify the extent of local autonomy or levels of centralisation and decentralisation suggest that Ireland is one of the most centralised countries in the developed world.[6] According to one measure used in an international study, Ireland emerges as *the* most centralised country in the study.[7] When drawing inferences concerning the degree of centralisation a number of factors must be borne in mind, including the size of the country and the voting system. While Ireland is one of the smaller European countries in terms of population, with just 5 million people, the population within the sphere of Dublin City Council is 550,000. This compares with 335,000 for Belfast City Council, while London is divided into 32 local boroughs with populations of between 150,000 and 300,000. In Ireland the proportional representational voting system means that local matters may be brought to the Dáil by TDs. However, none of these factors mitigates the reality of the relative growth in the importance of central rather than local government in Ireland.

The story of the growth in central government in Ireland is the story both of the growth in the provision of new services by central government, where none existed, and of the replacement of services previously provided by local authorities, or by voluntary workers in the home and the parish, and by religious organisations. In 1838 the Irish Poor Law Act was passed to assist the poor via the workhouse system or 'indoor relief'. The administration of the system was the responsibility of different civil parishes. The other local boundaries which existed at the time were counties, baronies and boroughs.[8] In 1872 the Poor Law Commission became the Local Government Board for Ireland and in 1898 the Local Government Act, which was introduced by the then Chief Secretary for Ireland, Gerald Balfour, established local government in Ireland on the same basis as in England, Scotland and Wales. In rural Ireland the grand juries, the bodies responsible for raising taxes and undertaking certain work, including road maintenance, were the precursors of county councils. They were mainly comprised of leading landlords in the area. The 1898 Act shifted control of local affairs away from the grand juries and therefore from landlords. The Act provided for the election of members of councils by the votes of those men on the local government electoral list, i.e., the middle class, professional, commercial and farming groups. Women were also included in the local government franchise. Suffragist Anna Haslam described the 1898 Act as 'the most significant political revolution in the history of women.'[9] Administrative counties with county councils were created. Six of the cities (two in Northern Ireland) were made county boroughs in which the corporations had almost all the functions of a county council as well as the functions of a borough corporation. The administrative county was divided into county districts, rural and urban.

James Meenan, in his classic study of the Irish economy, says that the extension of local government to Ireland by the 1898 Act was even more important politically rather than economically:

> This measure transferred local power (and patronage) from the landlords to elected bodies which, except in some counties of Ulster and a few areas elsewhere, would certainly be controlled by nationalists. In its own way, this was as far-reaching a transfer of power as the Treaty was to bring; and indeed the adherence of county councils and corporations to the Republican cause was to do a great deal to make the Treaty attainable.[10]

With independence the Local Government Board was replaced by the Department of Local Government. A guiding policy principle was that of subsidiarity. Where possible, decisions should be taken at a local, rather than a central, level. This principle had its roots in Catholic social teaching as first presented by Leo XIII in the papal encyclical *Rerum Novarum* (1891) and elaborated on by Pius XI in *Quadragesimo Anno* (1931). The proponents of subsidiarity maintained that it represented a bulwark against the State taking control of the lives of its citizens as could happen under a communist regime. According to sociologist Tony Fahey, 'Few places were more willing in principle to embrace Catholic social teaching than Ireland.'[11] For example, in the 1937 Constitution, while the State undertook to provide primary education, the primary educators of children were stated to be the parents. Surprisingly perhaps, local government did not merit mention.

Three factors have contributed to the curtailment of the subsidiarity principle in regard to the relationship between the State, local government, individuals and families. The first is the demands of citizens for the provision of more and better state services as funds became available. The second is the development of another strand of Christian teaching which gradually accepted the welfare state, where the strong care for the weak via taxation and public services. This strand was supported in the encyclicals of Pope John XXIII, notably *Mater et Magistra*. Concerning the relationship between the State and the local community, the thread of subsidiarity continues to run through the fabric of the European Union to the present day where community development is proposed as 'a true expression of the European principle of subsidiarity, ensuring that decisions, problems and issues are addressed at the lowest possible level'.[12] The third factor, possibly related to the first two, is the, at times, ad hoc approach to decision-making by government. Problems are dealt with on a case-by-case basis. For example, when it was considered that there were problems with the health services, the Health Service Executive (HSE) was established. In *Putting People First* (PPF), published by the Department of the Environment, Community and Local Government in 2012, it is stated that some traditional functions of local authorities have moved to specialist organisations in recent years 'due to necessities of scale, resources and expertise'.[13] The document suggests four areas where the functions of local government are being strengthened. These are an enhanced role in economic development and enterprise support, close involvement in community and local development, devolution of specific functions from central to local level and widening the reach of local government. With regard to devolution of functions from the centre, which is at the heart of local government, the document mentions areas such as the environment, water, food safety and housing but does not spell out precisely how much of these areas are to be dealt with at local level. This is important given that there are centralised bodies dealing with these areas; for example, the Environmental Protection Agency for the environment and Irish Water for water, while the Department of Health has overall responsibility for food safety.

In a comprehensive study of local government in Ireland, Mark Callanan quotes Article 1 of the Treaty of European Union:

> The treaty marks a new stage in the process of creating an ever closer union among the peoples of Europe, in which decisions are taken as openly as possible and as closely as possible to the citizen.[14]

The Lisbon Treaty (2009) included a more explicit reference to the principle of subsidiarity in the context of relationships between national and local governance. 'The principle of subsidiarity is also reflected in the Council of Europe's Charter of Self-Government, signed by Ireland.'[15] In the Lisbon

Treaty the right to local self-government was mentioned for the first time in one of the EU's treaties. Article 4.2 says:

> The Union shall respect the equality of Member States before the Treaties as well as their national identities, inherent in their fundamental structures, political and constitutional, inclusive of regional and local self-government.

In an essay on local government in the European Union, Marius Guderjan of the Humboldt University refers to the relevance of subsidiarity for local government.

Guderjan concludes:

> Local authorities are essential for executing EU legislation and this in turn allows them to shape EU policies … Subsidiarity and multilevel governance have become part of the EU's 'constitutional compound' but remain political rather than 'hard' legal principles.[16]

This would seem to be the case in Ireland, where it appears that political pull towards the centre has been stronger than towards the local. The development of the primary education system and the health services illustrates how voluntary work, often by religious orders, and local input have been largely replaced by the State. In the decades following independence the provision of State services in education and health, other than fairly basic provision, was thin on the ground. The dispensary service, a general medical service based on a means test, developed subsequent to the Poor Relief (Ireland) Act 1851. It was rooted in the dispensary districts of each poor law union – that is, a union of a number of civil parishes – and therefore administered locally. Although some new services for mothers and children under five years of age and treatment services for children attending national schools had been introduced by 1922, no further improvements were made in existing services and no new services were introduced until after the Second World War.[17] The dispensary system remained in operation until the introduction of the General Medical Services in 1972.

The role of the religious orders in providing healthcare services is acknowledged by Lee. Regarding the Catholic Church, Lee writes:

> Its administrative and managerial achievement, at home and abroad, in education, in health, in welfare, as well as in religion, owing much to women as well as men, deserves the highest recognition. The achievement at home has often been taken for granted, or even slighted, because of the over-politicisation of the perspective from which the role of the Catholic clergy has

tended to be assessed in conventional historiography, and because of the superficiality of much public comment on the church in society.[18]

The provision of hospital services by religious orders goes back to the nineteenth century. In 1835 St Vincent's Hospital was opened by Mother Mary Aikenhead, founder of the Sisters of Charity, in the former home of the Earl of Meath on St Stephen's Green in Dublin. Aikenhead was the first woman in Europe to found a hospital. Twenty years after the death in 1841 of their founder, Catherine McAuley, the Mercy Sisters opened the Mater Hospital in Dublin in 1861, and twenty years later, in 1883, the sisters opened a hospital in Belfast. Orders of nuns continued to open hospitals in Ireland until the mid twentieth century.

Greater centralisation developed in the 1980s when some of the smaller voluntary hospitals closed, including Baggot Street, Jervis Street, and the Meath and Richmond Hospitals in Dublin. Jervis Street and Richmond Hospitals were replaced by the large public hospital Beaumont, on the north side of the city. The move towards centralised State provision of education and health services was accelerated by the shift in emphasis towards economic growth as the dominant national objective in the years following the publication of *Economic Development* in 1958. This was followed in 1965 by the publication of the OECD report *Investment in Education*, which stressed the importance of education for economic growth. The introduction of free post-primary education and the building of new schools required considerable State investment. Regional technical colleges/institutes of technology, which developed from 1970 onwards, emphasised the meeting of manpower needs and proved to be effective engines of economic growth.

What's in a Name?

According to Article 28 of the Constitution, the 'Government shall consist of not less than seven and not more than fifteen members'. The titles of ministerial portfolios have evolved over time with the introduction of new portfolios – for example, 'Children and Youth Affairs' – or the introduction of a new element into an existing portfolio – for example, the inclusion of 'Skills' with 'Education'. In the hundred years since 1919 the Department of Local Government has undergone nine name changes and for a period of twenty years, from 1977 to 1997, the name 'Local Government' vanished from the titles of government departments.

From 1997 'Local Government' became an 'add-on' to a range of other ministerial responsibilities and never again ranked as the first name in the

Table 8a: Title Changes of Department of Local Government from First Dáil 1919–2020*

Title Minister/Department	Date
Local Government Board	1872–1921/2
Local Government	1919–24
Local Government and Public Health	1924–47
Local Government	1947–77
Environment	1977–97
Environment and Local Government	1997–2002
Environment, Heritage and Local Government	2002–11
Environment, Community and Local Government	2011–16
Housing, Planning, Community and Local Government	2016–17
Housing, Planning and Local Government	2017–20
Housing, Local Government and Heritage	2020–

* Under British administration, the title was Local Government Board for 1872–1922.

Table 8b: Other Government Departments with 'Community' in Title 2002–20

Department	Date
Community, Rural and Gaeltacht Affairs	2002–10
Community, Equality and Gaeltacht Affairs	2010–11
Community included with Environment and Local Government (see Table 8a)	2011–17
Rural and Community Development	2017–20

departmental title. It may be argued that names do not matter and that the work of local authorities crosses several departments, including, for example, Environment, Transport, Education and so on. But names reveal much about the policy priorities and focus of government. A Ministry of Local Government was established by the first Dáil in 1919, with W. T. Cosgrave as the inaugural minister. In 1924 a Ministry and Department of Local Government and Public Health was established. During the 1920s and 1930s the main focus of the department was to oversee the local authorities, which had previously come under the Local Government Board, and to promote the impressive local authority housing programme. In 1925 the poor law unions were abolished and their powers were transferred to county councils. In 1947 separate Departments of Health and Social Welfare were established and the former Department of Local Government and Public Health was renamed the Department of Local Government. Its responsibilities included housing, infrastructure and water. For thirty years, from 1947 until 1977, local government was the sole responsibility of a minister and government department.

Relevant departmental name changes are listed in Tables 8a and 8b. In addition to showing the twenty-year absence of 'Local Government' from the name of any department, the tables show the inclusion of the word 'Community' in the title of the Department of Environment, Community and Local Government from 2011 to 2016 and in the title of the Department of Housing, Planning, Community and Local Government for the years 2016–17. The word 'Community' had migrated from the Department of Community, Equality and Gaeltacht Affairs. It is also noted that 'Environment', which replaced 'Local Government' for twenty years, and continued to be linked with 'Local Government' for a further nineteen years, became part of a new Department of Communications, Climate Action and the Environment in 2016.

In the twenty year period 1997–2017 the name of the ministry which started as Local Government in 1919 changed five times. This could be interpreted in a positive way, as a reflection of changing policy priorities or to improve management. Or the changes might be interpreted in a more negative way, as reflecting a reduced commitment to local government or even some degree of confusion regarding its role. The Department of the Environment, which replaced the Department of Local Government in 1977, had 'Local Government' added back to its title twenty years later. This remained the position until 2002, when 'Heritage' was added. The Department of the Environment, Heritage and Local Government was in existence from 2002 until 2011, when 'Heritage' was replaced by 'Community'. The new Department of Environment, Community and Local Government became the Department of Housing, Planning, Community and Local Government in 2016. But in 2017 'Community' was dropped and the department became the Department of Housing, Planning and Local Government. However, one of the ministers of state at that department had responsibility for 'Communities and the National Drugs Strategy'. Between 2017 and 2020 a separate department was named 'Rural and Community Development'. While major departments like Finance and Health currently have a single designation, others have a multitude. Minister Catherine Martin presides over a department with six components in the title: Tourism, Culture, Arts, Gaeltacht, Sport and Media. Jack Chambers is the minister of state at the Department of the Taoiseach and government chief whip, but is also assigned as minister of state to the Departments of Tourism, Culture, Arts, Gaeltacht, Sport and Media, and of Defence. From the perspective of local authorities, it means that their energies are dispersed across a number of departments in search of funding, rather than a straightforward focus on the 'Custom House', the traditional seat of the Department of Local Government in bygone times. For example, in regard to climate action local authorities must look to the Department of the Environment, Climate and Communications, or with regard to transport they must look to the Department of Transport.

Some of the name-changing in regard to local government may have been influenced by changes in the titles of ministries in the UK. For example, in 1970 the Ministry of Housing and Local Government was combined with the Ministry of Transport to form the Ministry of the Environment. Then in 2018 the ministry was renamed Housing, Communities and Local Government. Name changes of departments reflect changing priorities of government. It must be assumed that for the twenty years when the name 'Local Government' did not have a place at the cabinet table, local government had fallen down the list of government priorities. And for the past twenty years Local Government has had to share a place with others, at times Environment, Heritage, Community, Planning and Housing.

Local authorities have had no role in the provision of health services since 1970. Arguments in favour of greater centralisation of services, for example, in health, have included grounds of equity and efficiency. It was argued that local authorities, which had extensive responsibility for health services prior to the introduction of regional health boards in 1970, but were relatively revenue poor, could not provide services as well as the better-off local authorities could. Originally, there were eight regional health boards but this number was increased to eleven in 1999. Five years later, on 1 January 2005, the HSE was established; when it was argued that a unified administration would increase efficiency and reduce costs. Over 100,000 persons are employed in the health services and in 2021 the HSE had a budget of over €20 billion. At present there are nine hospital groups and a number of community healthcare organisations. Further changes are due to be introduced under the Sláintecare plan,[19] although doubts have been raised concerning the future of Sláintecare following the resignation of the chief executive and the chairman of the advisory board in September 2021.[20] The plan proposes the re-establishment of six regional healthcare structures which would include all services – hospital and non-hospital – in each region. In essence this would be a move back in the direction of the old regional health boards which were in place before the establishment of the HSE. This move would seem to represent a significant acknowledgement of the limits of centralisation.

In education, too, the trend appears to be towards consolidation and greater centralisation. Under the Vocational Education Act 1930, thirty-three vocational education committees (VECs) were established to provide continuation and technical education for students aged fourteen to sixteen. Members of the VECs were selected by the relevant local authorities and the VECs were responsible for establishing and maintaining vocational schools. In 2013 the thirty-three VECs were replaced by sixteen education and training boards (ETBs), which include a number of local councillors on the boards. In making the announcement the then Minister for Education and Skills, Ruairí Quinn, said that the new ETBs would 'enhance the scale of local education and training'. Furthermore, 'This major reform will reduce the number of Chief Executive Officers in line with the number of bodies and full year savings are estimated at €2.1m.'[21] More recently, in 2018, the government decided to amalgamate ten of the fourteen institutes of technology into four technological universities.

Probably the most significant shift away from local authorities has been in relation to the direct provision of social housing, which is now 100 per cent funded by central government grants. Traditionally, local authorities acquired land for social housing and built housing units for rent to those who met defined criteria. In the early years of the twenty-first century there was a shift away from the direct construction of social housing units by local authorities to a system whereby local authorities would pay rent to private landlords or undertake long-term leasing in order to access accommodation for those requiring social housing.[22] A problem which Keegan has identified is that some local authorities no longer possess large tracts of land on which to build houses as they did in the past.[23] Another problem can arise due to planning permission delays but recently there has been a move to strengthen the role of local authorities in regard to the planning process. The Strategic Housing Development (SHD) planning application system was intended to speed up the supply of homes. Under SHD, planning applications go directly to An Bord Pleanála and decisions cannot be appealed. But the system has led to legal challenges and delays so it is to be replaced with a system which gives more say to local authorities and introduces time limits for making decisions.

Local authorities tend nowadays to rely more on voluntary approved housing bodies for the provision of social housing but as far back as the nineteenth century local authorities were providing large numbers of rental houses in rural and urban areas for low-income groups. This policy continued after independence, with a surge in building between the 1930s and early 1950s. For example, in the twelve months to 31 March 1953, 7,486 local authority houses were built. In the three decades from the end of the 1940s to the end of the 1970s nearly 150,000 local authority houses were completed. In the 1970s the annual number of local authority houses completed peaked at almost 9,000 in 1975, notwithstanding the severe economic difficulties encountered in the wake of the first oil crisis in 1973. The decades when a Department of Local Government existed, 1947–77, were the most fruitful in terms of local authority housing output and this period included the 1950s and the 1970s, when rates of economic growth were low. The building of local authority houses is different from the provision of housing by local authorities, because in recent years local authorities have purchased houses from the private sector for occupation by local authority clients. While this complicates comparisons over time, over 300,000 local authority homes have been built since the foundation of the State. Over two-thirds of these were sold off to tenants, reducing the local authority rental stock to around 100,000.

A scheme known as the 'Surrender Grant' scheme was introduced in the 1980s. It was an initiative of central government. Local authority tenants were offered a cash grant of Ir£5,000 to surrender their tenancy and move to the private sector. The objectives of the scheme were to stimulate the construction industry, to free up public housing stock in order to reduce waiting lists and to help former tenants to rent in the private sector or to buy a home. In the first fourteen months of the scheme in the Dublin area, 75 per cent of applicants came from three housing estates – Darndale, Ballymun and Tallaght. *A Study of the £5,000 Surrender Grant in the Dublin Housing Area*, by Iseult O'Malley (now a Judge of the Supreme Court), Fiona O'Toole and Aideen Hayden, showed that many of those who moved were identified as community leaders and their loss threw into crisis local organisations which had taken years to build up. Furthermore, an already fragmented community was required to absorb an increasing share of more marginalised people.[24]

An innovation in the 1960s was the establishment of the National Building Agency (NBA), a centralised organisation which it was hoped would build social housing at a more rapid pace than local authorities. The agency did produce housing output fairly rapidly. Among the best known social housing estates built by the NBA were those at Ballymun and Darndale in Dublin and Rahoon in Galway. However, it was generally agreed that while apartments and houses were built, amenities of every kind were lacking, leading to difficulties in developing real communities. A successor to the NBA was established in 2020. Called the Land Development Agency, it will promote a mixture of private and social housing and, hopefully, help to promote communities and not just provide shelter.

It is hardly a coincidence that in the year in which Local Government ceased to merit a ministerial position in cabinet a major change in the financing of local authorities occurred. In 1977 the government led by Taoiseach Jack Lynch abolished domestic rates and motor taxation for vehicles up to and including 16 h.p. The abolition of rates had also been mooted by Fine Gael but their intention was to spread the abolition over a longer period and to start with the abolition of rates on small farm holdings.[25] The loss of income from domestic rates was a serious blow to the independence of local authorities, as domestic rates contributed to the funding of housing, water and sanitary services as well as the collection of waste and other services. The motor tax, which would later be restored, went towards the Road Fund, which included provision for maintenance and repair of roads. The abolition of domestic rates, followed by the abolition of agricultural rates in the 1980s, limited the ability of local authorities to provide services. The local authorities introduced service charges for water and refuse in order to gather income but these proved unpopular, led to protests and were abolished by the government in 1997. Prior to the introduction of the Local Property Tax in 2013, local authorities derived their income from rates on commercial properties, housing rents and service charges, as well as from the Exchequer. In 2015 local government tax revenue in Ireland accounted for 3 per cent of total public tax revenue, compared with 6 per cent in the UK, 20 per cent in France and 26 per cent in Denmark.[26]

Before the abolition of domestic rates, a shift had taken place in the relative importance of the local authorities vis-à-vis central government in regard to the provision of education, health and social welfare services as well as housing. In the two decades between 1949 and 1970 the share of local authority expenditure in total public expenditure on these services fell from 48 per cent to 38 per cent (or from 40 per cent to 21 per cent when grants from central government net of transfers from local authorities are taken into account).[27] In the early 1970s rates amounted to 44 per cent of the income of local authorities, with 38 per cent coming from State grants and 18 per cent from miscellaneous receipts. In a research paper by Dr Mary Murphy in 2019 it was shown that 8 per cent of public spending was carried out by local authorities in Ireland compared with over 23 per cent in EU23 countries.[28]

In the debate on the Local Government (Financial Provisions) Bill 1977 Deputy Seán Treacy of the Labour Party was one of those who opposed the abolition of domestic rates and motor tax. He suggested, 'This is a sugar-coated Bill containing a deadly poison, a poison which connotes the ultimate destruction of the local authority system and the democratic basis on which it exists.'[29] Treacy doubted the capacity 'of a remote and elusive Department of State such as the Department of the Environment or the Department of Finance, and the ability of those Departments to make proper assessment of local requirements'. He suggested that it could be significant that the government had changed the name of the Department of Local Government to the Department of the Environment, implying a relative demotion of local government.

Over forty years later, in 2019, another case was made in defence of local government by UCC academic Dr Aodh Quinlivan, when he addressed the Joint Committee of the Oireachtas on Housing, Planning and Local Government.[30] Like Treacy decades earlier, Quinlivan stressed the importance of local government for democracy. Quinlivan said that local government exists for two main reasons: 'as a provider of local public services and as an instrument of local democracy to give expression to community self-government'.[31] Quinlivan said that local democracy was based on the idea of subsidiarity, which implied the devolution of the maximum number of powers and functions to the level closest to the citizen. Ireland, he said, had signed up to the principle of subsidiarity under the Council of Europe's Charter of Local Self-Government and the EU's Treaty of Amsterdam and under Article 21 of the Universal Declaration of Human Rights. Quinlivan said that local government in Ireland is extremely weak and, although it has received constitutional recognition, 'Staggeringly, it lacks constitutional protection.'[32]

Prior to the reforms introduced under the Local Authority Reform Act 2014 following PPF, there were 114 local authorities. Now there are thirty-one, namely twenty-six county councils, including three in Dublin – Fingal, Dún Laoghaire–Rathdown and South Dublin; three city councils – Cork, Dublin and Galway; and two city and county councils – Limerick and Waterford. Under the 2014 Act eighty town councils were abolished and the overall number of councillors was reduced by 40 per cent, from 1,627 to 949. The abolition of so many town councils echoed the abolition of rural district councils 100 years earlier, in 1925. Rural district councils had been introduced in 1898.[33] However, local government is relevant to regions of large population as well as small. Because of the importance of cities as hubs for economic, cultural and educational development and much else, increasing attention is being paid to city regions, or the metro. The idea of the metro includes the core city and its suburban and rural hinterland. Governance models include that of a directly elected mayor. In Limerick there is statutory provision for a directly elected mayor. Cork and Galway also have had the option of a directly elected mayor but have so far declined. The role of directly elected mayor, which comes with a salary, is not totally clear as it seems to envisage sharing of functions with the CEO. The role as envisaged in Ireland would seem to carry less authority than that of the Mayor of London, where, for example, Ken Livingstone wielded real power in the role. Michael Gove, Secretary of State for Levelling Up, Housing and Communities in the UK, has hinted at the devolution of more powers from Whitehall to elected mayors in the regions.[34]

Ninety-five municipal districts, increased to one hundred in 2019, were introduced following the 2014 Act. The municipal district structure is primarily based on town and hinterland, and operates within a unitary council. Most local authority areas are divided into two or more municipal districts. The only local authorities not to have municipal councils are Dublin, Cork and Galway City Councils and Dún Laoghaire–Rathdown, Fingal and South Dublin Councils. Municipal districts vary in size, with a small number having as few as five elected members.[35] For example, Co. Clare is divided into four municipal districts, centred on Ennis, Killaloe, Shannon and West Clare with 7, 5, 7 and 9 elected councillors, respectively. With just one city or county council for close to 150,000 people, Ireland has fewer municipalities than similar-sized European countries and they perform fewer functions than European counterparts.[36]

Alongside the decline in the relative importance of local authorities in the provision of services, centralisation has increased via the persistent growth of Dublin in terms of economic strength and population. Dublin is the seat of government and that will not change. Keegan points out that just over 40 per cent of national GDP is generated in Dublin, while less than a quarter of UK GDP is generated in London. The dominance of Dublin is also reflected in the growth in population. In 1926 Dublin, city and county, accounted for 17 per cent of the population of the Free State compared with 28 per cent of the Republic of Ireland in 2016. One in three citizens of the Republic lives in Dublin. At the general election in 2016, 43 of the 158 seats in the Dáil were in Dublin. Census data suggest that the lifeblood of rural communities is being diluted to strengthen urban communities, where the opportunities for work and study exist. The 2016 census was the first to include data on the 'daytime' population. The census provided these data for over 7,000 'workplace zones'. The results show that the night-time population of Dublin city, approximately 500,000, increased by over one-quarter to more than 700,000 during the day. Cork city showed an even bigger difference of 38 per cent between night-time and day-time population while Cork county and Meath showed large falls, no doubt because of their position in the commuter belt next to the cities of Cork and Dublin. The effects of Covid-19 on this situation are as yet unknown but it seems likely that there will be an increase in home-based work, which will reduce travel and may help to strengthen local communities.

In 1993 Dublin was divided into four areas – Dublin City Council, South Dublin County Council, Dún Laoghaire–Rathdown County Council and Fingal County Council. The division has worked well: each council has a number of area committees which provide an opportunity for councillors to pay close attention to their own particular area.

Some International Comparisons

A European perspective is provided by the European Charter of Local Self-Government and the principle of subsidiarity. The charter is an international treaty of the Council of Europe which Ireland ratified in 2002. It stresses the right of citizens to participate in public affairs and that this right can be most effectively exercised at local level. The concept of local self-government is defined in the charter as the right of local authorities, within the limits of the law, to regulate and manage a substantial share of public affairs under their responsibility and in the interests of the local population. The principle of subsidiarity is concerned with determining the appropriate competence at European, national or local levels.

Richard Boyle, in his study *Re-Shaping Local Government*,[37] says that a distinguishing characteristic of local government in Ireland is the relatively limited range of functions undertaken by these authorities. Many local authorities in other OECD countries have responsibility for a much broader range of social services. Alternative approaches internationally to local government reform fall into two main categories: amalgamation and merger on the one hand, and cooperation and coordination between authorities on the other. Boyle says that in many OECD countries there have been calls for larger local authority units which could yield greater economies of scale combined with collaborative planning and resource sharing. On the other hand it is argued by Callanan, Murphy and Quinlivan that larger authorities may be more bureaucratic.[38] A study in Denmark showed that citizen satisfaction with local services decreases slightly with an increase in the population size of the local authority.[39]

Northern Ireland falls into the category of merger and amalgamation where in April 2015 twenty-six councils were reduced to eleven. For example, Belfast City Council was expanded to include the surrounding urban area. This led to a population increase from 270,000 to 335,000. The new area now includes part of Lisburn City Council, Castlereagh Borough Council and North Down Borough Council. Economic development was one of the main drivers behind the decision to expand the boundary.

The alternative approach of cooperation and consolidation is exemplified by Greater Manchester, where the Greater Manchester Authority came into being in 2011. It is not a merger or a boundary change but a higher tier of government at the regional level whereby the ten authorities in Greater Manchester coordinate key economic development, regeneration and transport functions. The leaders of the ten councils meet monthly.

The *Routledge Handbook of International Local Government*[40] provides extensive coverage of local government worldwide. As would be expected of a study with such wide coverage, references to Ireland are sparse. However, in the final essay by NUI scholars Gerard Turley and Stephen McNena, comparative material on the financing of local government for the period 2000–14 is provided. Over that period local government current revenue as a share of GDP fell from 10 per cent to 3 per cent in Ireland. Turley suggests that the reduction was mainly due to the abolition of the health boards and the cessation of intergovernmental grants from central to local government to cover health expenditure when the HSE was established on 1 January 2005.[41] Of the twenty-eight countries of the EU at the time of the Turley and McNena study, only Cyprus and Malta had a lower share than Ireland in 2014. The highest share of 24.6 per cent was in Sweden while the UK share, at 10.5 per cent, was more than three times greater than the share in Ireland. Between 2000 and 2014 local government current revenue as a share of general government revenue plummeted from 28 per cent to 9 per cent. The share was lower only in Greece, Cyprus and Malta. By contrast, in the UK the share rose from 25 per cent to 27 per cent. The funding of local government worldwide depends as much, if not more, on political and institutional factors as on economic principles.

Turley and McNena suggest that the provision of services by local government can result in a better 'matching' of services with local needs. The trend to centralise contrasts, for example, with the situation in England where parish councils, which are the lowest rung of local government, cover more than 25 per cent of the population. They are responsible for areas described as civil parishes. Civil parish councils in England originated with the Local Government Act 1894. Parish councils are in the hands of unpaid councillors who are elected for a four-year term. The councils have quite a broad remit, including buildings for public use, cycle parking and the avoidance of litter. They have a right to be consulted on planning matters and to be appointed to the boards of primary schools and much else. The overriding objective of parish councils is to achieve what is best for their local area and parish.

The Irish local government reform programme based on PPF (2012)[42] envisages an enhanced role for local government. PPF was drawn up by the Department of the Environment, Community and Local Government against the backdrop of the financial crisis when financial caution was the necessary order of the day. The document accepts that the role of local government in Ireland is narrow by international standards. It states that some traditional functions have moved to specialist organisations due to necessities of scale, resources and expertise, although it does not analyse further why, for instance, such resources and expertise were lacking at a local level and yet made available to some more centralised body.

The emphasis in PPF shifts firmly on to economic development. Minister Hogan said: 'The Action Programme [PPF] empowers Local Government in an entirely new way, particularly in relation to economic development, and most importantly, sustaining and creating jobs.'[43] Local enterprise support is now provided through local enterprise offices. Also local government was given a central role in the oversight and planning of local and community development programmes. As noted, another significant change which followed from PPF was the establishment of municipal districts, which are based around principal towns augmented by their hinterlands. They go beyond the arrangement of town councils, which were abolished, and are closer to the arrangements in many European countries.[44] The aim of municipal districts is to engage with local communities in a variety of social and business activities. One significant recommendation of PPF, which has not been acted upon, is the devolution of more functions to local authorities.[45]

It may be that PPF heralds a move back towards stronger local government and a realisation that scale and centralisation come at a cost. Turley and McNena say that the challenge for Irish local authorities, as for similar authorities worldwide, 'is to provide a high level of public services while, at the same time, keeping taxes and charges sufficiently low to ensure the revenue base and, in general, economic activity continue to grow'.[46] This will be a difficult challenge.

6

Community, Local Amenities, Local Authorities

'Community Development can be tentatively defined as a process designed to create conditions of economic and social progress for the whole community, with its active participation and fullest possible reliance upon the community's own initiative.'[1] The main objective is to help people improve their economic and social situation. Community development encourages people to work as co-workers with a joint purpose rather than as individuals pursuing individual goals. Tony O'Grady, a community development practitioner, claims that a major imbalance has developed in government-supported community development, so that the more local and community-centred approach 'has been effectively obliterated in favour of the more centralised and prescriptive approach'.[2] In the 'local' approach, needs are experienced and identified locally by people who know the territory. There is local control and decision-making, and primary accountability lies with the local community in the form of an elected monitoring committee for each project. In the 'centralised' approach needs are defined centrally; there is central control and decision-making, and primary accountability lies with the taxpayer.

In October 2015 a conference was held at UCC on the theme 'The Changing Landscape of Local and Community Development in Ireland'. At the conference, researcher Brian Harvey provided an overview of the theme. Harvey suggested that community development began in Ireland in 1891 with the Congested Districts Board (CDB). The board worked in the west of Ireland, where it funded parish committees to work on community development and provided credit to help in the establishment of co-operatives. It also helped with the establishment of community-based nursing stations. According to Harvey, Nationalist MPs disliked the CDB because it bypassed the MPs into the community. The Nationalist Party managed to get the CDB to drop the focus on community development and to focus instead on land reapportionment.[3] The life of the CDB came to an end in 1923 and, according to Harvey, it was not until the 1960s that the practice of community development began again with new voluntary groups like Cherish (for single mothers) and Simon (for the homeless). Following Irish entry into the EEC in 1973, funds became available for community development from the European Social Fund. 'Community development was the method of choice for the first European programme against poverty, introduced in Ireland in 1975.'[4]

In Britain it was found that, despite an elaborate welfare state, large pockets of poverty persisted in many local communities. This awareness led to the establishment of the Community Development Foundation. This in turn had an influence on the community development programme established in Ireland by the Minister for Social Welfare, Michael Woods, in 1988. The programme eventually expanded into 180 projects and 107 family resource centres. Harvey explains how the networks associated with community development represented the emergence of social capital:

> The community development model in Ireland was locally-based action, targeted at both geographically and issue-based disadvantage … Networking was important for access to information, to people and power structures further up the line. These networks were the beginnings of what we now call the concept of social capital and building trust with institutions.[5]

In 2000 the government published a White Paper entitled *Supporting Voluntary Activity*. The White Paper affirmed the role of the community and voluntary sector and promised improved funding mechanisms. However, within a few years funding was cut and voluntary and community agencies were advised that their work was 'too political.'[6] In other words the agencies were not seen as neutral but rather as partisan in terms of political debate. Funding cuts continued as the economic downturn became severe from 2008. Just before the onset of the economic crisis, the Fianna Fáil/Green Party government elected in 2007 opted to abolish a number of social policy agencies in what became known as the 'bonfire of the quangos'. In December 2009, 19 of the 180 community development projects were closed. Harvey argues that the neutering of the community sector by the State was partly due to the State's opposition to the advocacy work of the organisations, which strayed into the political arena. Harvey claims that the State envisaged the task of community organisations as the provision of services rather than highlighting conditions of need and arguing against the status quo. Nor could the State satisfy the ceaseless demand for funds, especially in times of austerity. Former Tánaiste Michael McDowell claimed: 'There is hardly a major voluntary organisation in the country that didn't have its hand out for cash.'[7] Taken together, the observations of McDowell and Harvey imply government wariness, and probably wariness of civil servants and advisors, towards at least some voluntary organisations. Why would the government, or government officials, wish to fund organisations that are critical of government?

The Report of the Working Group on Citizen Engagement, chaired by Fr Sean Healy of Social Justice Ireland, was published in 2013. The findings contributed to the passing of the Local Government Act 2014. The *Report of the Working Group* recommended that a public participation network (PPN) be established in every local authority area to ensure input by citizens into the decision-making process at local government level. The establishment of PPNs was followed by the establishment of local community development committees (LCDCs) in each local authority area, each having three PPN representatives. A PPN is a formal network which facilitates the connection of local authorities with community groups. The three main community groups are (i) voluntary groups working in the community; for example, sports clubs, cultural groups, Tidy Towns; (ii) groups to protect the environment such as An Taisce and BirdWatch Ireland; and (iii) groups representing socially excluded persons, such as migrants, people with disabilities and Travellers. Although such groups are not mentioned in the report, a case could be made to include representatives of parishes, Catholic and Protestant, and representatives of other faith groups in PPNs, given the deep roots of parishes in the community.

The Department of Housing, Planning, Community and Local Government allocated each PPN up to €50,000 in 2017, to be matched with at least €30,000 by the relevant local authority. The funding should be used to employ a resource worker and to manage its operations. Time will prove the effectiveness or otherwise of the new system of PPNs. It appears to provide a mechanism for linkage between communities and local authorities. It also highlights the dependence of voluntary groups on public funding.

In light of the rapid growth in Dublin and some cities, together with the decline of many rural areas, it is important to look at the balance between urban and rural development and the associated impact on communities in a regional context. To an extent this is comparable to looking at the decline of parishes in a diocesan context. Fifty years ago a report was issued by Colin Buchanan and partners, a firm of English town planners who had been commissioned in 1966, the fiftieth anniversary of the Easter Rising, to propose a regional strategy for development. The Buchanan report examined four options. The first involved concentrating on Dublin; the second involved two other regional centres, Cork and the Limerick/Shannon area together with Dublin; the third involved developing a total of nine regions; and the fourth involved widely dispersed development.

The option chosen by government was the third one, to develop the nine centres of Dublin, Cork, Limerick/Shannon, Athlone, Drogheda, Dundalk, Galway, Sligo and Waterford. These would be designated growth centres for inward investment. However, initial enthusiasm faded and the Buchanan report started to gather dust. One cause of the neglect of the Buchanan report was, almost certainly, the very fact that it involved selection. Selecting certain centres meant that other potential centres were bypassed, and this led to discontent and objections in those centres.

The question of regional governance re-emerged twenty years after the Buchanan report when the Single European Act came into force in 1987. Structural Funds became available from the EU for purposes of industrial, agricultural and labour force development. In 1994 the government established regional authorities to supervise the distribution of EU Regional Funds and monitor public service provision. In 2015 the regional authorities were replaced by three regional assemblies – Northern and Western, Eastern and Midland, and Southern. The objective of these assemblies seems to be the coordination of the work of local authorities.

A further attempt was made at developing a regional strategy in the form of the *National Spatial Strategy*, which was launched in 2002. This recommended the development of 'gateway' towns for investment in addition to the main cities listed in the *National Development Plan 2000–2006*. The *Spatial Strategy* was to include decentralisation of government, whereby certain government institutions and jobs would be relocated outside Dublin. Politically, decentralisation was meant to compensate partially places not designated as 'hubs'.[8] The intention was to make the *National Spatial Strategy* more holistic. It did not necessarily imply that decision-making would be devolved to local level. In 2000 the Minister for Finance, Charlie McCreevy, announced that 10,000 civil service posts would be decentralised. By 2003 it was clear that the posts would be spread over fifty locations rather than allocated between designated growth centres. Breathnach, O'Mahony and van Egeraat speak of 'the failure of the NSS' and claim that it:

> had made little progress when it was effectively brought to a halt by the 2008 financial crisis which undermined the Irish government's finances, although its abandonment was not officially signalled by the government until early 2013.[9]

In September 2017 the Department of Housing, Planning and Local Government produced a draft plan – *Ireland 2040*. The draft plan highlighted 'five city regions' around Dublin, Cork, Limerick, Galway and Waterford. It is worth noting that according to the 2016 census, Dublin, Cork, Limerick, Galway and Waterford together accounted for 2.5 million people, or 52 per cent of the total population. Lobbying followed the publication of the plan. It was claimed that the plan had overlooked everywhere north of the Galway–Dublin railway line. In the event the government chose Sligo as the venue at which to launch the plan on 16 February 2018. Two elements in the project were unveiled. The *National Planning Framework* (NPF) aims to achieve balanced regional development so that the growth of Dublin will proceed more slowly than that of the cities of Cork, Galway, Limerick and Waterford. The second element is the *National Development Plan* (NDP), a ten-year programme to upgrade existing State infrastructure, and also to provide some new infrastructure at a cost of €115 billion.

Long-term vision over the next twenty years is desirable; but past experience suggests that twenty years or even ten years are very long periods over which to turn paper plans into practical realities. This is because the demographic, economic and social framework in which plans are framed changes continuously rather than every ten or twenty years. An example illustrates the point. Considerable investment is promised for school buildings, yet the Department of Education forecasts that the primary school population will fall by 100,000, or 20 per cent, by 2030. There is no forecast yet available for 2040. Second-level enrolments are expected to peak in 2025 and then fall back to current levels by 2030. As at primary level, there is no forecast for 2040. In the relatively stable 1960s, the second and third *Programme for Economic Expansion* did not last their terms. In the words of Joe Lee, 'The *Second programme*, scheduled to run from 1964–1970, was jettisoned in 1967 … The *Third programme* was quietly shelved in 1971.'[10] Longer-term vision and context is important and the planning horizon should not be unduly coloured by the next general election. Effective planning gets next year's plan right and then the year after and so on. Within the context of the longer term, Covid-19 makes this approach all the more necessary.

A feature of the NPF and the NDP is the strong focus on the economy. Balanced development requires that the building of physical infrastructure is accompanied by the building and strengthening of communities, as explained by Rajan in *The Third Pillar*.[11] Local communities, including the parish network, are important for identity and social stability and can also contribute to economic development. A number of priests have raised concerns about the NPF. Co. Clare priest Fr Harry Bohan maintains that urban development is favoured over the development of small towns and villages. Fr Eddie Gallagher, parish priest in Kilcar, Co. Donegal, believes that decentralisation should be aimed at small towns like Donegal (population 2,600). If an industry were located in Donegal it would help to develop the surrounding hinterland. He highlights the downward trend in numbers in three Donegal parish schools as warning signals for the future of the community. Twenty years ago the primary school in Kilcar had 218 pupils. Since then it has lost four teachers as the numbers have declined to 118. Over the same period the numbers in Cashel School in Glencolmcille fell from 166 to 68, while in Meenaneary school the decline was from 58 to 17. When a school closes, one of the collateral losses in the community is the fragmentation of parental networks linked to the school. Fr Bohan fears that Ireland might be a prosperous country, with a favourable balance of trade, but with people packed into a few cities, and a countryside filled with dead towns and villages.[12] An as yet unknown outcome of Covid-19 is the extent to which distance working might help to strengthen rural communities. The availability of broadband will be a factor.

The trend towards centralisation in State administration has been continuous, at least from the time of the abolition of domestic rates in 1977 and later the replacement of health boards by the HSE and the replacement of vocational education committees by a smaller number of education and training boards. Breathnach et al.[13] identify the paucity of functions devolved to regional and local levels, compared with other European countries, as a feature of subnational government in Ireland. Moreover, centralisation has not been confined to the public sector. For example, in banking it is acknowledged that the reduced input from branch managers and the centralisation of loan approvals contributed to poor lending decisions during the boom and subsequent crash. At a time when the sphere of local government has been reduced and central government, situated in the expanding capital city, Dublin, has tightened its grip, it could be argued that the need for local representatives to articulate local needs and to attempt to win resources, including from local charges, to meet those needs is not only reasonable but desirable.

A development which followed from the publication of *Putting People First* was the establishment of municipal districts together with municipal district officers. Boyle et al. describe how in Kerry the delivery of services is now achieved through engagement with local communities, 'for example, tidy towns, local voluntary festivals, and businesses, with a single point of contact in each municipal district through the municipal district officer'.[14] Municipal districts have the potential to bring together town, village and rural development and facilitate community engagement. It may also be that the State can learn something from the organisational structure of the churches, which is based on parishes within dioceses, bearing in mind the historical connection between Church parishes and civil parishes which were components and forerunners of local government.

The parish is a sphere which can provide positive connections. Frank Allen, chairman of Depaul Ireland,[15] which addresses the needs of homeless people, and former CEO of the Railway Procurement Agency, is in the atypical position of attending both a city and a rural parish. He lives in Dublin, where he attends a city parish, but on alternate weeks prior to the Covid-19 travel restrictions he attended a rural one in Cork. In his experience the rural parish is relatively stronger than the urban one and provides a different experience. The decline in attendance in the Dublin city parish has been 'precipitous' due to the absence of young people. In the rural Cork parish, where there is a better attendance of young people, non-church activities, including sporting activities, tend to be more closely linked to the church than they are in the city.[16]

Networks based on sports clubs and schools have survived in many rural areas, but many community amenities have closed, including small schools, post offices, Garda stations and local hospitals. Among the amenities to be closed or curtailed, small schools were probably the first to go, in the wake of the *Investment in Education* report in the 1960s. A 'No Doctor, No Village' campaign has been launched to increase the number of rural GPs.[17] Lack of rural GP services contributed to the election of an independent TD, Dr Michael Harty from Clare, in the general election in 2016. As a result of a Garda Station Rationalisation Programme, which took place in 2012 and 2013, 39 Garda stations were closed in 2012 and 100 were closed in 2013. In the decade 2008–18 close to 140 stations were closed in rural areas. Early in 2015 CIÉ announced its intention to reduce Expressway services between some rural towns, increasing the sense of isolation among rural residents. In 2016 CIÉ warned that certain train routes were proving uneconomic and would require further State subvention in order to remain open. The closure of post offices has added to the sense of isolation, and even neglect, in those areas where closures occurred. For many generations the post office provided employment and livelihood for thousands of people as well as providing the services of mail, telephone and social welfare payment provision which knit Irish society together. When radio was developed in the early years of the State it was the post office which oversaw the growth of Radio Éireann from the third and fourth floors of the GPO building in Dublin, long before the launching of Telefís Éireann and the move to Montrose.[18]

An Post directly operates fifty-one post offices, known as company post offices, but the vast majority of post offices are contracted, where services are provided under contract to An Post. While An Post operates the largest retail network in the country, two-thirds of all transactions occur in just 300 post offices. In the period 2007–14 there were 122 closures net, that is, taking account of a number of openings. In August 2018 An Post announced that it would close 161 post offices as part of a consolidation programme and voluntary retirement scheme agreed with postmasters and postmistresses. The closures will reduce the post office network from 1,111 offices to 950. According to An Post, they are committed to having a post office within 15 km of every community with 500 people. One of the post offices to close under the voluntary retirement package was in the village of Church Hill outside Letterkenny in Co. Donegal, where it had operated since the 1830s. Another to close was the office in Ballinafad, Co. Sligo, which had been run by the Carty family for almost seventy years.[19] One long-time resident of Ballinafad describes how, in the 1960s, there were four shops, three pubs, a Garda station and a post office in the town. The shops, the Garda station and the post office are gone. One pub remains 'and the church, and only we have a Filipino priest, the church would probably be gone too.'[20]

The response to post office closures has generally been negative. Some of those affected by the closures are angry, some devastated, some sad, while some take action. In the Co. Clare village of Kilnaboy:

> locals said that when the post office closed it felt like a dagger through the heart of the community. A place of conversation, of social intercourse had been removed, harming neighbourliness and a sense of belonging. Not to be deprived, and led by the artist Deirdre O'Mahony, they reclaimed the space, and it became an artistic and creative focal point for interrogating what it means to be part of a community in rural Ireland today. [21]

Fr Edward Gallagher, parish priest in Kilcar in Co. Donegal, described the closures as 'another sign of the death of rural Ireland'.[22] Fr Stephen Farragher in Ballyhaunis, Co. Mayo, says that the post office along with the church and school 'represent the heart of the community – and when you remove one of these you remove the heart'.[23] In Kilmovee in Co. Mayo, where the post office closed some years ago, services were maintained through an 'agency' in the parish community centre.[24] In that way the parish was filling the post office gap.

Historically, emigration has been a major contributory factor to rural decline. Emigration has come in cycles – in the 1950s, the 1980s and at the death of the Celtic Tiger in 2008. Lessons may be learned from the high emigration and rural exodus of the 1950s, which hit rural communities hard. Emigration posed a challenge to the GAA, which saw an improvement in the quality of rural life as vital. According to Cronin, Duncan and Rouse:

> The GAA shared with groups like Muintir na Tíre a commitment to the parish as the key unit of social organisation, to the role of the volunteer and the principles of community participation and self-reliance. The two organisations were also joined in the belief that the best way to combat the flight from rural Ireland was to improve the quality of life of the people who lived there.[25]

Following the emigration of the 1980s, a small group of farmers in the west of Ireland enlisted the support of a number of bishops to assist in the development of the west and to fight rural decline. This led to the establishment in 1994 of the Council for the West, which campaigns on behalf of the west in areas such as investment in infrastructure. The council has received support from bishops in both the Catholic Church and the Church of Ireland, as well as from business and community representatives. Despite the strong growth in total population in recent decades, some areas have experienced population decline; for example, the more remote parishes in the Diocese of Tuam, as well as some island parishes. Declines have also happened in some parishes in Sligo and Mayo in the Diocese of Killala. Some regard sport as a 'beacon of hope'. Aware of the fact that parts of rural Ireland have been losing population and services for a number of years, Fr Eamonn Fitzgibbon organised a conference entitled 'Building Rural Community – Lessons from Sport' in 2017. He believes that 'the world of sport is the one beacon of hope in rural Ireland at the moment'.[26] It is noteworthy that Fitzgibbon refers to sport rather than religion. Fitzgibbon's emphasis on sport supports the findings of the 2007 survey on active citizenship and the findings of sociologist Tom Inglis (2017), referred to in the next chapter. An unforeseen consequence of Covid-19 has been the growth in home working, with the result that many workers who normally would face long commutes on traffic-filled roads are being drawn to live in rural areas from where they can work remotely. This phenomenon has to have some effect on rural regeneration but it is too early to assess how strong the effect may be.

Bishop Fintan Monahan, who was appointed Bishop of Killaloe in September 2016, identifies 'a deep sense of loneliness among people in remote rural areas'.[27] He suggests that the reduced numbers of clergy and Gardaí, together with the reluctance of GPs to establish practices in rural communities, have contributed to the sense of isolation. The bishop's comments coincided with the results of the *Irish Examiner*/ICMSA poll which found that one-quarter of Ireland's farm-dwelling adults have felt lonely or isolated.[28]

One community decided to record its heritage before the village fades away. The population of Loch Con Aortha, a small village in Connemara, dwindled from ninety in 2004 to fifty in 2017, with only twenty under the age of sixty-five. In the 1970s there were nearly 100 pupils in the local primary school. Filmmaker and television producer Seán Ó Cualáin has worked with Seosamh Ó Suilleabháin, a village resident who is also a returned emigrant from England, to build a bilingual website that records place names, folklore, landmarks and other features of the village.[29]

Éamon Ó Cuív, whose ministerial portfolio included rural affairs, believes that the provision of fibre broadband in rural areas is vital and more important than the retention of post offices.[30] Broadband, which allows the transmission of multiple messages, and fibre broadband, which does so at speed, have transformed communication in a manner comparable to the transformation of travel in the nineteenth century due to the arrival of the railways.[31] At present, thousands of households and businesses do not have adequate broadband service. In November 2019 the government entered into a contract, on the basis of a sole tender, with a consortium led by an American businessman to bring the internet to 540,000 homes, farms and businesses in rural Ireland at a cost of €3 billion. Some communities, frustrated by the delays of the National Broadband Plan, have taken initiatives at local level. For example, in March 2018 Clare County Council took the initiative when the council established three digital hubs so that individuals and businesses would be able to rent desk space with high-speed broadband. The broadband officer with the council described the measure as 'connecting communities'. Similar hubs have been set up in Carraroe in Co. Galway and Gweedore in Co. Donegal.

Some of the areas in which local authorities shine brightest in local communities are the spheres of recreational and cultural services. These include public libraries, parks, playgrounds, swimming pools, and support for museums, theatres and other cultural venues. Libraries have been described as 'the public face of local authorities'. The public library service is provided by the 31 local authorities in 330 libraries nationwide. Callanan says that public libraries 'provide an important resource for local communities as a source of information, providing access to the internet, as a place for study, as a meeting place'.[32] Most libraries also contain archival material relevant to the area in which the library is located. One of the most remarkable stories of county librarians was that of Nora Niland (1913–88). Niland became Sligo County Librarian in 1945 and she started to take pictures on loan for art exhibitions, starting with three paintings by Jack B. Yeats. She founded the Sligo Municipal Art Collection, which now includes some hundreds of paintings.

Outstanding public libraries include the Lexicon in Dún Laoghaire and the recently opened library in Wicklow town. The new Library and County Archives is located in the historic old Ulster Bank building on Main Street. The overall cost was €6 million, which was co-funded by Wicklow County Council, the Department of Rural and Community Development and the Department of Housing, Local Government and Heritage. In addition to the library and a children's library, there is a dedicated community room which local groups can use for community activities. The origin of public libraries, like many local authority services, reaches back into history. The Public Libraries Act 1855 facilitated the provision of public libraries by empowering local authorities to levy rates for that purpose. In 1947 An Comhairle Leabharlanna was established to support local authorities as well as to advise the responsible minister on matters relevant to the public library service. These functions were transferred to the Local Government Management Agency (LGMA) in 2012. The LGMA provides a range of professional services to local authorities.

Local government is responsible for the development of the arts in its area. This may include among others the visual arts, film and theatre. Some local authorities run local museums. Each local authority has an arts plan and an arts officer who arranges displays and exhibitions and other cultural events. Together with local festivals, these can prove attractive to tourists and help to earn revenue for the local area.

The provision and maintenance of public parks by local authorities is of particular significance to those who live in built-up areas with little access to private open space. Many of the parks include children's playgrounds and sometimes sports pitches or tennis courts. Local authorities also often take charge of green spaces in housing estates. Local sports partnerships are developed to encourage participation in sport in the different local authority areas. Local authorities are also beginning to play a more significant role in the economic development of their areas since the establishment of local enterprise offices in each local authority region in 2012.

Early in 2017 the government published its *Action Plan for Rural Development*. Its aims for rural development are to support sustainable communities, to support enterprise and employment, to maximise rural tourism and recreational potential, to foster culture and creativity in rural communities, and to improve rural infrastructure and connectivity. The plan contains a total of 276 actions to be delivered by government or State agencies over three years, 2017–20. The plan envisages large expenditure from State and EU sources, some of which is covered by existing programmes. Expenditure includes €1.2 billion in payments to farmers under the Common Agricultural Policy, €4 billion under the *Rural Development Programme 2014-20*, €80 million on flood relief measures and €275 million under the National Broadband Plan. Local authorities are key partners in the development and delivery of the action plan. There is no mention of any input from parishes of any denomination, although the parish network spans the country. If the installation of rural broadband in every rural household proves difficult, might an interim measure of providing digital hubs in some parish premises merit consideration?

In 2018 the government announced a €1 billion Rural Regeneration and Development Fund, to be spread over ten years. Submissions were invited and the first programmes were sanctioned late in 2018. These included a social enterprise hub, café and 'men's shed' in Glenbrohane in Co. Limerick, an indoor sports facility in Claremorris, Co. Mayo, a Yeats Trail and surfing centre in Co. Sligo, and a community building in Murroe in Co. Limerick. The latter project echoes the Muintir na Tíre hall built in Murroe in the 1940s. Limerick is an example where the local authorities – city and county councils – have played an important role in regeneration and development. To take one example, Limerick City and County Council spent €10 million on a magnificent greenway for cyclists, which opened in 2021. This will increase tourism numbers and help the local economy. Likewise, Waterford City and County Council have developed an excellent greenway. Waterford Council has also been responsible for the development of important heritage and tourism venues, including the Viking Experience and the House of Waterford Crystal.

In 2018 the Society of Chartered Surveyors in Ireland published a report titled *Rejuvenating Ireland's Small Town Centres*. The report states that 'Local government has often been consigned to a minor role, while the national agenda is pursued.'[33] It also says that the Local Government Reform Act 2014, which provided for the dissolution of town councils, the creation of municipal districts and the merging of several separate local authorities, has resulted in 'claims of federalisation, where decision-making has become centralised or removed from where it is required'. At the top of the 'critical success factors' listed in the report is 'the importance of strong and visionary local authorities'.[34] As in the case of the government's *Action Plan for Rural Development* (2017), there was no mention of any church, although church buildings are present in most towns in Ireland. In England, by contrast, Greater Manchester and Suffolk are areas chosen 'for a government-funded pilot scheme designed to conserve places of worship'.[35] In many cases the churches are too big for the congregation and ways are being sought to utilise part of the property, for example, by the opening of a food bank, while the main area of the church is retained as a sacred space.

7

Parish as Social Capital

The poet Patrick Kavanagh says that great civilisations are based on parochialism – Greek, Israelite and English. He distinguishes parochialism from provincialism, claiming that provincialism is always beholden to the view of the metropolis but 'The parochial mentality on the other hand is never in any doubt about the social and artistic validity of his parish.' He describes how Irish emigrants in London sought the *local* Irish papers. 'Lonely on Highgate Hill outside St Joseph's Church I rushed to buy my *Dundalk Democrat*, and reading it I was back in my native fields. … Far have I travelled from the warm womb. Far have I travelled from home. So it is for these reasons that I return to the local newspaper. Who has died? Who has sold his farm?'[1] Parish is a defining element of identity. The 'local' is important not only for those who have emigrated, as shown by Muintir na Tíre officer and 'Save Rural Ireland' campaigner Bernard Kearney. Together with associates, Kearney has set up a community shop in Four Mile House, Co. Roscommon, which together with Derrane makes up Kilbride Parish. Among the items sold are groceries and newspapers which Kearney collects daily from Roscommon town, 10 km away. He says, 'Tuesdays are our busiest day, when local people come in to buy the *Roscommon Herald*.'[2] An example of a local urban newspaper that is reader-funded is the *Dublin Inquirer*, which is described as 'local, independent, different'.

Many from different walks of life have affirmed their connection with parish. Fifty years after Kavanagh wrote, Irish actor Denise Gough, winner of a Laurence Olivier Award, pinned the 'Ennis Parish Newsletter' to the notice board in her theatre dressing room in London. Gough, who was born in Wexford, moved to Ennis when she was four.[3] And at the height of the financial crisis in Ireland in 2008 the secretary general of the Department of Finance, Kevin Cardiff, recounts standing in a corridor in the Central Bank building, then in Dame Street, where he had a panoramic view of Dublin. He said, 'I always looked north, to the big red brick church which marked the parish where I grew up.'[4]

Identity with parish matters not only for rural dwellers and emigrants. In their book *Dublin: The Heart of the City*, Ronan Sheehan and Brendan Walsh describe how the parish is important to the identity of city dwellers. The catch-all 'Inner City' would have been an inconceivable term for those who identified by street or parish – Waterford Street, the Monto, the Pro-Cathedral Parish, the Diamond, Summerhill, Lourdes Parish, and the rest. 'East Wall was originally a parish-of-ease to cater for the overflow from St Laurence O'Toole's. Lourdes Church in Sean McDermott Street was likewise a parish-of-ease for the Pro-Cathedral in Marlborough Street.'[5] Sheehan says that people were aware of the ranking of parishes at a time when churches were full, not only for Masses but for devotions and parish missions also.

When residents identify strongly with the street or locality in which they live, for example, Pearse Street, the existence of a parish church and parish hall, in this case St Andrew's Church in Westland Row and St Andrew's Resource Centre on Pearse Street, provides an opportunity to bring people together and to strengthen community bonds. The resource centre at Westland Row[6] has been located in the former St Andrew's primary school on Pearse Street since 1985, when the Catholic Archdiocese of Dublin provided the premises as a resource centre for the Parishes of Westland Row and City Quay. Among the many facilities housed within the renovated building are meeting rooms, a job centre, a day centre for the elderly and a childcare centre.

Social Capital

One of the methods of building community, and of dealing with isolation and alienation, is by strengthening social capital. Jesse Norman, biographer of Edmund Burke, identifies the concept of social capital as an element of Burke's thought:

> Modern conceptions of social capital and human well-being have their proper place within his thought, and his vision of community, free institutions and civic virtue still has profound and unrecognised implications for politicians today.[7]

Today the concept of social capital is closely associated with the American sociologist Robert Putnam and his best-selling book *Bowling Alone*.[8] Not everyone subscribes to Putnam's approach, with some claiming that he has overlooked areas of community growth such as that attached to the development of youth soccer teams in the US. But Putnam's definition of 'social capital' – connections among individuals, social networks and the norms of reciprocity and trustworthiness that arise from them – is valuable. In that sense social capital is related to Burke's 'civic virtue'. 'The difference is that social capital calls attention to the fact that civic virtue is most powerful when embedded in a dense network of reciprocal social relations. A society of many virtuous, but isolated, individuals is not necessarily rich in social capital.'[9] Social connections are important for the rules of conduct which they sustain, fostering reciprocity.[10] Putnam says that faith communities in which people worship together are arguably 'the single most important repository of social capital in America'.[11] He quotes a pastor who says, 'The church is people. It's not a building; it's not an institution, even. It is relationships between one person and the next.'[12]

Faith communities include non-Christian faiths. For those of Jewish and Muslim faiths their place of worship is the synagogue and the mosque. In the 1820s the tiny Dublin Jewish community founded a synagogue at 40 Stafford Street, now Wolfe Tone Street.[13] By the middle of the twentieth century, when there was a substantial Jewish community in Dublin, there were a number of synagogues. For example, the Terenure Synagogue was completed in the 1950s when the Jewish community in Dublin numbered around 5,000. Buildings adjacent to the synagogue included a bath hall for ritual ablutions, a bungalow for a caretaker and a community hall. There was another synagogue on the South Circular Road with a large Jewish community living in the neighbourhood, which was known as 'Little Jerusalem'. At the 2016 census the total number of Jews in Ireland was just over 2,500, with 1,500 based in Dublin. Some of these had moved to Ireland on a temporary basis to work in high-tech industries. The 2016 census also reported there were over 60,000 Muslims, mainly Sunni, in Ireland. There are a number of mosques which provide a community focus as well as a centre of worship. The largest mosque is at Clonskeagh in Dublin, in a complex of buildings known as the Islamic Cultural Centre of Ireland. The cultural centre includes the Muslim national school, a State-funded primary school with an Islamic ethos. The religious department of the school is sponsored by the al-Maktoum Foundation. The centre embraces a community of all ages while the school has a special importance for families with young children.

Putnam suggests that there are three types of social capital: *bonding capital* – links to family, close friends and neighbours; *bridging capital* – links between socially heterogeneous individuals and groups, for example, some sports clubs and choirs; and *linking capital* – connections to the sources of power in society, including governmental bodies and private institutions.

Parishes include elements of bonding and bridging capital, forging links between friends and neighbours together with links with people from different social groups. The same individuals may form part of different groups and networks. The need to build bonding capital in some urban parishes where crime is rife, especially among young men, is urgent. For example, in the Dublin suburb of Darndale, two young men were shot dead in the early summer of 2019. As a result there were calls for increased Garda presence in the area. The response of the local curate and member of the Oblate Order, Fr Edward Quinn, was to praise the people of Darndale. He said that Darndale is made up of 'salt of the earth, true Dubs', who respond in times of crisis 'and who will respond to this as well'.[14] In early 2020 in Drogheda a teenager was murdered and his body dismembered as part of a drugs-related feud. At a prayer service in the Holy Family Parish Church, Ballsgrove, Bishop Deenihan, the Bishop of Meath, said that people had suffered and that 'violence leads nowhere'. By bringing the community together the prayer service was an exercise in bonding but that is just a start. Could, for example, parish visitation teams be assembled who would reach out, especially to young men, and invite them to use such parish facilities as are available, or put them in touch with services such as the Cuan Mhuire addiction centre in Athy?

Exclusion as well as Inclusion

Before highlighting examples where parishes built social capital, it is fair to point out that in some cases parishes failed to contribute to social capital and reaffirmed the social segregation and class division already in existence. In the 1950s when collections were made on entry to the church, for example, in St Agnes' Church in Crumlin, Dublin, the main door at the back of the church was known as the 'penny door' while the door further up at the side was the 'sixpenny door'. Poorer parishioners used the back door while the better off used the higher door. A similar policy operated in Westland Row, where there was a threepenny door and a sixpenny door.[15] This sort of segregation had long roots. When St Andrew's Chapel at Townsend Street, the precursor of St Andrew's, Westland Row, was built in the early nineteenth century, it had 'two separate entrances, one at Townsend Street for wealthy parishioners and another from Lazar Hill for the poor'.[16] According to Elizabeth Watson, author of a book on St Andrew's, the areas within the church were divided into sections for the wealthy and the poor.[17] In some churches the amount of dues paid by parishioners at Christmas and Easter was called out from the altar, starting with the biggest offerings and going down to the smallest. In his memoir of childhood in Kilkea in Co. Kildare, Micheál Ó Dubhshláine, later principal of Dún Chaoin national school in Co. Kerry, vividly recalls the ritual of the parish priest calling out the dues.[18]

One aspect of parishes related to class and economic strength concerned the contribution to church building funds which was expected of parishioners, rich and poor. Sometimes it was the poor who collectively contributed most handsomely. The Church of the Three Patrons (Patrick, Bridget and Columba) in Rathgar was known as the 'Maids' Church' or the 'Servants' Church' as the Catholic domestic servants in the homes of well-to-do Protestants in the vicinity often did not have enough time off to travel to Mass in nearby Rathmines. The Rathgar Church was built in the mid nineteenth century following a donation of £2,000 from a wealthy Catholic parishioner and nearly £5,000 contributed by the 'humbler classes' and from private fundraising.[19]

A painful example of where a parish in an economically disadvantaged area of Dublin sought to share in welcoming the Pope to their city, but was rebuffed, occurred nearly forty years ago. The visit of Pope (now Saint) John Paul II to Ireland in 1979 was regarded as a high point in Irish Catholicism, akin to the Eucharistic Congress in 1932. Parishes throughout Ireland were decked with yellow and white papal flags. But for the community in the Parish of Our Lady of Lourdes in Sean McDermott Street, named after a 1916 leader, it was what the Pope did not do that mattered. For weeks before the expected visit of the Pope, local residents had cleaned the church and scrubbed the streets. It was widely expected that the Pope would visit the shrine of Matt Talbot, the Dublin labourer who struggled with alcohol. The Pope was due to stop at Our Lady of Lourdes Church but the itinerary had fallen behind schedule, so the Papal cavalcade passed swiftly along Sean McDermott Street, but did not stop. The parish priest, Fr Peter Lemass, was so disappointed that he left Dublin to minister in South America soon afterwards. It was a stark moment in the life of the parish.

Nearly forty years later the care of Sean McDermott Street Parish was in the hands of Fr Richard Ebejer. Ebejer, who until 2017 was administrator of the parish, is a Salesian priest from Malta, who spent several years in Africa. The Salesians have a community house in the parish, Rinaldi House, where there is a support centre for young people at risk. In a letter to *The Irish Catholic* in October 2015 in the context of a possible visit to Ireland by Pope Francis, Ebejer described how Pope John Paul II 'was just driven past the church' in Sean McDermott Street. He said, 'The disappointment of the locals is still very palpable today, 36 years later.' A golden opportunity was lost to express solidarity with marginalised men, women and children. Ebejer claims that the Shrine of Matt Talbot was actually included in the itinerary of Pope John Paul but due to 'logistic reasons' the Pope did not stop. He suggested that if Pope Francis came to visit the Shrine of Matt Talbot he would surely also visit the Shrine of the Jesuit Venerable John Sullivan around the corner in Gardiner Street.[20] Since Ebejer wrote, John Sullivan was beatified in May 2017. In the event, during the brief visit of Pope Francis to Ireland in 2018 he visited the Pro-Cathedral and stopped at Our Lady of Lourdes church in Sean McDermott Street and met some of the residents. It was hardly by chance that the entrance to the Sean McDermott Street church was the location for the announcement in late December 2020 of the appointment of Bishop Farrell of Ossory as the new Archbishop of Dublin.

If parishes do not always resemble those faith communities which Putnam says are the single most important source of social capital in the United States, the evidence is nonetheless clear that parishes in Ireland have contributed to social capital and community life, and if parishes and associated volunteering fade, there will be a void. There is also a spiritual dimension to social capital: at times of trauma, the purely secular can seem limited. Rev. Trevor Sargent spoke of a memorial service organised by the Road Safety Authority for those killed on the roads. Imagery included butterflies on branches with some images borrowed from the church to fill a vacuum, but he felt there was a degree of 'clutching at a void'.[21]

Bonding and Bridging: The Liberties and Ballymun

An example of the creation of bonding capital is provided by the South Inner City Community Development Association (SICCDA) in Dublin, which covers the neighbouring Parishes of Meath Street (Saint Catherine's), High Street (Saint Audeon's) and Francis Street (Saint Nicholas of Myra). SICCDA, which was founded by local people, mainly women, set out to build a community in the Liberties. The Augustinian Order was given charge of Meath Street Parish and its members, especially Fr Michael Mernagh, have been involved with SICCDA for several years. Mernagh had studied community development and he helped to produce the report *When Day is Done*, on the challenges facing older residents of the Liberties. Among the results of SICCDA are a number of training and apprenticeship schemes in the Dublin 8 area and a thriving Liberties Women's Group.

A couple of decades before Jesuit Fr Peter McVerry started his work for the homeless, two other Jesuits, Fr Tom Scully and Fr Michael Sweetman, had begun the fight against poor housing and homelessness in the north inner city, where they lived in Gardiner Street Parish. In 1966 the Catholic

Housing Aid Society (CHAS), which created bridging capital, was founded by a group including Fr Scully, who was then a teacher in Belvedere College. CHAS was founded in response to dramatic events in Dublin in June 1963 when two pensioners died following the collapse of a tenement house in Bolton Street and when, some time later, two children were killed by a falling tenement in Fenian Street. CHAS decided to build apartments for the elderly poor at low rents. Dublin Corporation provided a large site at the top of Gardiner Street close to Mountjoy Square, where in 1969 a block of forty-five apartments was opened. The block was named after Fr Scully, who had died the previous year, aged forty-six. Fr Michael Sweetman also worked hard to tackle homelessness and helped to establish the Los Angeles Homes to house homeless boys.

In the late 1970s Archbishop Dermot Ryan asked the Jesuits to assume responsibility for one of the Ballymun parishes. Fr Kevin O'Rourke was the first Jesuit to live in Ballymun (Shangan) when he moved there in August 1980. He was aged thirty-one and newly ordained. In September 1982 he became parish priest of Shangan Parish. He was the youngest parish priest in Ireland at the time. St Pappin's Church, now a nursing home, was part of the parish's responsibilities. Shortly after O'Rourke's move to Ballymun, McVerry, who was on the staff of the newly established Jesuit Centre for Faith and Justice, came to live at MacDonagh Tower, where he opened a hostel for homeless boys.

Over the next couple of decades many Jesuits, both from Ireland and from overseas, lived and worked in Ballymun and contributed to bridging capital. In 1988 a second Jesuit community was founded in the flats at Sillogue Road. The new community was one in which Jesuits spent time in the years preceding ordination. Jesuits in Ballymun formed many bonds with the people. This was also true of the Jesuit associates – young laypeople based in Sillogue Road – also from Ireland and from overseas. They spent a year living together in community, undertaking a social placement in, for example, the Simon Community for the Homeless, or the Women's Refuge, while studying and sharing Jesuit spirituality. The Ballymun Job Centre was founded in 1987 with the financial support of the Jesuits. The Jesuits also supported adult learning, while the Jesuit university support and training programme has helped a number of young people to access third-level education. Also in 1987, the Ballymun Housing Task Force was created, comprising all of Ballymun's elected representatives, Eastern Health Board members, Dublin Corporation officials and, importantly, local community delegates. It was a model process, which led to refurbishment and regeneration in Ballymun.[22]

Although some Jesuits continued to work in Ballymun, the Jesuits formally handed back Shangan Parish to the Dublin Archdiocese in 2003. The handover was necessitated by lack of personnel. At the time half the Jesuits in Ireland were over seventy and very few were joining the order. Furthermore, the Jesuits wanted to deploy more personnel to Africa. When the Jesuits were leaving Ballymun after twenty-three years, Michael O'Sullivan, SJ, speaking at a farewell Mass in Our Lady of Victories Church, described the community-building work of the Shangan Jesuit community:

> There was the very visible sacramental ministry, which touched the lives of people here from birth to death, and offered sustenance on life's journey …
>
> The first meeting of the Youth Action Project (YAP) took place in the parish house in 1981. YAP was a local community response to the problem of drug abuse in Ballymun. St. Vincent de Paul Conferences held their meetings in the parish house …
>
> An AIDS resource group was convened in 1989 by one of the Jesuits … Other Jesuits took initiatives to do with the training and provision of counsellors through their involvement in the Ballymun Voluntary Counselling service in 1993 and bereavement counselling in 1994.[23]

One Jesuit priest who worked in Ballymun and then moved to Moyross, an economically deprived area in Limerick city, where he spent six years as parish priest, is Cork-born Fr Tony O'Riordan. When his assignment ended in Moyross in late 2016 he volunteered to join the Jesuit Refugee Service working in Aleppo and the refugee camps in Syria and Lebanon, where he spent several months before moving to the Maban region of South Sudan, where he worked on a school-building and teacher-training project. In 2018 O'Riordan's refugee compound was attacked by a mob during the ongoing civil war. 'Eventually, four members of the local parish council convinced the "mob" to desist and retreat.'[24] O'Riordan says that theirs was the only non-governmental organisation compound to escape total destruction.

One of O'Riordan's initiatives in Moyross was to liaise with local horse trainer Jim Bolger and others in the racing world to arrange work experience for young people from the area who were interested in horses, so that bridging capital was created. A special relationship developed between the parishioners of Moyross and the parishioners of Dalkey in Co. Dublin as a result of an appeal made by O'Riordan to parishes throughout the country in late 2014 to sell any valuable items which were not being used in order to fund a teacher in the parish primary school in Moyross. The parish was faced with employing a teacher privately because the Department of Education had reduced funding based on the number of pupils. Corpus Christi primary school in Moyross was then faced with the prospect of merging two junior infant classes into a single class of thirty-two. Inspired by the appeal, two parishioners in Dalkey contacted their parish council to help. O'Riordan and school principal Tiernan O'Neill came to Dalkey and spoke at Masses there. This led to Dalkey Parish raising funds to help the Moyross schools. Members of the Dalkey Parish Council visited Moyross. One of those on the parish council in Dalkey was Pat Keogh, manager of Leopardstown racecourse. He arranged for a group of young people from Moyross to attend the races at Leopardstown. Since then some of these young people have worked at Leopardstown's Christmas meeting and some have obtained work experience in Jim Bolger's stables.[25] O'Riordan believes that his experience in Ballymun and Moyross has had a positive effect on him:

> I just feel that I'm a better person for being here and what more can a community give.
>
>   That's the irony of a place like Moyross, or all of the other communities that I've been in and that are deemed poor: they are actually very, very rich in how they can make people better human beings.[26]

Bridging and Linking: Six Parish-Based Community Projects in Dublin

A number of projects, largely parish-based, undertaken some decades ago, involved the creation of both bridging and linking capital. Nearly thirty years ago, in 1992, Patricia Kelleher and Mary Whelan published a study entitled *Dublin Communities in Action: A Study of Six Projects.*[27] The study's six projects were the North City Centre Community Action Project (NCCCAP), Lourdes Youth and Community Services, Fatima Development Group, Ballymun Community Coalition, Tallaght Welfare Society and Greater Blanchardstown Development Project. Three of the projects were in Dublin's inner city and three in working-class areas on the periphery. Apart from the NCCCAP, the other five projects had local Roman Catholic Church links. The driving trio behind the NCCCAP were Tony Gregory, then a teacher, and later a councillor and TD; Fergal McCabe, a social worker; and Mick Rafferty, who became the full-time administrator. The Lourdes Project developed from efforts by the local parish to respond to the needs of young people. Early meetings of the Fatima Development Group, based in Fatima Mansions at Dolphin's Barn, were facilitated by a Holy Ghost priest who came to live in the Fatima Flats. The Ballymun Community Coalition, which was sparked by the withdrawal of banking facilities from Ballymun, was supported by the Jesuits living in the parish. The Tallaght Welfare Society, originally called the Community Welfare Service, was founded by the Dominican Prior of St Mary's Priory in Tallaght in 1969. The Greater Blanchardstown Development Project was an initiative of the Dublin Catholic Archdiocese with support from local parish personnel and other groups in the area.

Kelleher and Whelan suggest that the role of the Church in community-based work is well illustrated in the Lourdes, Tallaght and Blanchardstown projects, where the main initiators were connected with parishes and where the projects focused on the setting up of community-based services. In Ballymun and Fatima Mansions, one of the roles played by Church personnel was drawing on access to key contacts, thus creating linking capital. The Dominican prior in Tallaght and the parish priest in Sean McDermott Street established linking capital through their ability to gain access to State bodies and to negotiate public funding. The Blanchardstown Project was linked with six local parishes. Kelleher and Whelan said:

> The Church is a powerful force in Irish society. When its representatives play the role of broker between community groups and the state or support the efforts of groups in their negotiations, it undoubtedly improves their chances of being listened to.[28]

This reference to Church representatives playing the role of 'broker' between community groups and the State echoes what Putnam says about linking capital.

Doubtless it was more true of the past than of the present.

Linking Capital

The leadership role of the parish priest, in particular in rural parishes, at least until the 1960s, has been documented. In a survey completed in the early 1960s American Jesuit Bruce Biever found that 'for the Irishman, his church is his local parish priest, and more remotely, his bishop'.[29] There are many examples where a parish priest advocated with the civil authorities on behalf of his parishioners and so created linking capital. The parish priest appears as a figure of considerable formal authority and his church as the centre of a community. A striking example of the priest as provider of linking capital was reported in *The Irish Times* almost eighty years ago. Fr Donohoe, parish priest of Leighlinbridge, Co. Carlow, challenged the local health board's policy of forcing unmarried mothers to go into the county home against their will. He said that women were faced with the choice of going into the county home or being deprived of assistance. The chairman of the Carlow Health Board, Fine Gael TD James Hughes, said that the county home was a form of relief:

> We thought it was a wise policy to bring unmarried mothers into the County Homes for their own sakes. Why should we give them the right to refuse? They are living on the charity of people who pay for these services.[30]

When Fr Donohoe protested that the Board had no right to force these mothers into county homes, Deputy Hughes replied:

> I would expect, Father, that we would have your co-operation in trying to get girls like that into the County Home, where they are better looked after and safer than in their own place. Their children are sent out to decent homes, where they are properly looked after.[31]

Donohoe insisted:

> I say you are forcing people into the County Home which is against the law. By refusing assistance … you are taking the risk of allowing them to die of starvation. … If a girl refuses to go will you allow her to die?[32]

One of the most remarkable of the priests who advocated for their parish with the government was Msgr James Horan, the driving force behind the building of Knock Airport in Co. Mayo. Another important priest-advocate was Fr Peter Lemass, who, while working in the Lourdes Parish in Sean McDermott Street in 1979, issued a statement on housing needs in the area which was signed by priests in the parish. The statement referred to 'the inhuman living conditions in our area'. A practical response to this plea which brought a ray of hope to the area came with the 'Gregory Deal' in 1982 between Tony Gregory TD and the Fianna Fáil leader Charles Haughey. In return for Gregory's support on the vote for Taoiseach, Haughey promised, among other items, houses, jobs and a second-level school for the north inner city. Haughey's government fell before he had time to deliver on his promises. The school – the Larkin Community College – opened in 1999.

In his book *On the Edge – Ireland's Off-Shore Islands: A Modern History*, Diarmaid Ferriter provides many examples when island priests advocated strongly to the authorities on behalf of the islanders. These include An tAthair Diarmuid Ó Peicín, SJ, who strove to gain support for Tory Island and was ultimately successful in the 1980s, as well as Fr James Enright, who fought for improved communication between Valentia and the mainland in the 1950s. An tAthair Tomás Ó Murchú, who was based on Cape Clear in the 1960s and 1970s, was a staunch advocate for the Irish language and for the island co-operative.[33] Island priests were not 'sacristy priests'. Fr Paddy Gilligan, who was a curate on Inisheer in the late 1960s, reflected on the role of the island priest:

> I had a sense that my role as a priest was not confined to the altar or the pulpit but also to be involved in the social life of the parish, to build up a community to take responsibility for its own welfare.[34]

According to Ferriter, government files show that 'island priests also devoted much of their efforts to lobbying various government departments on non-religious matters'.[35] These included the decline in the fishing industry, problems with transport and food shortages. Priests helped the development of co-operatives and paved the way for development agencies with full-time managers. This, according to Fr Paddy Gilligan, saw 'the beginning of local government for the island'.[36]

Political scientist Tom Garvin points out that, besides his literary activities, Cork priest Canon Sheehan 'put his ideas on leadership into effect, becoming an organiser of his parish, helping to set up small factories and commercial concerns to keep the young of the parish at home, with particular emphasis on discouraging the migration of young women from the villages to the towns of Ireland, Britain and America'.[37] Garvin suggests that Sheehan was a forerunner of priests like Fr James McDyer of Glencolmcille in Co. Donegal. McDyer fought hard for the economic survival of his parish, challenging official neglect in the 1950s, 1960s and 1970s. In the 1950s he organised the building of a community hall, drawing on voluntary labour. A believer in 'meitheal', where each person would help with a neighbour's work, he established co-operative societies for the growing of vegetables and for knitwear, and a holiday village and a hotel to encourage tourism in the area. The hotel proved to be a loss-maker and liquidation resulted in 1980. Nonetheless McDyer's achievements were significant and in many ways his heir is a layman, Liam Ó Cuinneagáin, who established Oideas Gael, an organisation which provides Irish language and culture courses both for Irish people and for visitors from Northern Ireland and overseas.

Not all priests were benign, according to writers Patrick MacGill and Gerald O'Donovan, who said that some priests were divisive, with negative impact on their communities. In 1914, when he was aged twenty-five, MacGill's autobiographical novel *Children of the Dead End – The*

Autobiography of a Navvy was published. According to Corish, the book paints 'an acid portrait of the parish priest, who appears simply as an avaricious tyrant'.[38] Corish identifies the priest as James McFadden, known as An Sagart Mór, an authoritarian man who ruled his flock with an iron hand. But he defended them during the 'Plan of Campaign', a strategy operated by tenant farmers against landlords between 1886 and 1891 which aimed at reducing rents following poor harvests. It was some years later that McFadden was appointed parish priest of Glenties, where one of his parishioners was the boy Patrick MacGill.

Gerald O'Donovan published his first novel, *Father Ralph*, in 1913, having earlier left the priesthood. Corish summarises the priests in *Father Ralph*:

> Then there is the intellectual of the diocese, Father Magan, who came from Maynooth with a great reputation, though he is in fact an utter blockhead gifted with a prodigious memory; Father Sheldon, a thinking man who temporises, justifying it as 'an old man's weakness'; and the country priest, Father Duff, a farmer among farmers, who has substituted goodness for theology, not ineffectively.[39]

Volunteering and Social Capital

Many of the parish groups discussed in Chapter 3 have yielded a harvest of volunteers. This would coincide with Putnam's claim that half of all volunteering in the United States occurs in a church-related context. He cites a long list of social activities related to churches, drawing on the example of Riverside Church, a Christian inter-denominational church, in New York. Here the list stretches from AIDS awareness to the Chinese Christian Fellowship, Alcoholics Anonymous, martial arts, a family life centre with a swimming pool and much more. Putnam also believes that 'Churches provide an important incubator for civic skills, civic norms, community interests, and civic recruitment.'[40] The role of 'incubator' for civic norms was important historically in Ireland. As 'Catholic Ireland' was subject to British authority for so long against its will, it went against the grain to adopt British civic norms and the Catholic Church provided an alternative source.

Former Taoiseach Bertie Ahern believes that the decline in active church communities of all denominations has created a void in the wider community.[41] He gives an example of what has been achieved via cooperation between Church and community in the past. Probably the most famous football club for young people in Ireland, Home Farm, was founded on Dublin's north side in 1928 by Don Seery and Brendan Menton. At the start, the club was allowed to use a local farmer's field until the local parish gave permission for the club to have their pitch on church grounds and the parish priest became involved with the club.[42] Home Farm has been the nursery to some exceptional Irish footballers. The same is true of two north inner-city Dublin clubs – Stella Maris and Belvedere. Belvedere was founded 100 years ago by the Belvedere Union of past-pupils of the Jesuit Belvedere College and, named at the time, the Belvedere Newsboys' Club. Stella Maris was founded during the Second World War. A manager in the 'Belvo' [the Belvedere Newsboys' Club], which has numerous volunteers, spoke about the poverty and deprivation in the north inner city and praised the contribution by Dublin City Council and the Football Association of Ireland (FAI):

> In these circumstances, the work that goes on – in the football clubs, the youth clubs, by Dublin city council and the FAI – is pivotal. By focussing on the hyper-local, they're fixing fractured bits of the city.[43]

Ahern maintains that voluntary work, including in the sphere of sport, is vital to communities and that the State cannot afford to replace volunteers. It is scarcely by chance that Dáil deputies, including Maureen O'Sullivan and the late Tony Gregory, were active in their parishes before election to public office. According to an interview in *Hot Press* published in 2009, Gregory was a member of the Legion of Mary as a young person. Gregory belonged to St Agatha's, North William Street, and O'Sullivan belonged to the legion in St Joseph's, East Wall.[44] Parishes have been seedbeds for voluntarism.

When he was Taoiseach, Bertie Ahern established a Taskforce on Active Citizenship in April 2006 to lead to a 'national conversation' on the extent to which citizens engage in the issues that affect them and their communities. The taskforce, which was chaired by Mary Davis, chief executive of Special Olympics Ireland, reported in March 2007. The taskforce defined active citizenship as: 'how we play an active role in our families, neighbourhoods, communities, voluntary organisations, workplaces and political structures'.[45] The precept of Christianity to care for one's neighbour is the definition given by the Taskforce on Active Citizenship:

> In our view, being an active citizen means being aware of, and caring about, the welfare of fellow citizens, recognising that we live as members of communities and therefore depend on others in our daily lives.[46]

A survey carried out for the taskforce, summarised in Table 9, found that one-quarter of the volunteers surveyed said they were involved in sports organisations. This was followed by 14 per cent in community/residents' associations; 12 per cent in social welfare services (elderly, disability, deprived); and 11 per cent in religious or Church organisations. There was a sharp drop in participation in religious and Church organisations in the four-year period, from 20 per cent in 2002 to 11 per cent in 2006. The proportion of those involved in voluntary organisations associated with trade unions and professional organisations was low, at 1.7 per cent and 0.2 per cent, respectively, in 2006. In relation to trade unions the 'density ratio' or ratio of trade union members to employees has fallen sharply over the past twenty years, from 40.5 per cent in 1998 to 24.5 per cent in 2017. The high level of involvement in sports organisations is corroborated by Inglis's conclusion in his *Meaning of Life* study, which 'revealed the extent to which sport has become the new religion in Ireland'.[47] The *Report of the Taskforce* said: 'Religious organisations and Churches continue to play an important role in terms of social support, service delivery in key areas as well as altruistic behaviour at neighbourhood or family level – among the basic building blocks of civic behaviour and attitude.'[48] The work of the taskforce is now over twelve years old but no comparable survey with up-to-date data is available.

Research was conducted, and a document submitted to the Taskforce on Active Citizenship by the Council for Research and Development of the Irish Bishops' Conference. It dealt with active citizenship in faith-based communities. A survey of fifteen parishes/faith-based communities, including two Church of Ireland parishes and the Islamic Foundation of Ireland, was undertaken. Nine of the parishes/faith-based communities engaged with the research. A questionnaire was designed to gather data derived from the experience of volunteers in parish contexts. A related dimension concerned the means by which members of Ireland's migrant communities form networks.

The locations of the parishes/structures which engaged with the research are as follows: Roman Catholic – rural Galway, suburban Limerick, rural Tipperary, western chaplaincy for migrants, urban and suburban Dublin, suburban Cork; Church of Ireland – urban Dublin and suburban Wicklow; Islam – urban Dublin. A total of seventy-six people participated. The majority were over fifty years of age. Those who participated were clearly *active* members of their parish/group. The drop in the share of people who volunteer in many categories may be due to changing lifestyles which have made volunteering more difficult. The increase in the number of households in which both parents work, combined with increased time spent in travel and traffic, means that parents have less time to volunteer. Where grandparents mind children, the time available to grandparents to volunteer is reduced. The best way to recruit volunteers was found to be through personal contact rather than general appeal. One situation where volunteers were forthcoming was in relation to teaching English to immigrants. The report noted that among the 'New Irish' communities, finding out where the religious building, church or mosque, is located is important for other reasons as well as religious ones. Among the Polish community, one participant estimated that 20–30 per cent of those who come to church are doing so because they need help to find accommodation or employment: 'When the Polish church started, it was much easier to meet Polish people.'[49]

For those living alone, connection with a community may be of special importance. Although living alone does not necessarily equate with loneliness, there is likely to be a link in a proportion of cases. Brendan O'Carroll, star of the hugely successful television series *Mrs Brown's Boys*, and whose mother, Maureen O'Carroll, was a Labour Party TD in the 1950s, points to the role of the parish and Mass attendance in building social connections and combating loneliness:

> I think the Catholic Church and the parish system in general, particularly in rural areas, have been very, very good because to have a central place – like when Mass was really popular, before it went out of fashion – there was a central place that you went to every Sunday morning.[50]

O'Carroll says that sometimes neighbours realised that a person who lived alone was unwell because they had not been seen at Mass.

A few years before the survey on active citizenship a survey was undertaken by the Think-tank for Action on Social Change (TASC) regarding the organisations and individuals which impact on people. The media came first with 17 per cent, followed by the Dáil (16 per cent) and ministers (15 per cent). Next came the civil service (12 per cent), An Taoiseach (9 per cent) and the EU (8 per cent). Local councils were at 8 per cent while local councillors and local TDs were both at 6 per cent. Finally, community and voluntary groups were rated by 3 per cent.[51] Local councils being rated on a par with the EU, and local councillors on a par with local TDs, gives some indication of the relative importance of the local, although some questions regarding coverage might be raised. For example, were sporting clubs included in the voluntary and community groups? If so, the figure of 3 per cent is low.

When parishes fail, failure may be attributed not only to the decline in church attendance but also to a failure to provide a social dimension to parish life as well as a failure to provide pastoral accompaniment to those in

Table 9: Trends in Active Community Engagement 2002 and 2006

Organisational Type	2002 Per cent	2006 Per cent
Sports	26.4	24.8
Community/Residents' Associations	9.2	14.3
Social Welfare Services (Elderly, Disability, Deprived)	10.8	12.2
Religious or Church Organisations	22.2	10.9
Voluntary Organisations on Health	3.9	4.7
Education	0.7	4.3
Youth Work	3.9	4.3
Other Groups	3.0	4.3
Schools/Parents' Associations/Boards of Management	5.1	4.3
Recreation	3.2	3.0
Women's Groups	1.8	2.4
Political Parties/Groups	2.1	2.4
Third World/Human Rights	1.1	1.9
Trade Unions	1.6	1.7
Arts, Culture, Music	2.1	1.5
Local Community Action (Poverty, Employment, Housing, Racial Equality)	1.1	0.9
Professional Associations	3.4	0.2
Conservation, Environment, Ecology, Animal Rights	0.2	0.2
Missing/Don't Know	0.0	1.7
Total	**100**	**100**

Source: Taskforce on Active Citizenship (2007).

situations not endorsed by Church teaching. The chief executive of the charity Alone, Seán Moynihan, says that loneliness is a respecter neither of age nor of location. It can occur at any age in any place. 'Our natural view is that the country is more isolated than the city, but that's not always true. It's possible to be very isolated indeed in the city.'[52] The Irish Longitudinal Study on Ageing (TILDA), undertaken by researchers in Trinity College Dublin, showed that the problem of isolation is now worse in Dublin than in rural areas.[53] The late barrister and commentator Noel Whelan highlighted the report of a cross-party commission on loneliness in the UK, which reported in 2017 and which showed that loneliness affected young and old. The commission was set up by Labour Party MP Jo Cox and Conservative Party MP Seema Kennedy in 2016. Following Cox's murder later that year, it was decided to name the commission 'The Jo Cox Commission'. The commission worked with thirteen organisations, including Age UK and Carers UK, in an attempt to get ideas on how to tackle loneliness.[54]

In 2018 Keith Swanick, a GP and Fianna Fáil senator, together with Seán Moynihan of Alone, set up a taskforce to work out a response to the growing incidence of loneliness in Ireland. The taskforce members spanned a wide range of relevant experience. They sought submissions from the public and interested organisations and volunteer networks, North and South. The 310 submissions received helped to shape the report.[55] The taskforce recommended government funding of €3 million per annum towards combating loneliness, giving responsibility to a specific minister, specific research on loneliness, a public campaign, support for initiatives which alleviate loneliness and an action plan on volunteering. The taskforce concluded that 'Loneliness is the public health crisis of this generation.'

A study on the relationship between religious practice and the mental health of men and women aged over fifty years was carried out by TILDA at Trinity College over the period 2010–16 with a sample of 6,000 people. It was found that both men and women who attended religious services regularly had lower depressive symptoms. The size of an individual's social network was partly related to attendance at religious services. Professor Rose Anne Kennedy, principal investigator of the study, said that 'If religious attendance facilitates older people to maintain a larger social circle with continued social engagement, alternative ways to socialise will be necessary as we develop into a more secular society.'[56]

The ageing of Irish society is gathering momentum. In the fifty-five years of 1961–2016 the number of persons aged sixty-five years and over doubled from 315,000 to 624,000. It is projected that the number will double again to 1.38 million in the twenty-five years of 2016–41. Of the 400,000 persons living alone in 2016, 40 per cent, or 160,000, were aged sixty-five years and over. The provision of income and care for pensioners becomes even more challenging with the changes in family patterns that have occurred during the lifetime of those pensioners. The big increase in the number of people of all ages living alone is mirrored in the steady decline in the number of multigenerational households. In 1966 one in eight of the population aged sixty-five and over lived alone. Today the ratio is more than one in four. There is also an increase in the number of young, as well as older, people living alone, a fact which has consequences for housing policy and expenditure. For example, through relatives sharing, a housing unit might in the past have housed three people, whereas today three units might be sought. But with demand for housing outstripping supply, the average number of persons per household recorded in the 2016 census showed a slight increase for the first time since 1966, from 2.73 persons per household in 2011 to 2.75 in 2016. The decline in the number of dwellings built by local authorities, despite the rise in demand for housing, was highlighted in Chapter 5. In 1975, a year sandwiched between two oil crises, local authorities built 8,794 dwellings. Forty years later, in 2017, local authorities built 780 dwellings, a decline of over 8,000. This is a striking illustration of the diminution of the role of local authorities in this vital area.

One fact is certain: if social capital is to be developed in a manner which strengthens communities, central government on its own will fail. Robust local authorities embedded in local communities are needed. Given their track record of service in the community there should also be scope for parishes to play a role.

8

Renewal

It is difficult to resist the conclusion that the best days of the parish are past. Those were the days before the horror of clerical child abuse, when there were priests in abundance and churches were thronged for services, and when church weddings and church funerals were the norm. Now churches are relatively empty and alternative venues are often chosen for weddings and funerals. The decline of the parish is by no means a purely Irish phenomenon. Charles Moore, former editor of *The Spectator*, has spoken of the 'widespread sadness about parish decline' in England, which 'has galvanised those who value parish life to set up a campaigning group, Save the Parish'. Moore believes that the maintenance of church music is an important element in keeping parishes alive.[1]

Parishes always had aspects beyond the religious. The writings of Brian Friel and John B. Keane provide insights into how the concepts of 'parish' and 'community' became almost synonymous in twentieth century rural Ireland. Mark Phelan, lecturer in creative arts at Queen's University Belfast, wrote, following Friel's death, 'it's profoundly paradoxical that for all his global prestige and profile, all of Friel's work is set in Ballybeg: Baile Beag, literally the "small town": a dull, dreary Donegal parish'.[2] In Keane's writings the parish priest is a central character in plays as diverse as the comedy *Moll* and the tragedy *The Field*.

The parish has represented much more than an ecclesiastical unit. It has provided a community identity and a centre for activities and linkages. Many parish histories bear out this reality; for example, *Portumna: A Galway Parish by the Shannon*,[3] by John Joe Conwell, and *The Parish of Clontuskert*,[4] edited by Joe Molloy. Both show how family, religion, education, sport, culture and much else form a tapestry of community life within the respective parishes. The decline of the parish means more than a decline in religious services. Religion-based organisations have experienced declines in membership while links between the parish and, for example, political parties or the GAA have also weakened. Is there a loss to the community? Is there a loss of social capital?

The clearest reason for the decline in the parish as a focal point in Irish life, in both rural and urban areas, is the fall-off in active affiliation to religion. It is reasonable to assume that this reflects, in an increasingly secular world, a decline in faith, but the impact of the abuse scandals cannot be underestimated. Speaking of the lack of vocations to the priesthood, Bishop Dermot Farrell, then Bishop of Ossory, said:

> It is a faith issue fundamentally. If you look at the shortage of vocations the issue there is the faith, because people say 'why don't we ordain married men?' But if you look down the church on Sunday, you say 'well where are they going to come from?' … It is a crisis of faith we are dealing with fundamentally.[5]

The centrality of the parish in Irish life had probably begun to wane by the end of the Second Vatican Council in 1965 and a few years prior to the publication of *Humanae Vitae* in 1968. A serial drama on Telefís Éireann (RTÉ), based on rural life, contributed to a debate on traditional family values. *The Riordans* ran for 15 years and 500 episodes, from January 1965 to December 1979. Several situations at variance with the family of both the Church and the Constitution were examined. These included illegitimacy, mixed marriages (marriages between those of different religions), marriage breakdown, divorce, annulment and contraception. By the end of the series the clear message was that men, and notably women, were making up their own minds on these issues. The conclusion of Church of Ireland Bishop Harold Miller quoted earlier, 'We are losing young people after Confirmation', may be partly explained in the Catholic case by the fact that the teenage years are the years when sexuality comes to the fore. The introduction of post-primary education for all in 1968 may have contributed to the challenging by young people of the more traditional beliefs of their parents.

During the pontificate of Pope Francis there have been signs of a reaching out to those who are not in conformity with some Church teaching. For example, in *Amoris Laetitia* the Pope asks for pastoral discernment when dealing with Catholics who have remarried following divorce.[6] In addition to pastoral discernment there is to be accompaniment – striving to be with people in their everyday lives, especially in their family lives. Pope Francis has been reorienting the Church as a 'field hospital after battle'[7] so that the Church can better recognise the reality, and the frailty, of human lives as distinct from merely presenting a strict code of rules. In an interview early in his papacy Pope Francis referred to letters which he received from gay persons when in Buenos Aires. He said that these people felt wounded because the Church always condemned them. His response was that if a person is of good will and in search of God, 'I am no one to judge.'[8] 'By saying this, I said what the catechism says. Religion has the right to express its opinion in the service of the people, but God in creation has set us free: it is not possible to interfere spiritually in the life of a person.'[9] This emphasis on freedom of conscience echoes St Thomas Aquinas, St John Henry Newman and St John Paul II. In *Crossing the Threshold of Hope* John Paul II says:

> If man is admonished by his conscience – even if an erroneous conscience, but one whose voice appears to him as unquestionably true – he must always listen to it. … If Newman places conscience above authority, he is not proclaiming anything new with respect to the constant teaching of the Church.[10]

Clustering, Closure and Consolidation

The change in family patterns has consequences for the State and the voluntary sector as well as the churches. For example, in the 2016 census more than a quarter of families with children – 219,000 – were one-parent families.[11] Nowadays both the parents, or a lone parent, may be at work, often travelling long distances to their place of employment and requiring childcare for their children. This means that there is less time for involvement in the parish should the adults so desire. Reduced availability of laity has occurred at the same time as the fall in the number of priests. Proposals to deal with the lack of priests include the clustering of parishes[12] to share resources and personnel as well as the closure of churches. In the Dublin Archdiocese in 2018 there were nineteen team ministries, incorporating approximately sixty parishes. As now envisaged in Dublin, each parish will retain its own identity within each cluster or pastoral area and with at least one resident priest. Overall responsibility, and pastoral planning, will be shared according to a plan determined by members of the parish pastoral team. The work of each team will be coordinated by a priest moderator. Words matter and the word 'moderator' evokes a different image from that of 'parish priest', much as a 'director of nursing' or hospital 'CEO' conjures up a different image from 'matron'.

Clustering of parishes has also occurred in the Church of Ireland, where a priest may be allocated to more than one parish. For example, within the Mullingar Union of Parishes, Rev. Alastair Graham, who is in his eighties, has charge of four parishes – All Saints, Almoritia, Kilbixy and Killucan. In the Church of Ireland it is unusual to find two churches in the same parish.

An exception is the Parish of Taney in Dundrum in Dublin, which includes two churches – Christ Church and St Nahi's. In the Church of Ireland about half the services are morning services (prayer services), not Holy Communion, so an ordained clergyman or clergywoman is not required.

In the 1950s, when emigration from rural Ireland reached record levels and the population of rural parishes dwindled, but there were numerous priests, consolidation of parishes was not considered. In a survey published sixty years ago, in 1962, the Bishop of Limerick, Jeremiah Newman, observed that there might be more efficiency in rural parishes were several consolidated into one, but that such consolidation might damage the social status of rural communities since 'the village without a priest, like that without a post office or a garda station, is of an essentially inferior status.'[13] The days when the postmistress or postmaster, the bank manager and the Garda lived close to their places of work and were well-known figures in a locality are becoming memories. Senator Michael McDowell describes as an aspect of modern society the fact that the local Garda no longer lives locally – 'the danger is the garda force is becoming unrooted in the community.'[14] Michael Kelly, editor of *The Irish Catholic* newspaper, says that 'In many small communities the only constant has been the local parish church and the resident priest.'[15] At present there are close to 1,000 parishes in Ireland (1,365 on the island of Ireland), 950 post offices and 564 Garda stations. But the trend for post offices and Garda stations has been downwards. In the past twenty-five years about 800 post offices have closed.[16] In the two years of 2011–13, 139 Garda stations closed.

While few Catholic churches have so far closed in Ireland, the example of Finglas in Dublin could be an indicator for the future. There are two parishes with three churches in Finglas – the Parish of St Canice and St Margaret, which is in Finglas Village and in which St Margaret's is a chapel of ease,[17] and the Parish of the Annunciation, located on the Cappagh Road in West Finglas. St Margaret's is the oldest of the three churches, having been built in 1900 with a capacity of 300. It is adjacent to the remains of an earlier church which dates back to the late eighteenth century. Work began on St Canice's Church in 1920 and the church was extended in 1955 during the episcopacy of Archbishop McQuaid. The church has a capacity of 900. The Parish of the Annunciation was constituted from the Parish of St Canice in 1962 and the new church building was opened in 1967, so that it celebrated its golden jubilee in 2017. The capacity of the church is 2,000.[18] A survey in 2014 showed that the most popular Mass in the Church of the Annunciation was the Vigil Mass on Saturday, when the attendance of 284 amounted to less than 15 per cent of the capacity of the church. It was decided to demolish the existing church, which is in poor repair and difficult to maintain, and to replace it with a much smaller church with a capacity of 350. Provision will be made for meeting rooms, offices and a coffee dock. The final Mass in the big church was celebrated on 7 October 2018 by Archbishop Diarmuid Martin. The parish authorities have entered into discussion with Dublin City Council about the provision of social housing on the site.[19] These are the sort of discussions – between parish and council – which should bring benefit to the community.

In August 2021, in response to comments made by some bishops and clergy regarding the need to address the housing crisis, the Minister for Housing, Local Government and Heritage, Darragh O'Brien, suggested dialogue with the Church on the possible use of church lands and buildings in future housebuilding programmes. O'Brien said that some dioceses had already been engaging with local authorities with this objective in mind.[20]

The closure of Catholic churches has become increasingly common in some countries and may happen more frequently in Ireland in the future. One firm advocate of closures is the Cardinal Archbishop of Utrecht, Willem Eijk. Approximately 150 of the 400 churches in Utrecht have been closed, with more due to close in the coming years. Eijk believes that spending money on maintaining near-empty churches is unjustified and may limit the missionary outreach of the Church.[21] This view is shared by Bishop Cullinan of Waterford and Lismore, who believes that too many resources were deployed in the past on the maintenance of church buildings and insufficient resources on evangelisation.[22] He says that where we put our resources shows where our values and priorities are. Closures are happening on a notable scale in the Archdiocese of New York. Late in 2014 the archdiocese announced that it would merge 112 parishes, or about a third of the total, into 55 parishes. This will lead to the closure of over thirty churches within a year. Twenty-four of the merged parishes will continue to celebrate Mass at two sites.[23]

A striking example of closure and consolidation is found in the town of Widnes in the Archdiocese of Liverpool. In 1951 there were five parishes; by 1990 the number had increased to ten. In 2015 there were eight parishes with eight churches and just five priests. The decline in church attendance, combined with an average age of priests of seventy-two in the Liverpool Diocese, indicated the need for action. On the First Sunday of Lent in 2015, the existing eight parishes in Widnes, together with four churches, closed. One new parish was established with the five priests and the four remaining churches. The priests move around the four churches to say Sunday Mass and there is one weekday Mass in one of the churches. The steps taken by

Widnes could well be followed in areas of the world where the number of priests is declining.[24]

Closure raises the question of whether there is an ideal parish size or a viable parish size. Is there an ideal parish church size? Big churches built to accommodate large Mass-going congregations can provide anything but a sense of community for much smaller congregations today. What is the size, in terms of numbers of parishioners and geography, for which it is reasonable for a priest to take responsibility? Fr Eamonn Fitzgibbon, Director of the Institute for Pastoral Studies at Mary Immaculate College, St Patrick's Campus, Thurles, and Director of the Limerick Diocesan Synod in 2016, says:

> The challenge for today's priest is to avoid becoming a dispenser of sacraments divorced from a real experience of community and separated from other aspects of the role of the priest. … Because of the shortage of priests in Ireland today, the ministry of the priest tends to focus exclusively on the sacramental, with little opportunity for pastoral outreach.[25]

Various proposals have been made for the revitalisation of the parish. In April 2013 the 360 bishops of the biggest episcopal conference in the Church, that of Latin America and the Caribbean, met in Aparecida in Brazil. The theme of the conference was 'Community of Communities: A New Parish'. Shortly before the meeting in Brazil, in the first general audience of his pontificate, on 27 March 2013, Pope Francis urged his listeners to '*open the doors* … what a pity so many parishes are closed! … to "come out" in order to meet others'.[26] During his visit to Poland for World Youth Day in 2016, Pope Francis said that the parish 'had to remain as a place of creativity, a reference point, a mother, all these things'.[27]

In a document dealing with the formation of seminarians published by the Vatican in December 2016, the text says that seminarians should be educated so that they do not become prey to clericalism.[28] Pope Francis has frequently expressed concern about clericalism; for example, in a homily in 2016 he said, 'There is that spirit of clericalism in the Church that we feel: clerics feel superior; clerics distance themselves from the people'.[29] And the laity must not be 'clericalised'. Not long before he became Pope, he gave an interview with the Argentine Catholic News Agency in which he said, 'We priests tend to clericalise the laity. We do not realise it, but it is as if we infect them with our own disease.'

Engagement of laity, especially young people, is vital. Speaking in Rio de Janeiro in 2013, Pope Francis said, 'Young people are the window through which the future enters the world.'[30] Those who are only marginally, or not at all, engaged with the Church must be reached. 'Those young adults who do have an interest in practising their faith criticize the Christian churches for making so little effort to be relevant to their daily lives.'[31] Leaders in the Church must explore further the ordinary lives of people. For example, when the Church decrees there shall be no artificial contraception, will the Church set aside resources to nourish large families in poor households? How are individuals affected by economic recession? Parish life does not begin and end at the door of the church.

Surveys suggest that a majority of young people in Ireland have left the Catholic Church behind them.[32] It is striking, and a cause for thought, that in a survey of young people's attitudes to the parish carried out in the Dublin Archdiocese in 2017, 'A number of young respondents noted that it was people in parishes (priests and parishioners) who were the greatest obstacles for young people getting involved.'[33] There can be a tendency in some parish groups for those already *in situ* to continue in their roles unless there is a conscious effort to attract new faces. On the other hand some people may be anxious to relinquish those roles but suitable substitutes cannot be found. Archbishop Martin said that 'The report was one of the most disappointing documents that I read since becoming Archbishop.'[34] Significantly, responses were received from only two parishes in Dublin for collation into the final report in 2017 for the Youth Synod, compared with around 100 parish responses for the Synod on the Family in 2015. However, young people often engage in groups associated with the parish, especially the GAA, but also choirs or groups fundraising for charities.

Donal Harrington suggests four critical activities for the parish – caring, welcoming, listening and praying. He remarks that in the Irish language, the same word is used for both ministry and care – 'aire'. Everyone in the parish deserves to be noticed; yet some people spend their entire lives without being noticed by anyone.[35] Harrington asks, 'What will people see when they see "parish"?' He answers that 'It is possible they will see something that is on the way out – less and less people attending, less and less clergy, a part of a decaying institution.' Yet he 'sees tomorrow's parish as a place of hope'.[36] Every parish centres on its parish church and the celebration of Mass. But the parish, like the Church, is the *people*. Immigrants to Ireland, as well as visitors, sometimes comment on the lack of interaction in Irish parishes. The Church must go out to where the people are, to their homes, their places of work and recreation. This can only be done by the members of the Church. Above all, a parish should be a centre of friendship, friendship which both radiates within the parish and extends beyond the parish. Harrington suggests that one possible way of reaching out to those in the parish would be via an organised visitation in pairs. Such visitation might be preceded by a query on behalf of the parish as to who would welcome such visitation. Given the reality of an increasingly ageing population, such visitation might include visiting parishioners living in nursing homes, in a hopefully post-Covid world.

Strengthening Community Bonds

In the Old Testament love of God is mostly collective. Israel loves God; God loves Israel. But it becomes personal at times: Moses and Abraham are called friends of God. We can become friends of God through human friendship. The Quakers describe themselves as 'The Society of Friends'. Aelred of Rievaulx, a mediaeval abbot, in his *Treatises on Christian Friendship*, brought ancient ideals of friendship into the heart of Christian experience, while the poet Patrick Kavanagh gives us his insight into friendship when he tells us about his friend Michael,[37] for whom he worked for a few years after he left school at thirteen years of age:

> He is dead these number of years. I am sorry he is. He was a weak-kneed man, he side-stepped trouble when he could. He would have made a poor soldier. But he was my friend. He told me hard facts in soft words. He was kind. At his funeral the priest preached a fine panegyric over him. He was a near-saint, the priest said. I was glad.[38]

How might parishes be rebuilt so as to attract young and old, to make them places of both sacramental celebration and friendship? It is worth looking at some of the more vibrant parishes in an attempt to unlock their secrets. The Parish of St Thomas the Apostle, Laurel Lodge, in Dublin 15, is a good example. There are about 2,000 homes in the parish and a primary school, Scoil Thomáis, with 700 pupils and around 30 staff. The church was opened nearly thirty years ago, in 1993, following a couple of years when a prefab building was used. When the parish began, the parishioners were mainly young couples. The design of the church is extremely attractive. It is a single-storey building with a day chapel to one side and a courtyard where, in fine weather, people congregate spontaneously after Masses, funerals and other gatherings. The parish priest is Fr Brendan Quinlan. He has part-time help from a Capuchin priest from Raheny. Quinlan, who comes from Finglas, served in Ballygall before coming to Laurel Lodge. He has also served in Sean McDermott Street, with its shrine to Matt Talbot, and believes that Matt

Talbot is a wonderful example for those with addictions to alcohol and drugs. An active role for the laity is encouraged in Laurel Lodge. If there is no priest available, a layperson can arrange a liturgy.

At an early stage in the life of Laurel Lodge Parish, the Church donated land for a community centre, which has become a hub of parish life. Recently a Le Chéile Club for elderly parishioners was established by a group of young mothers. Meetings and outings are arranged which help to keep loneliness at bay. There are many other activities in the parish, ranging from GAA and soccer clubs to the St Vincent de Paul Society and several choirs. Music is important in the parish: there is a teenagers' choir, a children's choir, an adult folk group and two specialised choirs – Cana and Bealtaine. A new parish council was inaugurated and prayer forms an important part of each meeting. Quinlan says that ideas about the parish should come from the people and different members of the parish council have different perspectives on what should be done. The people of Laurel Lodge have earned a reputation for looking after the needs of others – for example, during the tenure of the previous parish priest, Fr Eugene Kennedy, the parish made a collective contribution towards financing St Francis Hospice in Raheny.

When a parish engages a community in a broad sense, attendance at religious services may increase. As described by Mags Gargan, writing in *The Irish Catholic*, at St Peter's, Little Bray, Dublin, there is a fine parish hall which is constantly busy 'with rooms booked out to facilitate local groups such as the Scouts and the Cubs and the Teach Failte group which provide English language classes to non-nationals'.[39] Balally Parish, which was constituted from Sandyford Parish in 1977, opened a parish pastoral centre in 2013. It has become a hive of activity. 'Staffed by volunteers; the centre hosts a number of classes, club meetings, youth activities and the weekly parish bingo. The coffee dock is a popular after-Mass venue on Sundays and on weekdays.'[40] A new parish pastoral centre opened in Foxrock Parish in 2009. It facilitates over forty groups who use it on a regular basis. The centre has a coffee dock, which opens each weekday morning after Mass. There is also a 'Mass café' on Sundays, which includes Bible stories for children.

There are many examples – a few will suffice – where initiatives were taken by people in a parish which strengthened community bonds and sometimes increased participation in related religious services. An example of community interaction in Sean McDermott Street was in evidence on 15 March 2016, when the pupils of Larkin Community College gave a performance based on the Six Days of the Easter Rising in 1916. Larkin College is adjacent to O'Connell Street, where the GPO was the central theatre of the Rising. The performance was a testimony to the talent of the young people, their parents and their teachers. One month later, in April 2016, a young Traveller man, Martin O'Rourke, was shot dead in a case of mistaken identity as he cycled along Sheriff Street. It proved to be a tipping point as the Taoiseach Enda Kenny attended the funeral and, following the funeral, asked industrial relations expert Kieran Mulvey for a report on the problems in the north-east inner city. Paschal Donohoe, local TD and Minister for Finance, became involved. A number of improvements to infrastructure, transport and amenities were recommended. An implementation board was established. One of the members of the board is Dublin footballer, and winner of five successive All-Ireland medals, Michael Darragh MacAuley.[41]

On 17 May 2016, three months after the killing in February 2016 of Eddie Hutch in a feud between gangs, residents set out from four north inner-city parish churches on a walk against violence. The four parish churches were St Agatha's on William Street, St Laurence O'Toole's on North Wall/Seville Place, Our Lady of Lourdes on Sean McDermott Street and St Joseph's on East Wall. The four groups processed to Buckingham Street to the monument by Leo Higgins entitled 'Home', which was erected in memory of those from the area who died as a result of drugs. The procession was organised by ICON (Inner City Organisations Network) because they believed that people in the community had become frightened by recent violence in the area. Archbishop Diarmuid Martin walked in the procession, as did local TDs and councillors. Archbishop Martin said, 'What the people of the inner city wanted was for their children to grow up safely and in communities of which they were proud.'[42] Maureen O'Sullivan, who represented the area in the Dáil from 2009 until 2020 and lives in East Wall Parish, said that the procession was very worthwhile and showed the strength of the local community.[43]

Each year for the past two decades a Service of Commemoration and Hope has been held in Our Lady of Lourdes Church in Sean McDermott Street in memory of all those who have lost their lives through drugs. A ceremony in 2017 included a reflection on grief by Fr Myles O'Reilly, SJ, an address by Archbishop Martin and music from the Gardiner Street Gospel Choir. A note of hope was sounded amid all the sadness.[44] Another example of community outreach is the initiative taken in 2018 by a group of university students in Dublin to re-establish regular worship in the Church of Ireland St Thomas's Church on Cathal Brugha Street, the street which connects Sean McDermott Street with O'Connell Street. The Student Gospel Music Services, called 'ONE' Dublin, started in October 2018. Music was led by the Discovery Gospel Choir and worship was led by members of the Anglican

Chaplaincy Team at Third Level, a network of Church of Ireland chaplains working in Dublin universities and other third-level institutions.[45]

Few parishes in the world have had to contend with the violence experienced in some parishes in Chicago. Chicago is a city with a high rate of violent crime, where the district of Pilsen has provided a remarkable example of community effort to tackle an epidemic of murders and gang feuds, and shows that no situation is hopeless. A non-governmental organisation, the Resurrection Project, was launched in the 1990s following the murder of a young man outside a church. Six local churches donated $5,000 each to help establish the project. The first task of the project was to keep the neighbourhood and streets clean and they did this by persuading local officials responsible for sanitation and garbage collection. The project undertook remedial education, after-school and job-training programmes. As the neighbourhood improved and educational and job opportunities increased, the project turned to helping the poor remain in their rented accommodation and so reduce homelessness. If possible, home ownership is encouraged; Raul Raymundo, director of the Resurrection Project, tells people when they buy a house, 'You're not buying a piece of property, you are buying a piece of the community.'

New Irish and Renewal

Writer Peter Costello has suggested that the Catholic Church in Ireland appears to lack the sense of community spirit displayed by the 'New Irish' communities, including the Sikh temple in Sandymount (based in a former cinema), the Chinese Grace Fellowship Church on Pearse Street, the mostly Nigerian Seventh Day Adventist Church in Ranelagh and the Methodists in Abbey Street.[46] Among the contributory factors to this situation, age of the congregation is relevant. Also it may be the case that a sense of identity and of family and community tends to be stronger among minority groups. Costello believes that the 'New Irish' work together in a closer way as families and communities because they need to rely more on their own networks, while the 'Old Irish' are able to access wider networks built up over longer periods.[47]

In 2011 a volume of selected poems written in Irish, and also translated into English, by Máire Mhac an tSaoi was published, titled *The Miraculous Parish/An Paróiste Míorúilteach*. The title refers to Dunquin in Co. Kerry, where the author spent much time as a child learning Irish. There can be few, if any, more powerful symbols of community than language.

In an increasingly multicultural society, people whose language of birth is, for example, Mandarin, Spanish or Polish may share the sentiments of

Mhac an tSaoi on the importance of parish. Many immigrants are Catholics. Immigrant groups usually have a chaplain who speaks their language and is, in a sense, their parish priest. Migrant inflows which have helped to build up the Church are a striking, if relatively new, phenomenon in Ireland. For so long, population movement was in the outward direction but that has changed. The Central Statistics Office estimates that the population in Ireland was close to 5 million in 2020 with non-Irish born amounting to 644,000, or just 13 per cent of the total. In the twenty-first century Ireland has welcomed thousands of immigrants from Poland, Romania, the Philippines, Nigeria, Croatia, Lithuania, Slovakia and many other countries. In the 2016 census there were 122,000 Polish people resident in Ireland while Lithuanians and Latvians together accounted for 57,000 and Romanians accounted for 29,000. In 2018 almost one-quarter of all women who gave birth in Ireland were of non-Irish nationality, as were almost one-quarter of the children's fathers. The Catholic Church has responded to the growing numbers of 'New Irish' and Masses are regularly celebrated in a range of languages. To give an example, in St Saviour's, Dominick Street, in Dublin, Masses are held for speakers of Polish, Spanish and Slovak. Church of Ireland priest Trevor Sargent has observed the contribution of immigrants to the life of the Church of Ireland. When Sargent was living in Balbriggan, many immigrants of Nigerian–Anglican and Pentecostal background made a vibrant contribution to parish life, especially in relation to choirs, in which adults and children played an active part.

In January 2005, in response to the inflow of immigrants and the resulting changing nature of community, Archbishop Diarmuid Martin initiated a 'Festival of Peoples' in Dublin's Pro-Cathedral. The Dublin Archdiocese has over a dozen international chaplains, led by Fr Gerry Kane, Chaplain for Foreign Nationals. The Poles form the largest group but there are also large numbers of immigrants from several African countries. Brazilian, Chinese, Filipino, French, Lithuanian, Romanian, Slovak, Spanish, Ukrainian, Croatian and Syro-Malabar immigrants are also numerous. Crosscare, the Catholic Support Agency of the Dublin Archdiocese, operates a Migrant Project to support immigrants in premises near the Pro-Cathedral. In parts of the Dublin Archdiocese, for example in the north inner city, the 'new communities' account for a substantial part of the total community.[48]

At St Andrew's Church, Westland Row, in Dublin, Masses are celebrated in Lithuanian, Polish and Mandarin for people of those communities. Because of the many Polish people in Ireland, there are thirty Polish chaplains working in over twenty dioceses throughout the country. St Audoen's Church in High Street in Dublin is home to the Polish chaplaincy in Dublin. Mass in Polish is celebrated daily and four times on Sunday (including the Vigil Mass). In the Diocese of Cork and Ross two Polish Masses are celebrated in Cork city each week. In Limerick, where there are an estimated 10,000 Poles, there are five Polish Masses each week. Five hundred Poles attend the Mass in St Michael's Church in Limerick every Sunday. The large Polish community in Limerick has a choir, Cantate Deo, which sings Leonard Cohen's 'Hallelujah' in Polish once a month.[49]

In an article in *The Irish Times* in May 2016 the Polish conductor of the Cantate Deo choir is quoted as saying that:

> There are still lots of Polish people who find it very hard being away from home and they miss Poland very much, so coming to Polish Mass is like getting a little piece of home and it also allows them to connect with other people and find support.[50]

Fr Andrzej, Polish chaplain at St Michael's in Limerick, says that people like to pray in their own language and he stresses the 'community-building' whereby Polish people can meet and pray together. Fr Stanislaw Hajkowski, head chaplain to the Polish community in Dublin believes strongly in faith communities for social survival:

> The life of all immigrants, especially those who want to keep their faith, resembles a caravan crossing a desert. Catholics outside of faith communities perish like people who attempt to cross deserts on their own.[51]

Fr Leo McDonnell, parish priest at St Michael's, says that the Polish people contribute hugely to parish life, including in practical ways such as maintaining the church or sorting out electrical problems. Bishop Brendan Leahy is impressed by the sense of community of the Polish people in Ireland:

> What strikes me always is their lively sense of community. I appreciate that's a little like the Irish abroad – there's a social bond that Sunday Mass supports. But we can still learn the lesson – when Sunday Mass is linked to a lively sense of community, it attracts people. [52]

In the Kerry Diocese a Polish chaplain, Fr Piotr Delimat, was seconded from the Archdiocese of Krakow at the request of the Bishop of Kerry, Dr Raymond Browne. Fr Delimat says: 'Polish Masses help people to have a connection with Polish practice and prayers. Especially in prayers people want to use their own language.'[53]

An alternative view suggests that integration might be preferable to segregation. A cautious note was struck by psychiatrist Dr Patricia Casey when she questioned the wisdom of separate churches for different ethnic groups and described such separation, and failure to assimilate with the local population, as bearing an implicit danger that people will become 'ghettoised'.[54] Questioning the wisdom of a separate church, St Audoen's, for the Polish community, Dr Casey said that if 'there would be no church identified with a particular ethnic group – they would all be shared in common'.[55] The opinion evoked differing responses, one of which was expressed in an article by Katarzyna Gmerek, a historical researcher. Gmerek attends Mass in a variety of churches and found the Latin Mass in Harrington Street very appealing. But she said that for a Pole in Ireland, 'having the Mass in their own language is a great comfort, improving their emotional well-being'.[56] Former Minister for Community, Rural and Gaeltacht Affairs Éamon Ó Cuív would agree. He says that there is a danger of losing identity if immigrants integrate completely. He cites the example of Irish emigrants who have maintained loyalty to their own GAA sports.[57]

Among the other immigrant groups is the Romanian Greek Catholic Church, whose chaplains in Dublin are Fr Muresan, also a curate in Aughrim Street Parish, and Fr Eugen Timpu, a curate in Sean McDermott Street. Fr Vasyl Kornitsky is chaplain to the Ukrainian Greek Catholic Church and also a curate in Donnycarney Parish. The Syro-Malabar Catholic Church has around 5,000 members in Dublin and their chaplain is Fr Abraham Pathackel. Other communities with international chaplains include the African, Brazilian and Chinese communities. Every Sunday a Mass is celebrated in Westland Row Church for the Lithuanian community by Fr Egidijus Arnasius and a Mass is celebrated in Mandarin twice monthly in Westland Row by Fr Anthony Hou. There is an attendance of around 60 people. An impressive feature of the Chinese chaplaincy is the number of Chinese people who have joined the Catholic Church. At the Easter Vigil in 2018, fourteen Chinese people received baptism.[58]

A study published in 2008, *Directory of Migrant-Led Churches and Chaplaincies*, by the All-Ireland Churches Consultative meeting on Racism, came up with interesting findings. The report states:

> There is a view that increasing secularisation is forcing many church buildings to close on this island, but here there is evidence of over 361 new local faith communities, congregations and chaplaincies being run by migrants and for migrants, bringing new life to our ecclesiological landscape. This new life is very diverse and may find expression in either existing or unused church facilities for worship.[59]

What is relatively new in Ireland has been part of American history since the late eighteenth century. At the beginning of the Revolutionary War in 1776, Catholics accounted for around 1 per cent of the population of the thirteen colonies, which then had a population of 2.5 million. The American nation was mainly Protestant. Between 1820 and 1860 the Catholic population exploded, because of waves of immigration from Europe, including Ireland. 'Each immigrant group rallied around their nationality-based parish and lobbied to be led by pastors who were members of the same immigrant group.'[60] The parish became a sanctuary, a gathering place for groups of immigrants and an oasis of support in a sometimes unwelcoming wider world. In the twenty years between 1880 and 1900, enrolment in parish-based Catholic elementary schools tripled.

A parish for a particular ethnic group helps to consolidate a sense of community within that group. This was the case with the immigrant flows into the United States, where parishes were founded for the Irish, the Germans, the Italians, the Poles, the Slovaks and others, together with associated parish schools staffed by Irish, German and Italian sisters and those of other nationalities. Over the decades some of those parishes have shed much of their ethnic identity, but an area, for example in Brooklyn in New York, may still be spoken of as the 'Italian area' because of its historical association with a strong Italian parish. The Catholic Church in the United States has vast experience of providing parish services in a wide range of languages. In 2010, 36 per cent, or over one in three parishes, of a total of 17,600, offered services for ethnic groups. By far the largest ethnic grouping was Hispanic/Latino.[61] English-speaking immigrants, including the Irish, gradually became part of mainstream, rather than predominantly ethnic, parishes.[62]

In the United States several nationalities may share the same parish. A survey in the Washington Archdiocese of immigrant faith communities in 2002 showed that three-quarters were part of multi-ethnic parishes while one-quarter worshipped in single-ethnicity parishes. The choice facing the churches is one between assimilation and pluralism. While assimilation has advantages, many immigrants may prefer their own space in their own language. According to Wittberg, studies of former Catholics among Hispanic immigrants have found that a big attraction of Evangelical and Pentecostal churches was the greater sense of community to be found in these churches.

Catholic parishes in the United States are larger than the parishes to which the immigrants had been accustomed in their home countries and, with the merging of parishes due to the clergy shortage they are becoming larger still ... In contrast, the average Protestant evangelical congregation contains two hundred members, all of whom know each other.[63]

Levels of practice in Ireland have fallen to such low levels as measured by Sunday Mass attendance that Ireland may be regarded as mission territory. It is possible that a number of parishes will be kept alive by the arrival of priests from overseas. The Archbishop of Cashel and Emly, Kieran O'Reilly, said that priests and religious coming to Ireland from oversees should be welcomed with open arms and given the opportunity to integrate into Church life.[64] In this regard the appointment of Archbishop Jude Thaddeus Okolo from Nigeria as papal nuncio might be regarded as a sign. As long ago as the 1980s, the late Cardinal Tomás Ó Fiaich said that the renewal of the Church in Ireland would come from Africa. The Society of African Missions, which for decades sent Irish priests to Africa, is now bringing African priests to Ireland.[65] A challenge similar to that which faced Irish priests working in foreign countries now faces African priests working in Ireland. They will have to develop fluency in the language and an understanding of the local culture and knowledge of the history of the parish in which they work. Okolo's ecclesial pedigree is directly linked to Ireland, as he was ordained bishop by Cardinal Arinze, in turn ordained bishop by Blackrock College alumnus Archbishop Charles Heerey. In turn Heerey was ordained bishop by another Irishman, Archbishop Shanahan.[66] Many parishes are already sustained by priests from abroad, including Marino in Dublin, which provided numerous vocations in the past.[67] It may be that the 'New Irish' will attract some more priests from their countries of origin to come and minister, and build up parishes, in Ireland.

Renewing Local Government

All member states of the Council of Europe – Ireland became a founding member in 1949 – are signatories to the European Charter of Local Self-Government 1985. Articles 2 and 3 of the charter state the following:

Article 2: The principle of local self-government shall be recognised in domestic legislation, and where practicable in the constitution.

Article 3: Local self-government denotes the right and the ability of local authorities, within the limits of the law, to regulate and manage a substantial share of public affairs under their own responsibility and in the interests of the local population.

Over forty years ago, Tom Barrington, founding director general of the Institute of Public Administration, argued that it was crucial for democracy to develop people's commitment to the community.[68] It is the role of the local authorities as well as the churches to build communities. With the void resulting from the decline in the churches, the role of local authorities in building communities has increased. John Tierney, former city manager with Dublin City Council, makes the following observation:

> A challenge at present is the creation of a sense of community in the numerous big housing estates springing up beside small villages or in suburban areas. Who needs to act as the 'primer' to knit those moving into the new houses into the community? The parish or the church does not occupy this space as it did in the past. ... More and more the local authority or local development bodies are occupying this space, using outreach facilities to build on the sense of place.[69]

Tierney holds the view that we look too much to the centre to solve problems: 'The local level provides the best opportunity for an active citizenship. Citizenship and community are the glue that binds society together, the real determinants of quality of life.'[70] Tierney quotes Jones and Stewart with approval:

> the public does not speak with one voice. A local community contains many communities with different demands, tastes and interests. The role of the elected representative is to seek to reconcile, or if that is impossible to balance and to judge.[71]

For elected representatives to do their job effectively, they must gain the trust of their constituents. Tierney points out that trust is fundamental in order to establish networks within communities and build social capital, as described by Putnam and Rajan.

Over the decades there have been several reports on local government as well as much research. The document *Putting People First* (PPF) was intended to set out a pathway for reform of local government. In his foreword to the document, Minister Phil Hogan said that it 'involves the most fundamental set of changes in local government in the history of the State'. The minister said that the reforms proposed dovetailed with the government's overall programme for government, which included making the political system more transparent, increasing the participation of women, reducing the number of TDs and establishing a Constitutional Convention. However, in the area of planning functions, Hogan proposed a curb on the role of councillors to direct the executive. This might be interpreted as a diminution in the role of councillors or it might be intended to reduce the pressure on councillors from local lobbyists. In any event balance is required. PPF admits that the role of local government in Ireland is narrow by international comparison and promises that its role will be refocused, particularly towards economic, social and community development, with an enhanced role for local enterprise offices.

In a valuable research paper published in 2020, Callanan highlights two key issues. The first issue is the service portfolio of local government, both the services provided and how they are provided. The second issue is the increased prominence given to city regions and the associated issues of metropolitan governance and local government leadership. In recent decades some important responsibilities have transferred to national bodies; for example, to Irish Water, Transport Infrastructure Ireland, the Road Safety Authority and the Environmental Protection Agency. On the other hand local authorities have taken more responsibility for economic development as well as climate change and social inclusion. The thirty-one local enterprise offices across the thirty-one local authorities are an important first-stop shop for small businesses. Callanan points out that the norm in other developed European states is a more extensive local government role in areas such as education, public transport, healthcare and childcare. To some extent the situation reflects the fact that Ireland's local government system resonates with the Anglo–Saxon administrative tradition in which local government does not have a strong political and legal status. However, Callanan rightly points out that even amongst the states in the Anglo–Saxon tradition, the role of local government service provision in Ireland is modest.[72]

Despite promises and probably good intentions, the centre continues to win out over the local in Ireland. The PPF document promised greater devolution and pledged that no separate structures of public service would be provided outside the local government system unless absolutely necessary. Local government was promised a central role in the provision of childcare in the discussions on the 2020 programme for government. But when the programme was published, the establishment of a new national body, Childcare Ireland, was announced. According to Callanan, this reflects a preference for establishing national single-purpose agencies to address what are often highly localised issues.[73]

A Community within the Community

When one looks back, one sees how remarkable it is that so many aspects of community life developed from parishes. In the Gospel, Christ emphasised the link between religious observance and service to others. In the words of Bishop Eamonn Walsh, emphasis on sacramental participation must be accompanied by 'reaching out' to the neighbours.[74] A very simple example is the initiative of Crosscare to collect unused Christmas gifts for redistribution to needy individuals and families. This has worked well because of the parish network whereby gifts are handed in to parish churches and then distributed via Crosscare. In the future, parishes are likely to grow to the extent to which they reach out and offer service. Many parishes retain and affirm links between parish and a broad range of groups. Finola Bruton, chairperson of Dunboyne Parish Council, described how at an affirmation ceremony in the parish a candle was lit to represent each group participating in the life of the parish and there were forty-two groups represented.[75] Many people who are involved in their parish are involved in other activities, including Civil Defence, GAA and Tidy Towns. In a survey undertaken in 2017, one of the respondents, a Limerick woman, said, 'Ireland couldn't function without its communities and volunteers. From plugging gaps in the public services to looking after the most vulnerable, we need strong communities to foster pride, activity, belonging, cohesion and societal vision.'[76]

In the words of Bishop Walsh, previously quoted in the Introduction, the parish is no longer identified with the community, but rather the parish represents a community, sometimes small, within the wider community. As parishes with their unique heritage dwindle in number and size, what, if anything, will replace them? The wider community in which the smaller parish community exists has become increasingly secular as religious values have weakened within the wider culture. But the parish has not been replaced as society has secularised; the parish continues as a basis of identity but not exclusively religious identity. Former Labour Party leader Eamon Gilmore believes that community life is as healthy as ever.[77] There is great participation, for example, in youth clubs and Tidy Towns projects. Gilmore suggests that within a parish area the church will play a role but not necessarily the leading role.[78] In Shankill, the Co. Dublin area in which Gilmore lives, there are Roman Catholic and Church of Ireland parishes. There is a parish-based community which is broader than the religious-based communities. This tallies with what Éamon Ó Cuív describes in Cornamona in Co. Galway, where he says the parish exists regardless of any church.[79] Whereas in the past the Church parish community was identified with the wider community, church communities are now smaller communities within the wider 'parish'.

Eamon Gilmore cites the example of the Shanganagh Park House Community Centre. The community centre was a project of Dún Laoghaire–Rathdown Council and represents valuable work by a local authority and an example of how a local authority contributes to community life, precisely because it is *local* and understands local needs. By coincidence, a previous owner of Shanganagh Park House donated the land on which St Anne's Catholic Church in Shankill was built in 1933. The community centre now contains meeting rooms, a community crèche, after-school provision, adult education and many other services. Local leadership for these activities is frequently provided by women. Críona Ní Dhálaigh made a similar observation about the strength of women's leadership in community services in the Francis Street and Meath Street areas of Dublin.[80]

An example of the conversion of a Catholic church to a cultural purpose, while maintaining intrinsic features of the church, is that of St Mary's Church in Inniskeen. This church, which the poet Patrick Kavanagh attended as a child, has been converted into the 'Patrick Kavanagh Rural and Literary Resource Centre'. The stained glass windows have been carefully preserved. Whenever there are surplus physical resources, these may be sold off and the proceeds may help to develop community centres; or buildings might be converted to provide housing for the homeless, as has been done on the Mater Dei site in Dublin. Apart from the church building itself, some form of parish centre, however modest, is valuable. Fr Paddy Byrne, a priest of the Diocese of Kildare and Leighlin and a curate in Portlaoise, is in no doubt of the value of the parish centre. He says: 'A parish centre is at the heart of our community. It presents a model of parish life; it is a place where the community gathers for various needs.'

Archbishop Diarmuid Martin's summary of his hopes for tomorrow's parish probably coincides with the hopes of many in the Church:

> I hope tomorrow's parish will be a place of welcome for all. … we have to be more welcoming and attentive to the young, embracing difference and open to exploring their questions and concerns. … I hope that tomorrow's parish will be a centre of learning where all find nourishment in faith and support in friendship. I hope that tomorrow's parish will also be confident and outward looking sending 'missionary disciples' to bring the presence of Christ into the world.[81]

The element of 'support in friendship', which implies the building of community bonds, could also be embraced by local authorities. A firm local base for some activity or organisation which is supported by the local authority might be one modest step forward. Solas Bhríde in Co. Kildare (St.

Brigid's Flame) is one example. In 1992 the Brigidine Sisters opened a small centre for Christian Celtic Spirituality named Solas Bhríde to explore the legacy of St Brigid of Kildare, including in the areas of education, ecology and spirituality. The interconnectedness of all creation and the need to care for the planet and community life are central concerns. In 2006 Kildare County Council commissioned a sculpture to house the Brigid Flame in the Market Square in Kildare town. A number of festivals and conferences followed and in 2011 Solas Bhríde hosted a visit by the Dalai Lama when he spoke in both St Brigid's Cathedral and St Brigid's Church. The centre organised a week-long event during 'The Gathering' in 2013, for which it was supported by a Kildare County Council grant. The centre is also the location for climate change workshops operated in conjunction with the Environmental Protection Agency and the local council. A new, enlarged centre was opened in 2015 by the Mayor of Kildare. Addressing the founders of the centre, the mayor said, 'Through you our lives are enriched, people are empowered, networks are developed and communities in Kildare grow closer together.' While small in scale, the example of the fruitful cooperation between a church group, Solas Bhríde, and a council, in this case Kildare County Council, proves the benefit of such cooperation to the local community and beyond.

Conclusion

Parishes in the past were not Paradise Lost. There was much that was good but there were also faults, sometimes severe. There was undue reliance and emphasis on clerical power and authority. Sometimes there was little connection between a priest-led parish and the daily lives of parishioners. Sometimes there was snobbery and class distinction between the better off and better educated and the poor and marginalised. The treatment of Travellers and of children born outside marriage, all of whom came under the umbrella of some parish, could be far removed from the Gospel. Any role for substantial lay leadership in the parish, other than perhaps in a fundraising capacity, was deemed unnecessary as there were priests in abundance. This abundance of clergy contained seeds of future problems because the need for lay involvement was obscured in a predominantly clerical church. There was also much that was good in parishes and there continues to be much that is good. In addition to the availability of Mass and the sacraments, there are many parish-based organisations, from choirs to the Society of St Vincent de Paul, which play a valuable part in the lives of people and which help to build up communities. Major organisations, not of religious inspiration, including the GAA, have parish roots. Despite the abuses, the weekly review *The Tablet* suggested in its Christmas edition in 2020 that 'churches are still among the most important manifestations of community networks, places where the nation stores its social and moral capital.'

Since the foundation of the State 100 years ago various goals have been held before the people by their leaders, including the unification of the whole island of Ireland and the restoration of the Irish language. For more than half the years since independence, from the time of the publication of *Economic Development* in 1958, economic growth has been presented as a dominant, if not the dominant, national goal. Although today local authorities are playing a role in local economic development, local government was not mentioned in *Economic Development*. There was a brief reference to the remission of local taxation on new factory buildings.

While neither the unification of the territory nor the restoration of the language has happened, a substantial degree of economic growth has been achieved. With growth, emigration has abated and been replaced by immigration. The relative importance of agriculture has declined so that the days when Ireland was 'an agricultural country' are a memory and there has been some decline in the fabric of parts of rural Ireland. The engine room of growth has been foreign investment attracted by a favourable tax regime and the availability of an educated, English-speaking workforce. Central government has grown stronger while local government has grown relatively weaker. But the Covid-19 pandemic highlighted the importance of local services for the welfare of individuals and communities. For example, the use of local response teams to develop testing and tracing has been significant and local authorities have played a role in coordinating these services. Richard Boyle believes that there is little likelihood of a significant increase in the remit or powers of local authorities in the future, but that they may have an enhanced role in coordinating services and community activities at a local level – for example, via municipal districts and municipal officers.[1] The 'power of the purse' may be the ultimate determinant of the functions carried out by local authorities. If they lack finance their functions will be constrained.

It might be said that a beneficial effect of Covid-19 was that it triggered action rather than a report. In both Church and State over decades there have been countless reports. In the case of the Church they were mainly due to the treacherous betrayal of child abuse. In the case of local authorities the context was often finance and revenue. Callanan mentions a former minister with responsibility for local government who referred to a 'small library' of reports published over a forty-year period making the case for a new form of local taxation. It took the financial crisis of 2008 and associated events to trigger the introduction of the Local Property Tax.[2]

The relative decline in the role of local authorities in providing social housing is clear from figures quoted by Michelle Norris, who says that 'Social housing accounted for 31 per cent of total housing output in the 1960s' but then contracted steadily 'to 10.8 per cent by the 2000s'.[3] In 2021 the report entitled *Housing for All*, which sets out an ambitious housing programme until 2030, was published by Darragh O'Brien, Minister for Housing, Local Government and Heritage. The report envisages an enhanced role for local authorities in relation to housing. In cooperation with the government the objective will be to increase the social housing programme to an average of

9,500 new-build social homes each year. A new Affordable Purchase Scheme, led by local authorities, will be launched in addition to an expanded Local Authority Home Loan. In addition, 36,500 local authority properties will be retrofitted to a high Building Energy Rating. There will be support for local authorities to purchase and resell up to 2,500 of the identified vacant properties in their areas. The planned maintenance and management of the existing local authority housing stock will also be crucial to addressing vacancy in social housing. There appears to be real commitment on the part of government, local authorities and the private sector to turn this report into reality.

Rising expectations associated with economic growth have fuelled rising demand for more and better State services. Looking to the future, difficulties in funding all the services sought are inevitable. The consequences of Brexit and possible changes in the system of corporation tax as suggested by the EU could make Ireland a less attractive location for foreign investment. These are factors which would contribute to slower growth and funding issues even before the costs of Covid-19 are reckoned. Total voted[4] public expenditure in Ireland in 2018 was approximately €61 billion, of which two areas, social protection and health, accounted for 57 per cent, or some €35 billion. In the same year, total expenditure by local authorities was €4.7 billion, less than 8 per cent of total public expenditure. A substantial part of local authority expenditure is now financed by grants from central government, which is an indicator of the constraints on the scope of local authorities to raise independent revenue. Since 2013 the Local Property Tax has been in operation. However, there are rules regarding how much is retained within a local authority area and how much is taken by central government. A case can be made for increasing the tax base of local authorities.

Despite a sharp spike in personal savings due to the decline in consumption during the Covid-19 pandemic, both the public and private sectors are heavily borrowed and public borrowing is due to rise further. The Exchequer deficit for 2021 was €7.5 billion, a breathtaking amount. In 1972, just before Ireland's entry into the EEC, Ireland's total national debt was €1.7 billion (£1.5 billion). In 2021 national debt stood at €240 billion, or 105 per cent of GNI*.[5] According to the Central Statistics Office, Ireland's general government debt per capita in 2020 was in excess of €45,000, or over €90,000 for every worker, one of the highest levels in the world. Economic growth, tax buoyancy and record low interest rates have facilitated the recent growth in public expenditure. As a result of Covid-19, tax buoyancy has at best stalled while demands on the public purse continue to grow.

Covid-19 has shown very clearly the limits of the market and highlighted the importance of community and volunteering. Two people with insight into both public finances and parish are former Ministers for Finance and former Taoisigh Bertie Ahern and John Bruton. Both agree that the fading of the parish has contributed to a weakening of community bonds and of volunteerism.[6] Someone who recognised the importance of volunteerism decades ago was former Department of Finance official and Legion of Mary founder Frank Duff. In 1966, as the national focus, expressed in the first and second *Programme for Economic Expansion*, shifted towards a greater role for government, Duff described it as a 'fatal error' to assume that the government could do everything itself. He wrote that no government, no matter if it had 'the wealth of Croesus and the might of the old Roman Empire', could satisfy all needs.[7]

At a time when housing and homelessness are central concerns, some degree of consultation between parishes and local authorities could prove valuable and perhaps proposals such as the 'Surrender Grant' scheme,[8] which led to potential community leaders leaving their areas, might be avoided. Even though it operated for a short period from 1984 to 1987, the Surrender Grant scheme had lasting consequences for some communities and parishes. Do the Churches, in particular the Catholic Church, discredited by the abuse scandals, have anything to contribute to building communities and strengthening social capital? Could parishes provide a framework for greater inclusion and solidarity? Christianity requires service of neighbour. The shedding of power can lead to the rediscovery of service. Regeneration can occur. In Westland Row Parish in Dublin many buildings which formerly served as homes are today in office use, meaning a reduction in potential parishioners, but the parish has important chaplaincies for the 'New Irish', including the Chinese and Lithuanian communities. St Andrew's Resource Centre on Pearse Street is busier than ever. The idea of grouping services 'to deliver them in an integrated and locally accessible way is not new'.[9] But St Andrew's is about more than co-location of services. 'It is about a commitment to human flourishing in the context of community'.[10] The Irish saying applies: Ar scáth a chéile a mhaireann na daoine – people are sheltered by each other.

Some years ago, writer Jon Anderson suggested that the Irish Catholic Church not only represented a religious denomination but was also 'a focus of national identity. [It was] the only Irish institution to stand outside the Protestant Ascendancy ... With its dense network of schools and its parishes at the centre of community life, it was almost a parallel society'.[11] Today Catholicism is no longer a badge of national identity and relations with the

Protestant Church are more mature and friendly. For a number of decades of the twentieth century, civic culture did mirror the culture of the majority Catholic Church, and there was much that was valuable in that culture. A potential danger to social cohesion lies precisely in the fact that Ireland did not develop a strong civic culture separate from the Catholic Church so that as the Church loses adherents, a void opens. A small example given at the outset concerned the fact that pubs in Ireland closed on Good Friday for over ninety years. This was largely due to the religious significance of Good Friday. The abolition of that restriction may be viewed as the dominant logic of the market.

The parish was a community of individuals and families who espoused common values stemming from a common faith. The parish priest was a leader in the parish and often in the wider community. Life's stages from birth to death were marked by sacraments which were conferred in the parish church. Many groups and associations of importance in Irish life were linked to the parish, ranging from those with a religious inspiration like the St Vincent de Paul Society to the chief sporting association, the GAA. In recent decades the number of priests and the numbers attending religious services have fallen dramatically and parishes are subject to clustering and closures. The pattern of family has changed. Notwithstanding economic growth and rising employment levels, many more families, including lone-parent families and the elderly, depend on State assistance and are not in a strong position to contribute voluntary service in the community, although the scope for faith-based volunteers is undiminished. According to Bishop Eamonn Walsh, the 'Pastoral Vision' for parishes is two-fold.[12] Anyone who engages with the parish should find a life-giving experience and members of the Church should go out with the Good News. This two-fold vision will remain an aspiration unless there are mechanisms to bring it to life.

As some churches are closed and others are linked in pastoral areas, and some parishioners opt to travel to other parishes, will it be possible to retain local connection with the people? Looking to the future, parishes can take heart both from substantial past achievements and from the reality that the scope to serve is undiminished. The potential of the internet to connect within parishes and to build community connections is considerable. Most parishes have at least basic websites. During the Covid-19 pandemic most parishes and monasteries broadcast Mass via webcam. 'YourParish App' is an app designed to build stronger Catholic communities and its use is growing. It is proving to be an invaluable aid to connect parishioners and share information. Its potential remains to be fully developed. In 1999 the Jesuits launched *Sacred Space* as a site for daily prayer and reflection. It has proved to be a success, with thousands of people availing themselves of the site, in many languages. On *Sacred Space*, one is not praying alone but as part of a global community.

Just as the monastic church gave way to the church based on dioceses and parishes, it seems that further change is on the way. Social media now provide a means of linking individuals. Where people once met at Mass, they now communicate/connect on the internet.[13] Facebook and Twitter have provided millions of people with a means to connect with each other, although they come with a health warning that not all interactions are benign. Fr Paddy Byrne writes a column for the *Laois Nationalist* and *Carlow Nationalist* and is aware of the importance of communication; he says that 'social media is part of all our lives'.[14] He has a Twitter account and compares his followers to 'an online parish'. He has large numbers of connections and has celebrated the marriage of several Twitter connections. In any event, the new media provide means of contact and sharing and also of praying.

There are two main ways in which parishes can help to build and strengthen the communities in which they are based. They can build up the groups which already exist in parishes and they can forge links with non-Church bodies, specifically, it is suggested here, with local authorities to determine local problems and needs and hopefully to find solutions. For example, parish representatives might have useful inputs to make in relation to local area plans of local authorities, which are land-use plans for any urban area in need of renewal.

One possible bright spot for rural towns and villages emerged in the form of remote working during the Covid-19 pandemic. In March 2021 the *Our Rural Future* plan was announced by the government. Worker-led decentralisation would see, among other changes, 20 per cent of the public sector working remotely. The plan includes a focus on the roll-out of high-speed broadband. Remote working hubs, together with tax incentives for remote working, are also part of the plan. The hope is to encourage those who are working remotely to move to rural areas and help in the regeneration of those areas.

In his book *Reimagining Britain*, Archbishop of Canterbury Justin Welby stresses the value of strengthening local communities:

> The process of developing and maintaining community health depends heavily on values such as subsidiarity and solidarity, and developing patterns of very local government that have both a broad enough range of responsibilities and adequate access to financial resources to permit action that increases

community well-being. To a large extent, especially in rural areas, such patterns of responsibility exist in the UK and across Europe in the form of parish councils and their equivalents.[15]

Ten years ago Conservative Prime Minister David Cameron promoted the idea of building a 'Big Society' which would give more power to the people. The idea was to give communities and citizens more control over their lives. Critics saw the initiative as a way to save public expenditure, but the goal of collaboration with the voluntary sector, faith groups, trade unions and businesses is attractive. Could there be a role for the Church parish or faith community in Ireland in such ventures? There is some degree of cooperation already; for example, in the area of housing the homeless, where voluntary bodies, often Church-related, play a role. Greater linkages at the local level would be beneficial to the economy as well as society, according to Raghuram Rajan, who argues convincingly that the economy is not just based on two pillars – markets and government – but also depends on the neglected third pillar – the local community.

Apart from cooperation with statutory bodies, there is scope for parishes to cooperate with a range of community groups as they have done in the past. One sort of community initiative which parishes might support is that of community bookshops. The new bookshop in Louisburgh in Co. Mayo might provide a template for similar initiatives in other parts of Ireland. A community bookshop called Books@One was set up in 2016 with the help of philanthropist Declan Ryan.[16] In addition to selling books – new and second-hand – the bookshop is a venue for book clubs and meetings. Creative writing courses are provided and a book festival has been held. There are also links with the local national school. Jane Feighery, head of strategy at the One Foundation, says their long-term goal is to have a Books@One in every county.[17]

If parishes are to help build and strengthen communities in the future, it will be important that they support other groups who are doing work in line with the mission of the Church. This can be achieved via individual church members and groups, as well as by formal engagement with the parish. One example is the Men's Sheds movement, which has an important objective of creating contact and friendship among people who might otherwise spend a good deal of time on their own. Contact and friendship contribute to positive mental health. In 2014 President Higgins expressed concern that over half of farming families are in some way affected by the impact of suicide in their communities. While those who take their own lives are not always isolated, good social connections are positive for mental health.

Psychotherapist Padraig O'Morain has written, 'As banks, post offices, Garda stations and schools gradually vanish from rural areas and towns, the opportunity to meet neighbours dwindles.'[18] Hence, he says that the importance of organisations like Macra na Feirme, the Irish Countrywomen's Association and the GAA need to be recognised in this context. One might add the parish.

A phenomenon which has developed since the 1980s is the growth of local and community radio stations, which can be of particular interest to those living in isolated areas and can help to strengthen local communities. Local radio provides an alternative to what some regard as the 'view from Dublin'. There is a special radio station for Gaeltacht areas – Raidió na Gaeltachta. There are around twenty-five commercial local radio stations around the country and a further twenty or so community radio stations, which are run on a non-commercial basis and cover the entire country, from Donegal in the north-west to Cork in the south. Both commercial and community radio stations have proved to be immensely popular at a time when a number of regional newspapers have gone out of business. It may be possible to forge links between parishes and some community radio stations; for example, through the broadcast of church choral recitals.

Community policing, which was launched in Ireland in 1987, provides another different example of an activity worthy of the support of parishes and parishioners. The object of community policing is to build relationships between Garda, members of the community, and statutory and voluntary organisations to prevent crime, to promote community problem-solving and to improve the quality of life in the community. With these objectives, community policing strategy involved the appointment of its own dedicated Garda to a community area. The Garda appointed would build a relationship with those in the community and help the residents to support crime prevention via the Neighbourhood Watch and Community Alert schemes. Community policing worked well for a number of years and helped to offset negative effects of the closure of small local Garda stations. It is acknowledged in the report *The Future of Policing in Ireland* that there is a shortage of frontline Gardaí and a need for more Gardaí in the community.[19]

Given the surplus and excess capacity of Church property as witnessed by the underutilisation of premises, it might make sense on economic, social and ecumenical grounds to consider sharing some Church properties to free up surplus property for sale and reinvestment in, for example, housing for the homeless. A recent example of sharing a church by members of the Church of Ireland and Catholics took place in Co. Monaghan: when St Mary's

Catholic Church in Castleblaney closed temporarily for essential repairs three years ago, St Maeldoid's Church of Ireland in nearby Muckno offered the use of its church to its Catholic neighbours. The parish priest in St Mary's described the generosity of St Maeldoid's as 'yet another example of the exceptional goodwill and wholesome spirit of Christian solidarity which we experience with our local Church of Ireland community'.[20] The ecumenical prayer breakfasts north of the border which were a feature of the later period of the Troubles were an important example of ecumenism, according to Dr Martin Mansergh, who played a significant role in the peace process. He remembers attending one breakfast presided over by Rev Martin Smyth, Grand Master of the Orange Order.[21]

There is also the possibility of complementary uses for churches which could enhance the facilities available to the community. Bertie Ahern suggested that churches might on occasion be used for concerts.[22] This is already happening in some churches, including St Michael's Church in Dún Laoghaire, St Andrew's Church in Westland Row in Dublin, St Peter's in Drogheda and Rowe Street Church in Wexford. Church of Ireland examples include the cathedrals in Limerick and Waterford, St Ann's Church in Dawson Street, St John's in Sandymount and St Iberius in Wexford, which are sometimes the venue for musical performances and talks. During the Kilkenny Arts Festival several ecclesiastical buildings are used. Haddington Road Church has a well-established lecture series. Events in University Church in Dublin have included book launches and lectures. But it is not just a question of complementary uses of Church property; it is also about building community. On the invitation of Archbishop Diarmuid Martin, the University of Notre Dame established the Notre Dame – Newman Centre for Faith and Reason at University Church. The organising vision for the centre 'is to create a space, a community really, in which a lively and intellectually rigorous engagement of faith and culture will occur',[23] inspired by the example of Saint John Henry Newman, who built the church which is home to the centre.

Looking ahead, given the fall in the number of priests, the fall in attendance at Mass and the decline in those receiving certain sacraments, including marriage, the closure of more churches and the clustering of parishes look set to continue. Inevitably, there will be effects on local communities. Attention in the Vatican is focused on decommissioning of places of worship which are surplus to needs and management of the Church's cultural heritage. Cardinal Gianfranco Ravasi, president of the Pontifical Council for Culture, says that decommissioned buildings should remain 'always within the community, with some value as a spiritual, cultural and social symbol' and, in the case of future profane use, any sacred artwork should be safeguarded, for instance, by transferring it to a diocesan museum.[24] When churches are put up for sale on the open market it is not clear how Cardinal Ravasi's criteria can be guaranteed. At a practical level, it can be argued that past and present parishioners contributed substantially to the cost of building and maintaining churches, and in some cases provided the sites. Does the present parish community then have any moral claim on the use to which the church building and surrounding grounds might be put – for example, for social housing or community use?

Further possibilities may arise through alternative uses for Church-related sites. In June 2017 Archbishop Diarmuid Martin announced that fifty new apartments for families would open on the former site of the Mater Dei Institute of Education on Clonliffe Road in Dublin. The facility would be run by Crosscare together with the Dublin Region Homeless Executive. Mater Dei closed in 2016 when DCU Institute of Education incorporated St Patrick's College Drumcondra, the Church of Ireland College of Education and Mater Dei Institute. At the present time, when Ireland is experiencing an acute housing shortage, could some more underutilised churches and other buildings owned by religious orders, but no longer in use, be converted to community and housing use? Already a number of such buildings have been given over for such purposes; for example, the Convent of Mercy in Naas has been converted into accommodation for older people together with tea rooms and a community centre.[25]

Caring for the environment is now high on the agenda of policymakers and citizens in Ireland and many other countries. Ireland's Climate Action and Low Carbon Development (Amendment) Act, which was signed into law in July 2021, sets Ireland on the road to a 51 per cent reduction in emissions by the end of the decade. Local authorities are asked to prepare climate action plans. Already many local authorities are taking steps to improve efficiency standards in buildings and to encourage and facilitate eco-friendly means of travel, such as cycling. Both local authorities and parishes could find common cause in the objective of caring for the environment with opportunities for fruitful cooperation.

In his encyclical *Laudato Si'* Pope Francis deals with the care of the earth, 'care for our common home'. The title *Laudato Si'* – 'Praise to you' (Lord) – is taken from 'Canticle of the Sun', written by Francis of Assisi. Environmental concerns tend to be very much on the agenda of the younger generation and were highlighted in the consultation with young people in the Dublin Archdiocese prior to the Synod on Youth.[26] One small change which would save large quantities of paper would be the installation of screens in churches showing the prayers for Mass and the resulting elimination of the need for approximately 5 million missalettes every year in Ireland.[27]

The 'care for our common home' requires local action as well as political leadership. Jonny Hanson, who was involved in setting up Jubilee Farm, a Christian environmental and agricultural project in Drumalis, Larne, Co. Antrim, has suggested that parishes are uniquely placed to take eco-action. He maintains that eco-action requires coming together in community and says that parishes have the facilities to host people and frequently have some land around their buildings. Where there is land available, a community garden could be established which would serve to bring people together in urban, suburban and rural areas.[28] As well as helping the environment, such a project would contribute to bridging and bonding capital, in Robert Putnam's terminology. The former Green Party leader Rev. Trevor Sargent continues his environmental work in Waterford with the provision of organically grown vegetables and general support for the environment. One example of a community garden, which was literally built on the site where the rubble gathered from the demolition of the old Fatima Mansion flats in Rialto in Dublin, is Flanagan's Fields. Flanagan was a market gardener in the area and a member of Dublin Corporation for many years. Dublin City Council was hugely supportive of the project, where locals, from schoolchildren to pensioners of mixed nationalities, grow a wide range of vegetables and flowers, as well as keeping bees. The site includes a grow dome, and environmentally beneficial technology includes harvested rainwater run by a solar-powered water pump.[29]

Care and conservation of the built environment is also growing in importance. With the support of the Heritage Council, local groups, including Tidy Towns and conservation groups, have adopted churches which have fallen into disrepair and require maintenance work. These include Knockboy Medieval Church in Waterford, Old St Peter's Church in Portlaoise and the Church of the Rath in Killeshandra.

The government has a plan which aims to make major reductions in carbon emissions by switching to green energy. The Sustainable Energy Authority of Ireland gives the example of two Catholic churches, the North Cathedral in Cork and St Oliver Plunkett in Dundalk, to show how this can be done. In both cases the churches received grants amounting to around 50 per cent of the cost of the work, which included the installation of solar panels and more energy-efficient heating and lighting systems.[30]

In the future one of the most interesting aspects of Irish life may be the degree to which representatives of the 'New Irish' gain greater representation at local level. To date there has been little, if any, breakthrough at national level. If the measure of a civilised society is how it treats its minorities, then increased representation at local level must be a step in the right direction. Diversity applies not only to people but also to places. One of the strengths of the local approach to policy over the central is that it can adapt more readily to, for example, the diverse needs of urban, suburban and rural areas.[31]

A final thought. Some suggestions were made in Chapter 8 about the possibilities for rebuilding parishes from a religious dimension where the sacraments are central. In this Conclusion a few suggestions have been made about reaching beyond the parish to the wider world. In that context, exploring and building on the connection between local government, which had its origins in the civic parish, and the Church parish could benefit both the secular and the sacred. The sphere of local government has declined in Ireland, in contrast to many EU countries which have vibrant local government. An endorsement of one particular role of local authorities is given by the Advisory Group on the Decade of Centenaries, which advocates a leading role for local authorities in supporting community-led commemoration augmented by State recognition. In speaking to the Joint Oireachtas Committee on Culture, Heritage and the Gaeltacht, the chairman of the advisory group, Dr Maurice Manning, spoke of the Soloheadbeg commemoration 'jointly organised by Soloheadbeg Parish Centenary Commemorative Committee and the Third Tipperary Brigade Old IRA Commemorative Committee'.[32] The plans were supported by Tipperary County Council. The ambush at Soloheadbeg in which two RIC constables were shot dead by members of the IRA is generally regarded as the start of the War of Independence.

The separation of Church and State in Ireland today means that mature cooperation is no threat to either Church or State and could benefit local communities. There is a growing body of scholarly opinion, as expressed, for example, by Putnam and Norman, that a range of communities and community life are important for the welfare of society and that a society of individuals overshadowed by a powerful central state is less than a true society. Prominent economists, including Raghurham Rajan, argue that strong communities contribute to sustainable economic growth.

During the visit of Pope Francis to Ireland in 2018, Taoiseach Leo Varadkar expressed the view that it was time to build a new relationship between Church and State in Ireland 'in which religion is no longer at the centre of our society but in which it can still play an important part'.[33] Could a starting point for the articulation of such a new relationship be found in dialogue between local authorities and churches of different denominations at the parish or local level? A number of researchers have pointed to the low turnout in local authority elections, a prime indicator of a lack of connectivity with the local citizens.[34] A simple but valuable contribution to local democracy, given the low turnout in local elections, might be the suggestion in parish newsletters that parishioners actually consider casting their vote. The location of the polling station, frequently in a national school, might also be indicated. If there is one conclusion to emerge from this study, it is the importance of the local both for Church life and for community life.

Appendix 1

Note on Ecclesiastical Provinces, Archdioceses and Dioceses

Ecclesiastical Provinces

The ecclesiastical province of Armagh includes the Metropolitan Archdiocese of Armagh, the Primatial See where the archbishop is Primate of All Ireland, and eight other dioceses: Ardagh and Clonmacnoise, Clogher, Derry, Down and Connor, Dromore, Kilmore, Meath and Raphoe. The ecclesiastical province is much more extensive than Ulster: it includes, in whole or in part, several Leinster counties – Louth, Meath, Westmeath, Offaly and Longford – as well as the Connacht county of Leitrim.

The Dublin province includes the Metropolitan Archdiocese of Dublin, the Primatial See of Ireland, and three other dioceses: Ferns, Kildare and Leighlin, and Ossory. The Dublin province resembles the civil province of Leinster but extends to only part of it – Counties Dublin, Kildare, Wicklow, Laois, Wexford, Carlow, Offaly and Kilkenny.

The province of Cashel and Emly includes the Metropolitan Archdiocese of Cashel and Emly (formerly the Diocese of Cashel and the Diocese of Emly) and the Dioceses of Cloyne, Cork and Ross, Kerry, Killaloe, Limerick, and Waterford and Lismore. The province of Cashel and Emly roughly corresponds to Munster.

Finally, the province of Tuam includes the Metropolitan Archdiocese of Tuam and the Dioceses of Achonry, Clonfert, Elphin, Galway and Kilmacduagh, and Killala. It is smaller than Connacht and includes, in whole or in part, Counties Galway, Mayo, Sligo, Roscommon, Clare and Offaly.

Archdioceses and Dioceses

Archdiocese of Armagh: Archbishop Eamon Martin
The Archdiocese of Armagh includes most of Co. Armagh and parts of Counties Tyrone and Derry in Northern Ireland. In the Republic it includes

Co. Louth and part of Co. Meath. Archbishop Eamon Martin was appointed in 2014. The origin of the See of Armagh goes back to the time of St Patrick. Over the centuries Armagh has been the scene of many conflicts and disputes. From the middle of the tenth century until early in the eleventh century the See of Armagh was ruled by a lay abbot, a member of the powerful Clann Sinaigh which claimed hereditary right to the abbacy of Armagh.

Table A1: Parishes, Active Diocesan Priests, Deacons, Churches and Catholic Population in Each Archdiocese and Diocese 2017

	Parishes	Priests	Deacons	Churches	RC Pop.
Armagh	61	96	10	152	228,474
Dublin	200	263	22	238	1,159,000
Cashel and Emly	46	80	–	84	81,609
Tuam	56	68	–	131	122,352
Achonry	23	30	–	47	34,826
Ardagh and Clonmacnoise	41	52	–	80	71,806
Clogher	37	66	–	85	86,047
Clonfert	24	32	–	47	36,000
Cloyne	46	77	6	107	151,711
Cork and Ross	68	92	–	124	220,000
Derry	51	70	–	104	237,747
Down and Connor	88	108	–	151	326,499
Dromore	23	27	3	48	63,400
Elphin	38	43	6	90	70,000
Ferns	49	76	1	101	101,244
Galway, Kilmacduagh and Kilfenora	39	44	4	71	105,707
Kerry	54	55	6	105	127,850
Kildare and Leighlin	56	74	8	117	205,185
Killala	22	30	1	48	38,715
Killaloe	58	70	–	133	114,525
Kilmore	36	64	2	95	57,024
Limerick	60	70	–	94	184,340
Meath	69	86	–	149	250,000
Ossory	42	58	–	89	84,244
Raphoe	33	56	–	71	81,250
Waterford and Lismore	45	61	–	85	136,029
Total	**1,365**	**1,848**	**69**	**2,646**	**4,375,584**

Source: Irish Catholic Directory (2018); Irish Catholic Bishops' Conference website.
Note: It is difficult to ensure that the number of active diocesan priests is up to date due to the numbers reaching the retirement age of seventy-five years.

This situation was ended when one of the members of the Sinaigh family, Ceallach (who would become St Celsus), had himself ordained in 1106. In 1129 Ceallach was succeeded by Malachy. Following the Anglo–Norman invasion, a series of Norman primates, of whom one of the best known was Richard FitzRalph (1346–60), assumed the leadership. One of the most famous archbishops of Armagh was Oliver Plunkett, who, in the post-Reformation era, was charged with high treason. Before he could mount his defence, due to a delay in witnesses coming from Ireland, he was convicted, imprisoned, and hanged in 1681.[1] He was canonised in 1975. In the nineteenth century Bishop William Crolly (1835–49) oversaw the building of the diocesan seminary and several churches as well as the start of the building of St Patrick's Cathedral, the 'mother church' in Armagh, which took decades to build and decorate.

In 2009 the parishes in the diocese were clustered into seventeen pastoral areas. Each pastoral area contains between three and five parishes. For example, the pastoral area 'St Colman's' contains the Parishes of Ardboe, Clonoe and Coalisland, while the pastoral area 'Dún Dealgan' contains five parishes, four in Dundalk and the fifth at Haggardstown, Blackrock. Each of the pastoral areas has a priest leader called a vicar forane. The vicars are supported by laypeople, who share leadership responsibilities with them. Both the total population of the archdiocese and the number stated to be Catholic have risen markedly since the mid twentieth century, while the number of priests, both diocesan and in religious orders, has declined. In 1950 there were 176 diocesan priests in Armagh, compared with 96 in 2017. This represents a decline of 45 per cent. In September 2015 the *Pastoral Plan 2015–2020* was launched following extensive consultation over the previous eighteen months with parish pastoral councils and other bodies.

Diocese of Meath: Bishop Thomas Deenihan

The Diocese of Meath, which belongs to the ecclesiastical province of Armagh, includes the greater part of Counties Meath, Westmeath and Offaly, and a portion of Counties Longford, Louth, Dublin and Clare. The cathedral of the diocese is named Christ the King and is situated in Mullingar.

The diocese has a fascinating history, which goes back to the old monastic settlements. It is thought that St Colmcille founded a monastery in Meath in the sixth century although the monks who created the Book of Kells are thought to have resided at the monastery on Iona. Edward Staples, once chaplain to Henry VIII, was appointed Bishop of Meath in 1530. At that time about half the parishes were in the care of monasteries. Within a few years the monastic lands were confiscated and Staples, who parted from Rome, helped to introduce the Protestant Reformation into Ireland. In his old diocese, as the Protestant Reformation took hold, the parochial structure collapsed and 'By the late sixteenth century Meath was a desolate religious landscape.'[2]

By the early seventeenth century, a number of Catholic gentry who had bought some of the monastic lands, and remained committed to the old Faith, 'established a network of domestic churches and priests, the latter drawn mostly from local families like the Plunketts, Cusacks and MacGeoghans'.[3] According to O'Connor, by 1622 there were over fifty secular[4] priests in Meath, many of them educated in colleges in continental Europe. They were supported by clergy from orders, mainly Franciscans, Cistercians, Capuchins and Jesuits. Tensions existed both between the secular clergy and the religious orders and between priests and laity. The laity, who had been used to running the church themselves since the 1530s, were reluctant to hand back power. Meath and its gentry families suffered in the wars of the seventeenth century, and after 1690 the Church had to struggle with the repressive legislation introduced by the Irish parliament following the Battle of the Boyne. By the time Patrick Plunkett became Bishop of Meath in 1779 a network of parishes extended throughout the diocese.

The Battle of Tara, fought on 26 May 1798 between Irish rebels and government forces, resulted in a decisive defeat of the rebels. Following the rebellion, the Catholic Church in Meath took the shape that is recognisable today. The clergy were drawn mainly from farming, professional and shopkeeping families. By the twentieth century, according to O'Connor, 'the structures and practices inherited from the previous century grew frayed.'[5] There were highlights like the construction of the Cathedral of Christ the King in Mullingar, completed in 1939, and the success of the Legion of Mary and the Pioneer Total Abstinence Association, but new challenges were evident.

Following Vatican II a programme of reordering church buildings took place under Bishop McCormack. In addition there was further church building and a massive school-building programme. The changes following Vatican II were dwarfed by the changes from the early 1990s when the pace of economic growth increased. The eastern seaboard of the diocese, the Dublin–Kildare borderlands and the towns in general became engulfed in a frenzy of building activity. Migrants returned and new immigrants poured into the diocese. O'Connor sums up the outcome:

> Vocations to the priesthood declined; attendance at Mass faltered; recourse to the sacrament of penance collapsed; religious education lacked direction.

Table A2: Bishop/Archbishop in Each Diocese 2019

Province of Armagh	Bishop/Archbishop
Armagh	Eamon Martin
Ardagh and Clonmacnoise	Francis Duffy
Clogher	Laurence Duffy
Derry	Donal McKeown
Down and Connor	Noel Treanor
Dromore	Eamon Martin (with Armagh)
Kilmore	Msgr Liam Kelly (Administrator)
Meath	Thomas Deenihan
Raphoe	Alan McGuckian
Province of Cashel	
Cashel and Emly	Kieran O'Reilly
Cloyne	William Crean
Cork and Ross	Fintan Gavin
Kerry	Raymond Browne
Killaloe	Fintan Monahan
Limerick	Brendan Leahy
Waterford and Lismore	Alphonsus Cullinan
Province of Dublin	
Dublin	Diarmuid Martin
Ferns	Denis Brennan
Kildare and Leighlin	Denis Nulty
Ossory	Dermot Farrell
Province of Tuam	
Tuam	Michael Neary
Achonry	Paul Dempsey
Clonfert	Michael Duignan
Elphin	Kevin Doran
Galway, Kilmacduagh and Kilfenora	Brendan Kelly
Killala	John Fleming

> While the laity still contributed to the church financially it became more difficult to entice them into long-term, structured commitment to parish service. … a growing indifference to religion and church life was perceptible.[6]

At the time of the survey of the Meath Diocese undertaken by Mac Gréil in the early twenty-first century 115 priests were serving in the 69 parishes of the diocese. Many parishes had just one priest. The vast majority of the parishes had two churches, usually at different ends of the parish, and built before the arrival of the motor car, with Masses also offered in convents and hospitals. The three very large Parishes of Mullingar, Navan and Tullamore also involve hospital and school/college chaplaincies. A pointer to the future may be seen in the announcement in 2015 by Bishop Michael Smith that the Parish of Ballymore would have no full-time priest because Fr Philip Smith was retiring. Ballymore Parish has two churches – Ballymore and Boher – and at one time had two priests. Fr Oliver Devine of the neighbouring Parish of Drumraney assumed responsibility for Ballymore.

Archdiocese of Dublin: Archbishop Dermot Farrell

The Archdiocese of Dublin includes the city and county of Dublin, nearly all of County Wicklow and portions of Counties Carlow, Kildare, Laois and Wexford. It is estimated that there were over one million Catholics in the archdiocese in 2017. The diocesan cathedral is that of the Immaculate Conception of the Blessed Virgin Mary, known as St Mary's Pro-Cathedral.

An era of church building in Dublin developed under Archbishop Murray (1809–52) when ninety-seven churches were built, and continued under his successor, Archbishop Cullen. During the tenure of Archbishop Walsh from 1885 to 1921 the number of parishes in Dublin grew from sixty-four to seventy-seven. According to Thomas Morrissey, SJ, when Edward Byrne succeeded Walsh as archbishop in 1921, eighteen of the seventy-seven parishes were in Dublin city.[7] Over 85,000 Catholics lived in the city area between the Royal and Grand Canals. London-born Herbert George Simms was appointed temporary architect to Dublin Corporation in 1925 and in due course was responsible for the Crumlin and Cabra estates as well as the south inner-city flat complex known as Oliver Bond.

The tenure of Archbishop John Charles McQuaid, commencing in 1940, ushered in a further period of extensive church building and growth in the number of parishes. Between 1940 and 1972 McQuaid oversaw the creation of sixty new parishes and the building of eighty churches. In addition, 250 Catholic primary schools were opened. By 1972 there were over 130 parishes in the Dublin Archdiocese.

In 1972 Archbishop Dermot Ryan succeeded Archbishop McQuaid and during his tenure 54 more parishes were founded, so that by 1984 there were 188 parishes serving 1.1 million Catholics in the archdiocese. Partly because of the recession in the 1980s and partly because of a drop in demand, church building and the formation of new parishes slowed under the tenure of Archbishop Kevin McNamara, who was archbishop from 1984 to 1987. The tenure of Archbishop Desmond Connell from 1987 to 2004 was wracked with child abuse scandals and declining church attendance. Dealing with the consequences of child sexual abuse by clergy was to the forefront of the diocesan agenda during the period when Archbishop Diarmuid Martin was in charge (2004–21). Archbishop Martin was succeeded by Archbishop Dermot Farrell in 2021, who, in an effort to deal with the multiple problems facing the archdiocese, set up a working group under Msgr Ciarán O'Carroll, former head of the Irish College in Rome, to review the situation.

The 200 parishes which exist in the archdiocese (2017) are divided into sixteen deaneries: Blessington, Bray, Cullenswood, Donnybrook, Dún Laoghaire, Fingal North, Fingal South East, Fingal South West, Finglas, Howth, Maynooth, North City Centre, South City Centre, South Dublin, Tallaght and Wicklow.

Archdiocese of Tuam: Archbishop Michael Neary

The Archdiocese of Tuam, which is served by sixty-eight diocesan priests, includes half of Co. Mayo, half of Co. Galway and a small part of Co. Roscommon. The archdiocese extends from the island Parish of Moore on the River Shannon to Achill on the Atlantic coast. The cathedral of the archdiocese, situated in the town of Tuam, is that of the Assumption of the Blessed Virgin Mary. Tuam has the largest Gaeltacht area of any diocese, with four Gaeltacht parishes: Aran, Spiddal, Carraroe and Carna. The archdiocese includes six island parishes as well as national pilgrimage centres at Knock, Croagh Patrick, Ballintubber Abbey and Máméan. In addition to the parishes with their churches, there are a number of 'Mass centres' in schools and convents. Thirty-five years ago, in 1986, there were twenty-one such centres in use; ten years later the number had been reduced to fifteen.[8]

In the mid 1990s Micheál Mac Gréil was invited by the Archbishop of Tuam, Dr Michael Neary, to undertake a survey into the 'pastoral needs and resources of the archdiocese.'[9] Mac Gréil, who had recently retired from his position as senior lecturer in sociology at Maynooth, and who was a native of Tuam Archdiocese, was well fitted for the task. He decided to send a detailed parish enquiry form to each of the fifty-six parishes in the archdiocese. This form was filled in by clergy and laity over the period of March to December 1996. The initial report, *Quo Vadimus?* (*Where Are We Going?*), documented the pastoral needs, resources and level of participation of parishioners throughout the archdiocese. Religious observance and practice emerged as remarkably healthy. Mass attendance (Vigil and Sunday) was down from ten years earlier, in 1986, but nonetheless very high compared with some other parts of the country.

At the time of the survey, when much of the rest of the country was experiencing economic growth, serious socio-economic challenges existed in the archdiocese, with employment and job opportunities a dominant issue in all fifty-six parishes. Thirty-eight of the parishes were exclusively rural and some of these had lost population to the extent that their viability was threatened. Other parishes showed growth, especially those within the orbit of strong urban centres. A question emerged over the extent to which effort should be directed towards building up communities and parishes that were weak and failing, or to concentrate on the more urbanised areas. A similar issue arises in other dioceses where a majority of parishes have suffered a decline in attendance if not in population. In the future it is likely that choices will be made either to close some parishes or to consolidate them into 'clusters'.

Inland parishes in East Mayo and East Galway as well as some parishes in the more remote western areas – Achill, north-west Connemara – were suffering serious population decline. Mac Gréil says, 'One of the positive outcomes of this finding was its influence on Minister Éamon Ó Cuív, TD.'[10] Ó Cuív later launched the CLÁR (Ceantar Laga Árd-Riachtanais/Weak Regions High Need) national programme, which singled out communities that had suffered a 50 per cent or more decline in population between 1926 and 1996 for favourable treatment in relation to small-scale infrastructural grants.

The decline in vocations to the priesthood and religious life was reported throughout the archdiocese. At the time of Mac Gréil's study in 1996, one of the most valuable grassroots liturgical structures was the practice of station Masses, whereby Masses were celebrated in people's homes with perhaps neighbours from the adjoining twelve to fifteen houses attending. Church funerals continued to remain important. Almost all parishes reported that families of deceased were visited by a priest. Visitation to the housebound by a priest was widespread, while many received Holy Communion from lay ministers of the Eucharist.

Mac Gréil also examined lay involvement in liturgy and in Church organisations. Nearly 5 per cent of the Catholic population were involved in liturgy; for example, as lay readers or ministers of the Eucharist. He noted the importance of Church-based organisations if the laity were to embrace issues such as ecumenism in a collective manner. There had been a decline in participation in such organisations since the Second Vatican Council, indicating a 'privatisation of religion'. Eleven of the parishes had no organisation recorded. Of the six organisations which featured in at least some of the parishes, the organisation with by far the largest membership was the Pioneer Total Abstinence Association, with 2,682 members. Mac Gréil suggested that this number needed to be treated with considerable caution. The other organisations (members in brackets) were the Apostolic Work Society (493), Vincent de Paul (202), Order of Malta (200), Legion of Mary (191) and St Joseph's Young Priests Society (84).

Mac Gréil says that it is difficult to assess the impact of *Quo Vadimus?* He says that it raised awareness of the current state of the parishes. But it was not easy for some clergy to accept the decline of their administrative and pastoral supremacy. Clearly, there is a role for greater lay involvement. He believes in the need for better training for the laity to avoid 'fundamentalism', on the one hand, and, on the other, a lack of self-confidence. He also favours the permanent diaconate. Following the publication of *Quo Vadimus?*, Mac Gréil invited comments. He interviewed most of the parish priests and some of the curates from the fifty-six parishes. He wrote a follow-up report entitled *Ar Aghaidh Linn* (*Let Us Go Forward*), which contained a definite set of recommendations. He says, 'Surprisingly, I received no reaction after delivering the texts (copies) of the Report to Father Brendan Kilcoyne, secretary to Archbishop Neary, at the end of June 2000 (or in early July). I assume the priests read the documents and discussed it among themselves.'[11]

One parish in the Tuam Archdiocese, St Mary's, Headford, has recently published a book, entitled *Roots of Faith: A Journey of Hope*, to celebrate 150 years of the parish church. At present the parish has around 700 homes and 3,000 residents, compared with a little over 200 homes when the church was built. The book delves into the remote past and deals with holy wells and Mass rocks as well as the more modern grottos. Local graveyards are examined also. In reviewing the book, the writer Peter Costello says, 'the heart of the book is devoted to the creator of the church, Fr Peter Conway … He brought the Presentation Sisters to the area … Today the Presentation College in Headford is the largest of its kind in the Western region.'[12] While praising the book, Costello expresses regret that like so many local histories that he has read, this parish history stops in the early 1920s. In any event the Parish of Headford seems to be in a vibrant state, to judge by the activities listed on its website, which include adult and children's choirs, Comhaltas Ceoltóiri Éireann (Society of the Musicians of Ireland) and Solstice Arts Group. Headford Parish also has GAA, soccer and rugby clubs.

According to a report by Cathal Barry in *The Irish Catholic* in September 2015, an upcoming 'cluster mission' was planned in Galway (Tuam Archdiocese). Fr Paddy Mooney, the parish priest in Glenamaddy and Williamstown, is quoted as saying that the mission 'will give people a greater awareness of their need to travel to neighbouring parishes'. The parish cluster of Glenamaddy, Dunmore, Kilkerrin–Clonburne and Williamstown hosted a Redemptorist mission on 4–11 October 2015.

The cluster secretary, Breda Kavanagh, told *The Irish Catholic*:

> The church is going to change and people have to get out of their comfort zones and realise it might not be possible to have Mass in their own church.
>
> With the reality of the shortage of priests people will have to get used to travelling. I know each parish wants its own identity but unfortunately the situation is that it will have to change.[13]

Diocese of Limerick: Bishop Brendan Leahy

The diocese, which belongs to the ecclesiastical province of Cashel and Emly, includes the greater part of Co. Limerick, part of Co. Clare and one townland in Co. Kerry. The diocesan cathedral is named St John the Baptist and is located in the city of Limerick. Limerick city has some striking family-related features. The city has the highest percentage of births outside marriage, 58.6 per cent, compared with the national average of 36.1 per cent. Limerick city also has a relatively high rate of marital breakdown and divorce.

Ten of Limerick's parishes are served by non-resident and retired priests. Already a number of parishes have been gathered together in clusters and a Mass rota is established among the available priests, who may or may not be resident in the parishes. For example, three parishes in the Kilmallock area no longer have a resident priest: Bulgaden/Martinstown, Glenrue and Castletown/Ballyagran. It is inevitable that the total number of Masses will be reduced but it is hoped that churches will remain open for weddings and funerals.[14] Smaller parishes fear that they will lose their identity. Fr Frank Duhig, the parish priest of Newcastle West and administrator for the two Parishes of Monagea and Feohanagh/Castlemahon, expresses the worry of smaller parishes:

> The biggest fear the smaller parishes would have is losing their parish identity. For example in Newcastle West there are 7,200 people, while there is only 1,300 in the Feohanagh/Castlemahon area and 800 in Monagea. Smaller parishes feel threatened and their biggest fear is losing parish identity, but it is up to them to take ownership of their pastoral council and we have people doing that.[15]

In addressing the problem of the decline in the number of priests, the Diocese of Limerick decided to take a group of priests on a study visit to Évry–Corbeil–Essonnes, a diocese in the Latin rite, and a suffragan diocese of the Archdiocese of Paris, to see how the Church there is dealing with the problem of vanishing vocations. It is likely that stronger participation by the laity will be an essential component of the way forward.

Limerick took an important initiative to review the past and plan for the future by convening a diocesan synod in April 2016. It was the first diocesan synod in Ireland in fifty years and the first in Limerick for eighty years. The last was held in a very different Ireland in 1936, just four years after the Eucharistic Congress of 1932. Based on the fruits of the synod, the *Limerick Diocesan Pastoral Plan 2016–2026* was published in December 2016. Six themes were identified to provide a framework for diocesan strategy over the course of the plan. A total of 100 proposals divided over the six areas were listed as means of fulfilling the goals associated with each theme. The six themes were: Community and Sense of Belonging; Pastoral Care of the Family; Young People; Liturgy and Life; Faith Formation and Education; and New Models of Leadership. Specific proposals included the establishment of lay parish visitation teams; the establishment of family life centres which would try to support many needs of families, including for food; the setting up of a youth café; better recognition for hymns and prayers in Irish; parishes to follow Sunday school model for purposes of evangelisation of children; and a review of sources for parish income. The plan covers a broad territory. A recurring motif is the need for lay involvement – both volunteers and paid workers. There is also frequent reference to training. For example, two laypeople from the diocese have been assigned to Maynooth for liturgy training. As a pointer to the future, in order to facilitate a day-long conference of clergy, every parish in Limerick held a lay-led liturgical service on Tuesday 25 April 2017.[16]

Notes on Other Dioceses

Archdiocese of Cashel and Emly: Archbishop Kieran O'Reilly
The archdiocese includes most of Co. Tipperary and parts of Co. Limerick. It includes forty-six parishes, eighty-four churches and eighty diocesan clergy. The 'mother church', or the cathedral church of the archdiocese, is the Cathedral of the Assumption, which is located in neither Cashel nor Emly but in Thurles. The suffragan dioceses of the province of Cashel and Emly are Cloyne, Cork and Ross; Kerry; Killaloe; Limerick; Waterford and Lismore; and Kilfenora. Kilfenora is administered by the Bishop of Galway in the province of Tuam.

In preparation for the World Meeting of Families 2018 the archdiocese organised a Family Fun Day at Tipperary Racecourse at the end of April 2018. A range of activities were organised and parish groups, including parish cells, the Society of St Vincent de Paul and the Legion of Mary, were featured. The event was very well attended.

Diocese of Achonry: Bishop Paul Dempsey

The diocese includes parts of Mayo, Roscommon and Sligo. The diocese has twenty-three parishes, forty-seven churches and thirty priests. The mensal[17] Parish of Ballaghadereen comes directly under the bishop and is the location of the Cathedral of the Annunciation of the Blessed Virgin Mary and St Nathy. The other twenty-two parishes have their own parish priest. After the appointment of the former Bishop of Achonry, Brendan Kelly, to the Diocese of Galway in late 2017, the diocese remained vacant until early 2020. There had been some speculation that the Dioceses of Achonry and Galway might be merged.

One of the most popular devotional events in the diocese is the Annual Knocknacarra Parish Novena to Our Lady, held in the month of May. Speakers each day include both priests and laypeople.

Diocese of Ardagh and Clonmacnoise: Bishop Francis Duffy

The diocese includes nearly all of Co. Longford, the greater part of Co. Leitrim, and parts of Counties Cavan, Offaly, Roscommon, Sligo and Westmeath. The diocese has forty-one parishes, including the mensal Parish of Longford, where the Cathedral of St Mel is located. It has eighty churches and fifty-two diocesan priests.

The diocese contains one of the most important religious sites in Ireland – Clonmacnoise, where St Kieran established a monastic settlement in the sixth century. The visitor centre at Clonmacnoise attracted over 150,000 visitors in 2018.[18] The diocese also contains the village of Ardagh, where in the nineteenth century the Ardagh Chalice, which dates from the eight century, was found. The original Sam Maguire Cup, which was first presented for inter-county GAA football in 1928, was based on the design of the Ardagh Chalice.

Diocese of Clogher: Bishop Laurence Duffy

The diocese includes Co. Monaghan, most of Co. Fermanagh and portions of Counties Tyrone, Donegal, Louth and Cavan. Clogher Diocese contains thirty-seven parishes with eighty-five churches and has sixty-six priests. The diocesan cathedral of St Macartan is in the town of Monaghan.

Castleblaney in Co. Monaghan set a striking example in ecumenical cooperation when the Church of Ireland St Maeldoid's Church facilitated Catholic services when the Catholic church was under renovation.

Diocese of Clonfert: Bishop Michael Duignan

The diocese includes portions of Counties Galway, Offaly and Roscommon, and contains twenty-four parishes, forty-seven churches with thirty-two priests. Edward Martyn, novelist, playwright and president of Sinn Féin, was born at the home of his maternal grandfather, James Smyth, in the Parish of Loughrea. Financial support from Martyn and from the Smyth family ensured high-quality work in the cathedral in Loughrea, including that by John Hughes, the foremost sculptor in the country at the time, and by Michael Shortall, a student of Hughes. The Yeats sisters, Lily and Elizabeth, who together with their friend Evelyn Gleeson set up the Dun Emer Guild, embroidered twenty-four banners of Irish saints for the cathedral. Jack B. Yeats and his wife, Mary, designed the banners. The superb stained-glass windows came from An Túr Gloine studio under the direction of Alfred E. Child.

Diocese of Cloyne: Bishop William Crean

The diocese covers most of Co. Cork and contains 46 parishes with 107 churches, 77 priests and 6 permanent deacons. The cathedral church is St Colman's in Cobh. One of the most famous priests born in the diocese was Thomas Croke, Archbishop of Cashel and Emly, after whom Croke Park, the headquarters of the GAA, is named. Croke was born at Castlecor (Parish of Kilbrin, Co. Cork) and spent some time as parish priest of Doneraile. Another famous parish priest of Doneraile was the writer and novelist Canon Patrick Sheehan. Croke accompanied the Bishop of Cloyne to the First Vatican Council.

From the mid 1990s a series of complaints of child sexual abuse by clergy were made in Cloyne. This resulted in the establishment of a Commission of Investigation, led by Judge Yvonne Murphy, to examine how both Church and State handled allegations of abuse by clergy in the diocese. The commission found that the diocese was ignoring the Church's own guidelines, and that Bishop John Magee had failed to report complaints against priests and had given an incorrect account to a previous inquiry as to how he was handling allegations. The report was published in 2011. In March 2009 Pope Benedict XVI appointed Archbishop Dermot Clifford of Cashel and Emly as apostolic administrator of the Cloyne Diocese. Bishop Magee was replaced by Bishop Crean in 2013.

Diocese of Cork and Ross: Bishop Fintan Gavin

The diocese includes Cork city and part of Co. Cork and contains 68 parishes and 124 churches with 92 priests. The cathedral church of St Mary and St

Anne is in Cork city. The first cathedral was opened in 1808 as the parish church of the single parish, then on the north side of the city – hence the popular name: the North Chapel. Local historian Roger Herlihy explains that much earlier, in 1635, Bishop William Tirry established two parishes, one in the north of the city based around a church in Coppinger's Lane, now called St Rita's Place, and the other on the southern side based around a church on Cat Lane, now known as Tower Street.[19] The present-day South Parish, although still large, has been greatly reduced through subdivision with the formation of other parishes, including Saints Peter and Paul, St Finbarr's West [the Lough] and St Michael's [Blackrock]. In addition to the diocesan churches and the churches of religious orders, many other denominations have been present in the South Parish over the years. Roger Herlihy lists these as Anglicans, Presbyterians, Episcopalians, Unitarians, Quakers, Jews, Anabaptists and Jehovah's Witnesses.[20]

As in almost every parish, education has played an intimate role in parish life. Among the orders who established education centres in the South Parish were the Presentation Order and the Ursuline Sisters at Douglas Street, the Presentation Brothers at Douglas Street and Greenmount, the Christian Brothers at Sullivan's Quay and Deerpark, and the Mercy Sisters, first at Rutland Street and later at Sharman Crawford Street. There was also the Church of Ireland Blue Coat School on St Stephen's Street, so called because the boys wore a blue uniform; St Nicholas' National and Industrial Schools on Cove Street; and the Cork Model National School, open to all denominations, on Anglesea Street.

Diocese of Derry: Bishop Donal McKeown

The diocese includes areas in Northern Ireland and the Republic – almost all of Co. Derry, parts of Counties Donegal and Tyrone, and a very small area across the River Bann in Co. Antrim. The diocese contains 51 parishes with 104 churches and 70 priests. The cathedral church of St Eugene is in the city of Derry.

The Catholic Boys' Grammar School, St Columb's College in Derry, has a number of well-known alumni. They include writers Seamus Heaney and Brian Friel, statesmen Patrick McGilligan and John Hume, and Ireland football manager Martin O'Neill.

Diocese of Down and Connor: Bishop Noel Treanor

The diocese includes Co. Antrim, the greater part of Co. Down and part of Co. Derry, and contains 88 parishes with 151 churches and 108 priests in diocesan ministry. The cathedral church of St Peter's is in Belfast. The continued increase in the number of Catholics in and around Belfast accounts for the position which Down and Connor holds as the second-largest diocese in Ireland, with a Catholic population in 2017 of 326,499. In 2013 Bishop Treanor initiated a pastoral review based on the 2011 census. A regular practice rate of 20 per cent was ascertained across the diocese.

Diocese of Dromore: Archbishop Eamon Martin (Appointed as Administrator in 2019)

The diocese includes portions of Counties Antrim, Armagh and Down. It contains twenty-three parishes, which have been divided into five pastoral areas since 2012. There are forty-eight churches with twenty-seven priests and three permanent deacons. The cathedral church of St Patrick and St Colman is in Newry.

As in a number of other dioceses, sexual offences by priests have occurred in Dromore, including the case of a young girl who was abused by the parish priest of Donaghmore in 2001. He was convicted in 2012.

Diocese of Elphin: Bishop Kevin Doran

The diocese includes portions of Counties Roscommon, Sligo, Westmeath and Galway, and contains thirty-eight parishes, ninety churches, forty-three priests and six permanent deacons. The cathedral church of the Immaculate Conception of the Blessed Virgin Mary is in Sligo. In autumn 2015 Fr Raymond Brown, who had been parish priest in Kilbride, Co. Roscommon, for close on thirty years, retired. There was no priest available to replace him so he will continue to live in the parish priest's house and share duties with Deacon Seamus Talbot. His non-replacement illustrates the increasing scarcity of priests and the growing importance of permanent deacons.

Diocese of Ferns: Bishop Denis Brennan

The diocese includes almost all of Co. Wexford and part of Co. Wicklow, and contains 49 parishes, 101 churches, 76 priests and one permanent deacon. The cathedral church of St Aidan is in Enniscorthy.

The Ferns Diocese and some of its parishes have become virtually synonymous with clerical sexual abuse. In 2002 the Bishop of Ferns, Brendan Comiskey, resigned. One of the auxiliary bishops of Dublin, Bishop Eamonn Walsh, was appointed administrator. In 2003 retired Supreme Court Judge Frank Murphy was appointed by the government to lead an inquiry into clerical sexual abuse in the diocese. The report published in 2005 identified more than 100 allegations of child sexual abuse against 21 priests in the 40 years between 1962 and 2002. The report pointed to serious failures by

Bishop Comiskey in responding to the allegations. Denis Brennan was appointed bishop in 2006.

Diocese of Galway, Kilmacduagh and Kilfenora: Bishop Michael Duignan (Appointed in 2022 to Succeed Bishop Brendan Kelly)

The diocese includes portions of Counties Galway, Mayo and Clare and contains thirty-nine parishes, seventy-one churches, forty-four priests and four permanent deacons. The diocesan cathedral of St Nicholas and Our Lady Assumed into Heaven is in Galway city.

The best-known Bishop of Galway in recent decades was Eamon Casey, who was bishop from 1976 to 1992. He resigned in 1992 when it became known that he had fathered a son some years earlier. Bishop Casey died in 2017.

Diocese of Kerry: Bishop Raymond Browne

The diocese includes Co. Kerry (except Kilmurry) and part of Co. Clare, and contains 54 parishes, 105 churches, 55 priests and 6 permanent deacons. The cathedral church is that of the Assumption of the Blessed Virgin Mary in Killarney.

In an item on the Sean O'Rourke RTÉ radio programme on 21 July 2016, reporter Brian O'Connell highlighted the shortage of priests in the diocese. At the time five parishes in the Kerry region were without a parish priest. This number would increase to six following the death of Fr Pat Moore. Fr Moore was described as being like a 'community outreach worker who could organise a cup of tea and a singsong'. In the Clare region of the diocese there were eight parishes in 2018 without a parish priest. In Labasheeda Fr Tom McGrath became parish priest following the death, at a relatively early age, of the local parish priest Fr Kelly. Fr McGrath set up a liturgy with laypeople – all women – a first for the diocese.

Diocese of Kildare and Leighlin: Bishop Denis Nulty

The diocese includes Co. Carlow and parts of Counties Kildare, Laois, Offaly, Kilkenny, Wicklow and Wexford, and contains 56 parishes and 117 churches with 74 priests and 8 permanent deacons. The cathedral church is that of the Assumption of the Blessed Virgin Mary in the town of Carlow.

In 2017 the Diocese of Kildare and Leighlin, in what is thought to be a first for a diocese, organised a family picnic at Punchestown Racecourse. There was a large attendance of 4,000. It was organised in preparation for the World Meeting of Families that took place in Dublin in 2018. A number of other dioceses, including the Archdiocese of Cashel and Emly, have followed with similar initiatives.

Diocese of Killala: Bishop John Fleming

The diocese includes portions of Counties Mayo and Sligo, and contains twenty-two parishes, forty-eight churches and thirty priests. Killala also has one permanent deacon. The cathedral church is St Muredach's in Ballina. The Newman Institute, based in Ballina, provides adult religious education and faith formation. The population of the diocese fell from 49,000 in 1950 to 39,000 in 1990, or by 20 per cent. It recovered slightly to 40,000 in 2016. Of the total population, 38,000 are listed as Catholic. In response to the population decline in the 1990s, the western bishops took an initiative called 'Developing the West Together'. This led to meetings in a number of venues and was followed by a government initiative to develop the west.

Diocese of Killaloe: Bishop Fintan Monahan

The diocese includes portions of Counties Clare, Laois, Limerick, Offaly and Tipperary. There are 58 parishes divided into 12 clusters, 133 churches and 70 priests. The cluster system has generated increased cooperation between clergy and between parish pastoral councils. The last 'new' parish to be founded was the Parish of St Senan's at Shannon in the 1960s, to accommodate the growth of Shannon Airport and the surrounding area. The cathedral church is St Flannan's in Ennis.

Diocese of Kilmore: Msgr Liam Kelly (Administrator)

The diocese includes almost all of Co. Cavan and a portion of Counties Leitrim, Fermanagh, Meath and Sligo, and contains thirty-six parishes. Thirty-three of the parishes are in the Republic and two are in Northern Ireland. The diocese has ninety-five churches, sixty-four priests and two permanent deacons. The cathedral church of St Patrick and St Felim is located in the town of Cavan. A diocesan assembly was held in 2014 and a pastoral plan drawn up. Four main areas of pastoral and missionary activity were identified: youth ministry; liturgy, sacraments and prayer; diocesan structures; and support for priests.

Diocese of Ossory: Administrator Dermot Farrell

The diocese includes most of Co. Kilkenny and portions of Counties Laois and Offaly, and contains forty-two parishes, eighty-nine churches and fifty-eight priests. The cathedral church is St Mary's in Kilkenny. A pastoral plan has been put in place following consultation.

Following the resignation in 2016 on health grounds of Bishop Séamus Freeman, a member of the Pallottine Order, Msgr Michael Ryan, parish priest in Castlecomer, was appointed as diocesan administrator prior to the appointment of Bishop Dermot Farrell, former parish priest of Dunboyne and Kilbride, in January 2018. In March 2019 Bishop Farrell said that the number of Masses would have to be reduced in his diocese because of the fall in the number of priests. From 1 December 2019 Sunday Masses in Ossory were reduced from 140 to 92.[21] He referred to an inconclusive papal investigation established by Pope Francis in 2016 into whether there were women deacons in the early Church,[22] while Msgr Ryan suggested that married priests should be considered: he pointed to the fact that many married Anglican priests had joined the Catholic Church. Since the Church of England's decision to ordain women in 1992, large numbers of Anglican clergy have been ordained Catholic priests, with special permission being given for married men to do so.[23]

Diocese of Raphoe: Bishop Alan McGuckian, SJ

The diocese includes the greater part of Co. Donegal and contains thirty-three parishes, seventy-one churches and some fifty-six priests. The cathedral church is of St Eunan and St Colmcille in Letterkenny. Bishop Alan McGuckian, a member of the Jesuit Order, was appointed bishop in 2017. He is the first Jesuit ever to have been appointed bishop in Ireland. Bishop McGuckian comes from Northern Ireland and is a fluent Irish speaker.

Diocese of Waterford and Lismore: Bishop Alphonsus Cullinan

The diocese includes the city and county of Waterford, a large part of Co. Tipperary and a small segment of Co. Cork. The diocese contains forty-five parishes and eighty-five churches and has sixty-one priests. The cathedral church is the Most Holy Trinity in the city of Waterford. The parishes are grouped as Waterford city, Waterford county and Tipperary.

Appendix 2

Parish Groups not Included in Chapter 3

Active Retirement Groups

Active Retirement Ireland (ARI) was established following a retirement exhibition in Dún Laoghaire in 1978. There are about 500 ARI groups across the country, with over 20,000 members. The revenue of ARI comes from membership subscriptions as well as funding from the HSE. Some professional staff are employed. There are no formal links between parishes and ARI groups but many groups meet in Church premises, both Roman Catholic and Church of Ireland.

Apostolic Work Society

The Apostolic Work Society, originally named the Catholic Women's Missionary League, was founded in Belfast in 1923. It was the idea of a young woman from Enniskillen, Agnes McAuley. At the first meeting ten women were present and Fr Edward Crossan from St Malachy's College presided. The aim of the association is to help the overseas missions of the Church through the offering of prayers and Masses as well as through material aid. The latter includes, for example, the supply of Mass kits and vestments. While the society brings together groups of women in parishes in order to support the missions, its focus is primarily on the overseas missions rather than domestic parishes.

Bethany Bereavement Support Groups

Bethany Bereavement Support Groups are parish-based voluntary groups which give support to the bereaved and their families. Fr Myles O'Reilly, SJ, who had worked at Columbia University Hospital in New York in the 1970s, was very impressed by the approach to death and dying that he encountered there. He started giving retreats in Milltown Park, Dublin, on the Christian response to death. Gradually, Bethany Bereavement Support Groups were formed, taking the name from the visit by Jesus to Mary and Martha when their brother Lazarus died.

Confraternities and Sodalities

The best known confraternity in Ireland, the Confraternity of the Holy Family, was founded in Limerick city by the Redemptorists in January 1868.[1] The Confraternity of the Holy Family had been founded in Belgium in 1844 by Henri Belletable, a military engineer, to support a Christian way of life among men working on the railways.[2] When the Belltable Arts Centre was opened in Limerick in 1981, it was located in the former Redemptorist Confraternity Hall. The centre was called after Belletable (without the middle 'e'). The confraternities, which comprise groups of laypeople seeking to develop personal piety and to undertake charitable works, spread across Europe as the Redemptorists preached parish missions. A weekly Mass, exclusively for men, was celebrated for the confraternity for 150 years until 2017 when, because of falling numbers of attendees, the Mass was opened to women, possibly with the hope of increasing the number of attendees. The world had changed. Ger O'Brien, who attended the men's Mass for sixty-three years, said their Mass was also a social outlet for many. 'It was a lovely men's club. Everyone would congregate in the church yard afterwards and talk about sport.'[3]

Sodalities are confraternities or associations, generally divided into men's sodalities and women's sodalities, that meet at regular intervals for religious devotions. Members usually say certain daily prayers and undertake some activity like visitation of the sick. The name 'sodality' comes from the Latin *sodalitas*, meaning comradeship or fellowship, *sodalis* being the Latin word for companion or comrade. Parish sodalities and confraternities were a prominent feature of parish life in Ireland until the 1960s.

In addition to parish sodalities the Jesuit Sodality of Our Lady frequently existed in schools. The Jesuit Sodality was founded by a Belgian Jesuit, Jean Leunis, who had known Ignatius Loyola. The sodality was rooted in Ignatian spirituality and involved attendance at a weekly meeting and the undertaking of some apostolic activity. According to Professor James Donnelly, there were 823 local sodalities of Our Lady in Ireland in 1958; by 1975 approximately 82 branches were in existence.[4] Following the Second Vatican Council, and an initiative taken in France, the Jesuit Sodality found new expression in 'La

Vie Chrétienne' so that the Sodalities of Our Lady would re-emerge as Christian Life Communities.

Men's Breakfast Initiative

Close to 100 men meet for breakfast 6 times a year in the parish hall in the Johnstown/Killiney Parish of Our Lady of Good Counsel in South Dublin. The idea for the breakfasts came from a similar venture in a Catholic parish in Baltimore in the United States. A voluntary donation of between €2 and €4 is suggested. There is a fifteen-minute talk by someone from the local community who speaks about their own experience, often with reference to their faith. To date speakers have included a dentist, an accountant and a Church of Ireland businessman. The breakfasts have resulted in bringing the community closer.[5]

Parish Cells

Parish cells were started by an Irish priest in Florida in the 1980s. Fr (later Msgr) Mike Ivers from Longford drew inspiration from the Pentecostal Churches and travelled to Korea to see cell groups in action among non-Roman Catholic believers. The cells encourage the laity to take on a missionary role and encourage priests 'to turn the parish into a community of ardent faith, where members are "agents of evangelisation" and the parish is a "constant center of missionary outreach" '.[6] The cells spread from Florida to Milan in Italy, and in 2015 parish cells received official Vatican approval.

Fr Michael Hurley, who was parish priest in Ballinteer in Dublin, introduced cell groups to Ireland. Cell groups are small faith groups of between four and twelve people who meet each fortnight in the home of a participant. According to Matt Gleeson, a long-time member of a cell group in Ballinteer, in addition to developing the relationship of the individual member with God, cells look outwards. They seek ways in which to help in the parish through looking out for others who may be experiencing difficulties, or by visiting the elderly and isolated. Cell groups help to foster a better community spirit. Cell members also play a role in parish ministries; for example, as members of parish funeral teams.[7] It is suggested that the system of parish cells 'not only benefits lay people, but also priests who are able to clarify and renew their faith by providing the biblical readings for each Cell.'[8]

Scouts

The Boy Scouts were founded by Robert Baden-Powell in 1907 and within a year the scouts were established in Ireland. In 1910 Baden-Powell's sister, Agnes Baden-Powell, helped establish the Girl Guides. In the 1970s mixed scouting was introduced. While scouting is independent of any religion, Baden-Powell emphasised the practice of Christianity. However, some in Ireland regarded the Baden-Powell scouts as having a British and Protestant ethos. Following independence two priests, Fr Tom Farrell and his brother Fr Ernest Farrell, considered the possibility of a Catholic scouting organisation and, with the approval of the hierarchy, Fr Farrell founded the Catholic Boy Scouts of Ireland (CBSI) in 1927. Most of the scout troops were associated with parishes and met in church halls. This was true of Protestant and Catholic troops. The scouting groups operated separately – the CBSI on a 32-county basis, while the Scout Association of Ireland (SAI), for the Baden-Powell scouts, operated in the Free State/Republic, and the Scouting Association Northern Ireland operated in Northern Ireland.

Following the Good Friday Agreement in 1998, the climate towards cooperation between Catholics and Protestants improved in Northern Ireland and, as a more ecumenical approach had been developing in the South since Vatican II, it was decided to explore the possibility of a merger. Twenty years later, in 2017, the SAI and the CBSI merged in the Republic. In his book on the history of the CBSI in Donnybrook from 1927 until the birth of Scouting Ireland in 2017, Dermot Lacey shows how central the parish was to the life of scouting.[9] Prior to the establishment of the CBSI in Donnybrook, there was already a scout group there under the patronage of the Church of Ireland Parish of St Mary's. When the Catholic parish priest in Donnybrook, Msgr Daniel Molony, founded a scout unit in 1927, it was named the Sacred Heart Unit after the Parish of Donnybrook. According to Lacey:

> Another interesting aspect regarding the name of the unit is how members from those early years inevitably referred to it as the Sacred Heart Unit, or the SHU, as opposed to the numerical description [the 3rd Dublin]. This has all but disappeared now and reflects a changing Ireland.[10]

From the 1930s through to the 1950s and 1960s the relationship between the CBSI and the Catholic Church was strong. Lacey gives examples of the close connection between Church and Catholic scouts in Donnybrook, which would have been typical of other parishes also. There were monthly parades to Sunday Mass until the 1990s. Until the mid 1960s the parades were led by the units' own pipe and drum band. Lacey pays tribute to the contribution made to scouting in Donnybrook by a series of priests, some of whom acted as unit chaplain, starting with Msgr Molony.

Support Groups for Victims of Domestic Violence

It has been suggested by a number of priests that churches are in the front line of reaching out to those suffering from domestic violence. Cork-bask Redemptorist Fr Gerry O'Connor says that in certain parts of Ireland 'it would be a big part of your [a priest's] ministry, and not an easy one.' In one parish in which he worked, O'Connor said that one weekend each year would be dedicated to the theme of domestic violence 'with support groups being set up for women who suffered from the issue, and also for men inclined towards violence'.[11]

Marriage Introductions

A special initiative was launched in the parish at Knock, Co. Mayo, by Fr Michael Keane – the Knock Marriage Bureau – now known as Knock Marriage Introductions Bureau. The bureau was started in 1968, partly because young women were leaving the Mayo area due to a lack of opportunity for marriage and because of the low marriage rate in rural Ireland in general. Since 1968 over 900 marriages have taken place with the help of the bureau, which was led by Canon Joe Cooney, who succeeded Fr Keane until 2015. In 2015 five marriages took place through the bureau. Fr Stephen Farragher took over in 2017, and in 2019 he announced the closure of the bureau. The internet, online dating and apps, as well as financial pressures, led to the closure.

Notes

Introduction

1. *La Croix*, 17 May 2016. Interview took place in Rome on Monday 9 May 2016.
2. Ibid.
3. Anne-Marie McGauran, *Community Call: Learning for the Future*, NESC Secretariat Papers, Paper No. 22, Dublin: National Economic and Social Council, 2021.
4. Derek Scally, *The Best Catholics in the World*, Dublin: Penguin, 2021, p. 14.
5. Micheál Mac Gréil, *Our Living Church*, Maynooth: NUI Maynooth, 2005, p. 27.
6. Coordinator of Catechetical Formation in the Dublin Archdiocese.
7. Donal Harrington, *Tomorrow's Parish: A Vision and a Path*, Dublin: Columba Press, 2015, p. 16. No analogy is perfect – *omnis analogia claudicat*. A bypass, by reducing congestion in a town, may also increase the space and the calm for the creation of a community within the town.
8. Raghuram Rajan, *The Third Pillar*, London: William Collins, 2019, p. xx.
9. Harrington, op. cit., p. 91. Quotation is from Pope Pius X, *Vehementer Nos*, Rome: Vatican Publishing, 1906, p. 8.
10. Harrington, op. cit., p. 92.
11. Matthew Schmitz, 'The Unnameable Violence', *Catholic Herald*, 9 August 2019, p. 16.
12. Ibid.
13. 'Thieves on the Run after French Cathedral "Sacrilegious Robbery"', *The Irish Catholic*, 7 November 2019.
14. Scally, op. cit., p. 16.
15. Patsy McGarry, 'Mary McAleese says "Game is Almost Up" for All-Male Catholic Church', *The Irish Times*, 11 March 2019.
16. Hugh Brody, *Iniskillane: Change and Decline in the West of Ireland*, London: Allen Lane, 1973, p. 175.
17. Tom Inglis, 'Church and Culture in Catholic Ireland', *Studies*, 106, 421, 2017, p. 24.
18. Ibid.
19. Pope Francis, *Amoris Laetita* (57), Rome: Vatican Publishing, 2016.
20. Chai Brady, 'Stark Choices for Parishes as Boundary Restructure Possible', *The Irish Catholic*, 15 March 2018.
21. William King, *A Lost Tribe*, Dublin: Lilliput Press, 2017.
22. European Union Community Development Network, *Including the Excluded: From Practice to Policy in European Community Development*, Bristol: Policy Press, 2005.
23. Dermot McCarthy, 'Community Commitment in Heart of Dublin', *The Irish Times*, 10 December 2019.

24 Rajan, op. cit. p. xiv.

25 Meeting with Bishop Walsh, 20 March 2017.

26 Meeting with Deputy Maureen O'Sullivan, 20 March 2017.

27 The county was originally introduced as an area of local government following the Norman invasion.

28 Meeting with Deputy Éamon Ó Cuív, 6 October 2016.

29 William E. Simon Jr, *Great Catholic Parishes*, Notre Dame, Indiana: Ave Maria Press, 2016, p. 7.

30 Richard Boyle and Joanna O'Riordan, *Capacity and Competency Requirements in Local Government*, Dublin: Institute of Public Administration, 2013, p. 7.

31 Richard Boyle, *Re-Shaping Local Government: Overview of Selected International Experience with Local Government Reorganisation, Mergers, Amalgamation and Coordination*, Dublin: Institute of Public Administration, 2016.

32 Meeting with Owen Keegan, 24 September 2021.

33 Meeting with Richard Boyle, 20 September 2021; Boyle and O'Riordan, op. cit.

34 Suggested in conversation with Ger Turley, 28 September 2021.

35 Gerard Turley and Stephen McNena, 'An Analysis of Local Public Finances and the 2014 Local Government Reforms', *The Economic and Social Review*, 47, 2, 2016.

36 Meeting with Owen Keegan, 24 September 2021.

37 Norma Prendiville, 'Council Calls for an End to Irish Water', *Limerick Leader*, 9 October 2021.

38 Ronan Smyth, 'Proposal to Redraw Waterford–Kilkenny Boundary will "Leave a Very Bitter Taste"', *thejournal.ie*, 14 February 2017.

39 Barry Roche and Marie O'Halloran, 'Turnout Typified by Empty Ballot Box', *The Irish Times*, 2 December 2019.

1. The Parish Landscape

1   Description given by Deacon Dermot McCarthy, meeting, 13 September 2016.

2   Liam Irwin, 'The Irish Parish in Historical Perspective', in Eugene Duffy (Ed.), *Parishes in Transition*, Dublin: Columba Press, 2010.

3   Paul MacCotter, *The Origins of the Parish in Ireland*, Dublin: Royal Irish Academy, 2019, pp. 44–5.

4   Ibid., p. 45.

5   N. J. G. Pounds, *A History of the English Parish*, Cambridge: Cambridge University Press, 2000, p. 4, quoted in MacCotter, ibid., p. 45.

6   European People's Party, *EPP Manifesto: 'Let's Open the Next Chapter for Europe Together'*, Brussels: European People's Party, 2019.

7   Patrick Corish, *The Irish Catholic Experience*, Dublin: Gill and Macmillan, 1985, p. 42.

8   Thomas O'Connor, 'Summary of the Diocese of Meath', in Micheál Mac Gréil, *Our Living Church*, Maynooth: NUI Maynooth, 2005, p. 1.

9   Patrick Corish, *The Catholic Community in the Seventeenth and Eighteenth Centuries*, Dublin: Helicon, 1981.

10 Kevin Whelan, 'The Catholic Parish, the Catholic Chapel, and Village Development in Ireland', *Irish Geography*, 1983.

11 Desmond Roche, *Local Government in Ireland*, Dublin: Institute of Public Administration, 1982, p. 70.

12 Niamh Nic Ghabhann, 'How the Catholic Church Built its Property Portfolio', *RTÉ Brainstorm*, 2018.

13 Hugh Brody, *Iniskillane: Change and Decline in the West of Ireland*, London: Allen Lane, 1973, pp. 65–6.

14 Horace Plunkett, *Ireland in the New Century*, Dublin: Maunsel, 1904, pp. 169–75.

15 Whelan, op. cit. A barn chapel generally comprised a simple barn-like structure with four walls, a clay floor and a thatched roof. There were no side chapels and no pillars.

16 Jean Blanchard, *The Church in Contemporary Ireland*, Dublin: Clonmore and Reynolds, 1963.

17 Possibly as a result of the clerical abuse scandals it is judged wiser to appoint bishops to dioceses where there is more distance between the bishop and the priests.

18 Whelan, op. cit.

19 Corish, *The Irish Catholic Experience*, op. cit., p. 233. In *Knocknagow*, Mat Donovan is engaged in a sledge-throwing contest with Captain French. His inspiration to succeed is drawn from the old mud walls and thatched roofs of his village, and as he prepares to throw the sledge, he exclaims, 'For the credit of the little village!' (Charles. J. Kickham, *Knocknagow, or the Homes of Tipperary*, 26th edition, Dublin: James Duffy & Co., 1887, p. 453).

20 Gene Kerrigan, *Another Country: Growing Up in '50s Ireland*, Dublin: Gill and Macmillan, 1998, p. 72.

21 Archbishop Dermot Ryan, 'The Lessons of the Past', Lecture given in Lyon and Paris, 8 and 9 January 1983.

22 Austin Flannery, OP, 'Introduction', in Richard Hurley and Wilfred Cantwell, *Contemporary Irish Church Architecture*, Dublin: Gill and Macmillan, 1985, p. 14

23 Quoted in Flannery, ibid., p. 13.

24 Our Lady features prominently in the stained-glass windows in the chapel of the college, whose full title is 'King's College of Our Lady and St Nicholas'.

25 Flannery, op. cit., p. 22. The Constitution on the Sacred Liturgy was a document of the Second Vatican Council.

26 Flannery, op. cit., p. 23.

27 Flannery, op. cit., p. 27.

28 Flannery, op. cit., p. 28.

29 Christopher Moriarty, 'The Church of the Holy Spirit, Greenhills', *The Messenger*, June 2017, p. 23.

30 Ibid., p. 23.

31 See www.stmarysbelfast.org

32 Elena Curti, 'Preserving Northern Ireland's Churches', *The Tablet*, 21 July 2021.

33 Meeting with Críona Ní Dhálaigh, 9 October 2018.

34 Brody, op. cit. pp. 175–7.

35 Brendan Walsh, 'The Shock of the New', *The Tablet*, 17 February 2018.

36 See https://www.bbc.co.uk/religion/religions/christianity/holydays/motheringsunday_1.shtml

37 Interview with Fr Mac Gréil, 29 October 2015.

38 Colm Fitzpatrick, 'Travelling with the Chaplain on the Move', *The Irish Catholic*, 4 October 2018.

39 'Making Parishes Work', *Catholic Herald*, 12 August 2016, p. 3.

40 Donal Murray, 'Parish Life: Facing a Challenging Future', in Eugene Duffy (Ed.), *Parishes in Transition*, Dublin: Columba Press, 2010, p. 76.

41 Meeting with Msgr Dolan at the Chancellery, Archbishop's House, 6 March 2015.

42 Meeting with Rev. Trevor Sargent, 29 November 2018. Sargent wrote his MA dissertation on the subject.

43 Meeting with Rev. Sargent, 29 November 2018.

44 Meeting with Rev. McKnight and two members of his circuit, Sandra and Ken Cardwell, 25 January 2019.

45 Quoted in William King, 'An Endangered Species', *The Tablet*, 9 December 2017.

46 *The Irish Times*, 18 March 2017.

47 Patsy McGarry, 'Priest Numbers "on Edge of Cliff", says Nuncio', *The Irish Times*, 18 March 2017.

48 Ryan, op. cit.

49 Noel Baker, 'Diocese by Diocese: The State of the Catholic Church in Ireland Today', *Irish Examiner*, 3 April 2018.

50 Cathal Barry, 'Church Must Meet Challenge of 70% Drop in Priests in Dublin', *The Irish Catholic*, 21 January 2016.

51 Sarah MacDonald, 'Priest Shortage Will Mean End of Regular Weekend Masses – Bishop', *Irish Independent*, 3 July 2017.

52 Jeremiah Newman, 'Priestly Vocations in Ireland', Paper given to the First International Conference on Priestly Vocations in Europe, Vienna, October 1958.

53 Meeting with John Bruton, 15 May 2017.

54 Association of Catholic Priests, 17 April 2013.

55 Richard Power, *The Hungry Grass*, London: The Bodley Head, 1969.

56 Cited in León Ó Broin, *Frank Duff: A Biography*, Dublin: Gill and Macmillan, 1982, p. 58.

57 Duff to McGrath, 13 March 1948, Legion of Mary Archives.

58 Tom Inglis, *Moral Monopoly: The Catholic Church in Modern Irish Society*, Dublin: Gill and Macmillan, 1987, p. 42.

59 James S. Donnelly, 'A Church in Crisis', *History Ireland*, 8, 3, 2000.

60 Vatican statistics.

61 Claire Simpson, ' "Silks" to Become Men of the Cloth', *The Irish News*, 4 October 2018.

62 Data for 1955 provided by Ian d'Alton; data for 2017 provided by Peter Cheney, Representative Church Body, Church of Ireland.

63 Robert MacCarthy, 'The Future of Ministry in Ireland', *The Irish Catholic*, 20 November 2014.

64 Ibid.

65 *Church of Ireland Census 2013*, presented to General Synod 2015.

66 Quoted in Corish, *The Irish Catholic Experience*, op. cit., p. 7.

67 Corish, *The Irish Catholic Experience*, op. cit., p. 32.

68 Greg Daly, 'Mapping a Church Fit for Mission', *The Irish Catholic*, 20 June 2019.

69 Michael Kelly, 'Merger of Dioceses Already Under Way – Papal Nuncio', *The Irish Catholic*, 12 December 2019.

70 The See where the bishop ranks first among the bishops.

71 Alan Harper, 'Foreword', in Malcolm Macourt, *Counting the People of God. The Census of Population and the Church of Ireland*, Dublin: Church of Ireland Publishing, 2008.

2. Celebration, Commemoration

1 John O'Donohue, *Divine Beauty: The Invisible Embrace*, New York: Bantam, 2003.

2 Speaking with Ray Darcy, RTÉ, 6 October 2018.

3 Kevin Whelan, 'The Catholic Parish, the Catholic Chapel and Village Development in Ireland', *Irish Geography*, 1983.

4 Paul Andrews, SJ, 'Why the Mass Should be Called Mass, not Eucharist or Liturgy', 2007, retrieved from https://www.jesuit.ie/news/371/ [24 March 2022].

5   Kieren Fallon, *Form: My Autobiography*, London: Simon and Schuster, 2017, p. 11.

6   H. Murphy, 'The Rural Family: The Principles', *Christus Rex*, 6, 1952, pp. 3–20.

7   Vincent Ryan, OSB, *The Shaping of Sunday*, Dublin: Veritas, 1997, p. 8.

8   Louise Fuller, *Irish Catholicism since 1950 – The Undoing of a Culture*, Dublin: Gill and Macmillan, 2002, p. 270 and p. 275. The data for 1973–74 are from Research and Development Unit, *A Survey of Religious Practice, Attitudes and Beliefs in the Republic of Ireland, 1973–74*, Dublin: Research and Development Unit, Catholic Communications Institute of Ireland, 1975. The data for 1988–89 are from Micheál Mac Gréil, *Religious Practice and Attitudes in Ireland 1988–1989*, Maynooth: Survey and Research Unit, 1991.

9   A request was made to all twenty-six dioceses; the data were available for six dioceses at the time.

10   *The Irish Catholic*, 13 July 2017.

11   Meeting with Bishop Walsh, 20 March 2017.

12   Ryan, op. cit., p. 61.

13   John Scally, 'The Station Mass', *The Messenger*, October 2017, p. 18.

14   Communication to friends from the late Justice Dermot Kinlen, 2016.

15   John Horgan, 'Babette's Feast Shows us Value and Future of the Eucharist', *The Irish Times*, 13 December 2016.

16   A celebration whereby the congregation is blessed with the Eucharist by the celebrant following a period of prayer. Hymns are sung.

17   Ciarán O'Carroll, 'Pius IX: Pastor and Prince', in James Corkery and Thomas Worcester (Eds), *The Papacy since 1500*, Cambridge: Cambridge University Press, 2010, p. 139.

18   Patrick Corish, *The Irish Catholic Experience*, Dublin: Gill and Macmillan, 1985, p. 234.

19   Ibid., p. 234.

20   Cathal Barry, 'The Death of the Removal', *The Irish Catholic*, 25 February 2016.

21   Meeting with Deputy O'Sullivan, 20 March 2017.

22   Fiona Fitzsimons, 'Catholic Parish Registers', *History Ireland*, 23, 2, March/April 2015, p. 21.

23   Request from the author to each of the dioceses.

24   Frank McFerret, 'A Theologian Has Suggested that *Humanae Vitae* Was the Main Reason that the Catholic Church Has Lost its Dominance in Irish Secular Life', *Irish Medical News*, 24 January 2000.

25   Patsy McGarry, 'Priest says Confession Ended When People No Longer Saw Sex as a Sin', *The Irish Times*, 18 February 2017.

26   Ibid.

27   There are sixteen deaneries, or groups of parishes, in the Dublin Archdiocese. Each deanery is the pastoral responsibility of an auxiliary bishop or episcopal vicar. The Maynooth Deanery includes ten parishes.

28   Fuller, op. cit., p. 226.

29   Patsy McGarry, 'Parents Spend an Average of €845 on First Communion', *The Irish Times*, 26 June 2017.

30   Interview with Regina Doherty, *Sunday Business Post*, 29 October 2017.

31   Jill Kerby, 'Make Saving a Rite of Passage', *Sunday Business Post*, 28 April 2019.

32   Corish, op. cit. p. 107.

33   'First Communion "an Orgy of Materialism" ', *Catholic Herald*, 2 June 2017, p. 8.

34   *Irish Independent*, 27 September 2018.

35   Alan Shatter, *Life is a Funny Business*, Dublin: Poolbeg Press, 2017, p. 53.

36   Eva O'Brien, 'Faith in Irish Schools', *Trinity News*, 1 December 2015.

37 Colm Fitzpatrick, 'Teenagers Leaving Church at a Higher Rate', *The Irish Catholic*, 27 December 2018.

38 Central Statistics Office, *That was Then, This is Now*, Cork: Central Statistics Office, 2000, p. 54.

39 'We're the Marrying Kind', *The Irish Times Magazine*, 9 May 2015.

40 Patricia Wittberg, SC, *Catholic Cultures*, Collegeville, Minnesota: Liturgical Press, 2016, p. 80.

41 Kathy Sheridan, 'Marie Heaney: "I Had a Very Public Grief" ', *The Irish Times*, 10 September 2016.

42 *The Irish Times*, 11 July 2016.

43 'Ireland Sees More Funerals Move Away From Church', *Catholic Universe*, 26 February 2016, p. 5.

44 Archdiocese of Dublin, *Funeral Ministry Policy*, Dublin: Archdiocese of Dublin, 2016, p. 1.

45 Sarah MacDonald, 'Lay People to Perform Funeral Duties', *Irish Independent*, 9 February 2019.

46 Rosita Boland, 'A Day That's Alive with Meaning', *The Irish Times*, 18 August 2008.

47 Ibid.

48 St James is the English for Santiago.

49 John G. O'Dwyer, 'Time to Unlock Tourism Potential of Pilgrim Paths', *The Irish Times*, 6 April 2018.

50 Archdiocese of Dublin, *Consultation on the Presentation of the Preparatory Document of the XV Ordinary General Assembly of the Synod of Bishops*, Dublin: Archdiocese of Dublin, 2017.

51 The phenomenon of 'believing without belonging' implies a degree of faith without commitment to a particular religion. The concept was first proposed by sociologist Grace Davie in 1994. 'Belonging without believing' implies remaining a nominal member of a religion.

52 Suzanne Behan, *The 50 Francis Street Photographer*, Dublin: Hachette Ireland, 2017, p. 149.

53 Church of Ireland, *Church of Ireland Census 2013*, Dublin: Church of Ireland Publishing, 2013.

3. Parish Groups

1 Some of these groups are listed in Appendix 2.

2 Commission for Pastoral Renewal and Adult Faith Development, *Parish Pastoral Councils: A Framework for Developing Diocesan Norms and Parish Guidelines*, Dublin: Veritas, 2007, p. 18.

3 Ibid., p. 22.

4 Meeting with Bishop Walsh, 26 June 2015.

5 *The Irish Catholic*, 11 May 2017, p. 3.

6 Greg Daly, 'Ask not What Your Parish Can Do for You …', *The Irish Catholic*, 9 February 2017.

7 See www.siamsatire.com/about/history

8 'Priest, Scholar, Poet and Linguist who Founded An Díseart', *The Irish Times*, 20 August 2016.

9 Andy O'Mahony, *Creating Space: The Education of a Broadcaster*, Dublin: The Liffey Press, 2016, p. 32.

10 Ibid., p. 33.

11 Ibid., p. 61.

12 Ronan Sheehan and Brendan Walsh, *Dublin: The Heart of the City*, Dublin: Lilliput Press, 2016, p. ix.

13 Patsy McGarry, 'In a Word … Bazaaar', *The Irish Times*, 17 December 2016.

14 Catherine Conroy, 'Passion Project: The Greatest Story Ever Told in Ballyfermot', *The Irish Times*, 8 April 2017.

15 Peter Finnegan, 'A Passion Play for Our Times in Ballyfermot', *The Irish Times*, 4 April 2017.

16 The Men's Sheds movement started in Australia. It invites individuals to come together and engage in activities such as woodwork, gardening and community work. It has been successful in overcoming loneliness and promoting mental health. Men's Sheds in Ireland was the subject of a *Nationwide* programme on RTÉ in March 2020.

17 Michael P. Murphy, *The Frederic Ozanam Story*, Waterford: Society of Saint Vincent de Paul, 1976, p. 6.

18 Gerry Martin, 'The Society of Saint Vincent de Paul: The Early History', in Bill Lawlor and Joe Dalton (Eds), *The Society of St Vincent de Paul in Ireland*, Dublin: New Island, 2014, p. 6.

19 Ibid., p. 8.

20 Ibid., p. 18.

21 *The Rule of the Society of Saint Vincent de Paul*, 1976, p. 5.

22 Ibid., p. 7.

23 Meeting with Rev. Trevor Sargent, 29 November 2018.

24 Kieran Murphy, 'Expressing, Experiencing and Exploring Connections', in Bill Lawlor and Joe Dalton (Eds), *The Society of St Vincent de Paul in Ireland*, Dublin: New Island, 2014, p. 69.

25 Fiona Reddan, 'Charity Shops: Just How Much Do Your Unwanted Goods Get for Those in Need?' *The Irish Times*, 28 February 2017.

26 Bill Lawlor, 'Editor's Introduction', in Bill Lawlor and Joe Dalton (Eds), *The Society of Saint Vincent de Paul in Ireland*, Dublin: New Island, 2014, p. xx.

27 Murphy, 'Expressing, Experiencing and Exploring Connections', op. cit., p. 71.

28 Liam Fitzpatrick, 'Fifty Years a Vincentian: A Personal Journey', in Bill Lawlor and Joe Dalton (Eds), *The Society of Saint Vincent de Paul in Ireland*, Dublin: New Island, 2014, p. 79.

29 Murphy, 'Expressing, Experiencing and Exploring Connections', op. cit., p. 73.

30 Interview with Elizabeth Watson, 9 November 2018.

31 Dermot McCarthy, 'Community Commitment in Heart of Dublin', *The Irish Times*, 10 December 2019.

32 Legion of Mary, *Handbook*, 2005, pp. 11–12.

33 Mags Gargan, 'One Third of New Priests Inspired by Legion of Mary', *The Irish Catholic*, 17 August 2017.

34 Duff to Firtel, 20 February 1961.

35 Author's interview with Bill Caulfield, 11 March 2009.

36 *Irish Independent*, 7 February 1959.

37 Duff to Duffy, 26 June 1954, Legion of Mary Archives (LOMA).

38 Frank Duff, 'The Faith, the Nation', Talk to An Réalt, 1971 (Tape 91, LOMA).

39 Pioneer Archive, University College Dublin, *The Context*, p. 1.

40 Conversation with Fr Mac Gréil, 15 February 2016.

41 Elizabeth Malcolm, *'Ireland Sober, Ireland Free'. Drink and Temperance in Nineteenth-Century Ireland*, Dublin: Gill and Macmillan, 1986, p. 185.

42 Quoted in Diarmaid Ferriter, *A Nation of Extremes*, Dublin: Irish Academic Press, 1999, p. 232.

43 Ibid., p. 180.

44 Ibid., p. 180.

45 Ibid., p. 217.

46 Ibid., p. 394

47 Ibid., p. 216.

48 Ibid., pp. 190–1.

49 Gerard Gallagher, *Are We Losing the Young Church? Youth Ministry in Ireland*, Dublin: Columba Press, 2005, p. 127.

50 Ibid., p. 139.

51 Gerry Adams, *Before the Dawn*, Dublin: Brandon, 2017, p. 181.

52 Ibid., p. 257.

53 Gallagher, op. cit., p. 135.

54 The course has been successfully used in Richhill in Co. Armagh according to the minister there, Rev. Nick McKnight. Meeting with Rev McKnight, 25 January 2019.

55 Martin Maguire, ' "Our People": The Church of Ireland in Dublin and the Culture of Community since Disestablishment', in W. G. Neely and R. Gillespie (Eds), *"All Sorts and Conditions": The Laity and the Church of Ireland, 1000–2000*, Dublin: Four Courts Press, 2002.

4. Branching Out

1 Feichín McDonagh, 'What Constitutes a Catholic School in 2019? A Legal Perspective', *Studies*, Spring 2019, pp. 8–19.

2 The village was named 'Auburn', also known as Lissoy, Co. Westmeath.

3 Tom Inglis, *Global Ireland: Same Difference*, London: Routledge, 2008, p. 208.

4 INTO Education Committee, *The Place of Religious Education in the National School System*, Dublin: Irish National Teachers' Organisation, 1991, p. 7.

5 The Presentation Sisters, founded in Cork by Nano Nagle; the Ursuline Sisters, developed by Elizabeth Coppinger; the Mercy Sisters, founded by Catherine McAuley; and the Loreto Sisters, founded by Frances Ball, were mainly engaged in education of young boys and girls and of older girls. The Christian Brothers were concerned with the education of boys.

6 E. G. Stanley, Letter from Chief Secretary of Ireland to His Grace, the Duke of Leinster, on the Formation of a Board of Commissioners for Education in Ireland, October 1831. The full text of the letter is published in Richard Aldous and Niamh Purseil, *We Declare – Landmark Documents in Ireland's History*, London: Quercus Publishing, 2008.

7 Séamas Ó Buachalla, *Education Policy in Twentieth Century Ireland*, Dublin: Wolfhound Press, 1988, p. 20.

8 Donald H. Akenson, *The Irish Education Experiment*, Oxford: Routledge and Kegan Paul, 1970, p. 157. A number of synonyms were used at the time for 'undenominational', including 'general', 'united', 'combined' and 'mixed'.

9 INTO Education Committee, op. cit., p.7.

10 INTO Education Committee, op. cit., p. 8.

11 INTO Education Committee, op. cit., p. 8.

12 Martin Maguire, ' "Our People": The Church of Ireland in Dublin and the Culture of Community since Disestablishment', in W. G. Neely and R. Gillespie (Eds), *"All Sorts and Conditions": The Laity and the Church of Ireland, 1000–2000*, Dublin: Four Courts Press, 2002.

13 The patron is a representative of the owners and can be an individual or a group.

14 Catholic Primary Schools' Management Association, *Board of Management Handbook 2016*, Maynooth: Catholic Primary Schools' Management Association, 2016, p. 15.

15 Department of Education and Skills, *Governance Manual of Primary Schools 2015–2019*, Dublin: Department of Education and Skills, 2015.

16 Interview with Peter Mooney, 26 April 2015.

17 Maurice Garvey, 'Ballyfermot Parents Fearful over Future of Local Schools', *Echo.ie*, 9 June 2016.

18 Greg Daly, 'Dozens of Catholic Schools at "Breaking Point" Due to State Cuts', *The Irish Catholic*, 24 May 2018.

19 Ibid.

20 Neil C. Fleming, 'Lord Londonderry and Education Reform in 1920s Northern Ireland', *History Ireland*, 9, 1, Spring 2001.

21 Quoted in Mike Cronin, Mark Duncan and Paul Rouse, *The GAA: A People's History*, Cork: Collins Press, 2009, p. 209.

22 Ibid., p. 40.

23 'A Step into the Unknown', *Meath Chronicle*, 3 January 2018.

24 D. Vincent Twomey, *The End of Irish Catholicism*, Dublin: Veritas, 2003, pp. 8–34. The trophy referred to is the Sam Maguire Cup, named after the west Cork Republican, GAA player, Church of Ireland member and London resident Sam Maguire.

25 Cronin, Duncan and Rouse, op. cit., p. 243.

26 Sean Cavanagh on *Today with Sean O'Rourke*, 13 September 2018.

27 Obituary, *The Irish Times*, 25 April 2015.

28 Obituary, *The Irish Times*, 2 February 2016.

29 'The Priests Were on the Ball', *Galway Advertiser*, 12 November 2009.

30 John Scally, 'The Sunday Games', *The Messenger*, August 2017.

31 Ida Milne, ' "The Jersey is All that Matters, not Your Church": Protestants and the GAA in the Rural Republic', in Ian d'Alton and Ida Milne (Eds), *Protestant and Irish*, Cork: Cork University Press, 2019, p. 180.

32 Ibid. p. 180.

33 Paul Rouse, 'GAA Can No Longer Cling Blindly to the Rules', *Irish Examiner*, 27 July 2018.

34 20 July 2018.

35 Diarmaid Ferriter, *A Nation of Extremes*, Dublin: Irish Academic Press, 1999, p. 5.

36 Ibid., p. 115.

37 Ibid., pp. 197–8.

38 Patsy McGarry, *The Irish Times*, 30 August 2000.

39 Micheál Mac Gréil, *The Ongoing Present*, Dublin: Messenger Publications, 2014, pp. 290–1.

40 Joe Brolly interview with Barry J. Whyte, *Sunday Business Post*, 23 July 2017.

41 Keith Duggan, 'Discredited Banks No Longer Share the Ethos or Values of the GAA', *The Irish Times*, 21 October 2017.

42 *Sunday Independent*, 28 August 2011.

43 Conversation with John Costello, 15 November 2017.

44 Peter McGuire, 'Strength in Diversity', *The Irish Times Magazine*, 25 August 2018.

45 Cathal Barry, 'Faith and Sport the "Matrix" for Strong Parishes', *The Irish Catholic*, 25 February 2016.

46 John Harrington, 'GAA Plans to Tackle Rural–Urban Demographic Shift', 26 April 2019, retrieved from www.gaa.ie [24 March 2022].

47 Patrick Corish, *The Irish Catholic Experience*, Dublin: Gill and Macmillan, 1985, p. 248.

48 Mark Tierney, *The Story of Muintir na Tíre 1931–2001 – The First Seventy Years*, Tipperary: Muintir na Tíre, 2004, p. 31.

49 Ibid., p. 26.

50 Ibid., p. 39.

51 M. Morrissey, 'Canon Hayes – Pioneer of the Community Idea in Ireland', *Rural Ireland*, 1959, p. 18.

52 Ibid. p. 18.

53 *Muintir na Tíre Handbook*, 1943, p. 19.

54 Tierney, op. cit., p. 67.

55 G. Maher, *Muintir na Tíre*, p. 13, quoted in Tierney, op. cit., p. 67.

56 Tierney, op. cit., p. 50.

57 From 1904 a French Catholic Forum movement had begun holding 'Semaines Rurales' or Rural Weeks.

58 The oldest penny dinners in Ireland were started in Cork in the 1840s.

59 Muintir na Tíre, *Rural Ireland*, Tipperary: Muintir na Tíre Rural Publications, 1959, p. 91.

60 Ibid., p. 96.

61 Kevin Whelan (1983) has drawn attention to the ESB collection of parish maps deposited in Maynooth College Library.

62 Maurice Manning and Moore McDowell, *The History of the ESB*, Dublin: Gill and Macmillan, 1984, p. 129.

63 Tierney, op. cit., p. 82.

64 Michael Shiel, *The Quiet Revolution: The Electrification of Rural Ireland*, Dublin: O'Brien Press, 2003, p. 183, quoted in Tierney, op. cit., p. 86.

65 *Dáil Debates*, 9 July 1948.

66 Tierney, op. cit., p. 98.

67 Quoted in Tierney, op. cit., p. 107. *The Programme for Economic Expansion*, known as the *First Programme*, was largely based on *Economic Development*, produced by T. K. Whitaker and civil servants in the Department of Finance.

68 *Economic Development*, p. 116.

69 United Nations Bureau of Social Affairs, *Social Progress through Community Development*, New York: United Nations Bureau of Social Affairs, 1955.

70 Tierney, op. cit., pp. 136–7.

71 Tierney, op. cit., p. 176.

72 Warner Moss, *Political Parties in the Irish Free State*, New York: Columbia University Press, 1933, p. 99.

73 Basil Chubb, *The Government and Politics of Ireland*, Oxford: Oxford University Press, 1970, p. 89.

74 Meeting with John Horgan, 23 June 2016.

75 See www.finegael.ie

76 Harry McGee, live blog, 2 June 2017.

77 Archives of the Fianna Fáil Party, p. 176, UCD Archives.

78 Conor Lenihan, *Haughey: Prince of Power*, Dublin: Blackwater Press, 2015, p. 42.

79 William Murphy, 'The Spring Tide of Irish Nationalism', *Sunday Business Post*, 5 April 2018.

80 Diarmaid Ferriter, *The Border: The Legacy of a Century of Anglo–Irish Politics*, London: Profile Books, 2019, p. 47.

81 Bryce Evans, *Seán Lemass: Democratic Dictator*, Cork: Collins Press, 2011, pp. 186–7. In the 1957 general election Loughman regained the seat which he had lost in 1948.

82 Ibid., p. 203.

83 Meeting with Councillor Ní Dhálaigh, 9 October 2018.

84 R. K. Carty, *Party and Parish Pump: Electoral Politics in Ireland*, Ontario: Wilfred Laurier University Press, 1981, p. 146.

85 Ibid., p. 142.

86 Ibid., p. 143.

87 Ibid., p. 59.

5. Local Government

1 J. J. Lee, *Ireland 1912–1985*, Cambridge: Cambridge University Press, 1989, p. 547.

2 Diarmaid Ferriter, 'Why Irish Local Government is Absolutely Useless', *The Irish Times*, 23 November 2019.

3 Michael McDowell, 'Daft Rafting Plan Shows Absence of Local Democracy', *The Irish Times*, 4 December 2019.

4 Meeting with Owen Keegan, 24 September 2021.

5 Communication from Owen Keegan, 26 October 2021.

6 Mark Callanan, *Local Government in the Republic of Ireland*, Dublin: Institute of Public Administration, 2018, p. 340.

7 Ibid., p. 341.

8 Desmond Roche, *Local Government in Ireland*, Dublin: Institute of Public Administration, 1982, p. 39.

9 Quoted in Joyce Padbury, *Mary Hayden: Irish Historian and Feminist 1862–1942*, Dublin: Arlen House, 2021, p. 110.

10 James Meenan, *The Irish Economy since 1922*, Liverpool: Liverpool University Press, 1970, pp. 14–15.

11 Tony Fahey, 'The Catholic Church and Social Policy', *The Furrow*, April 1998.

12 European Community Development Network, 2017.

13 Department of the Environment, Community and Local Government, *Putting People First: Action Programme for Effective Local Government*, Dublin: Department of the Environment, Community and Local Government, 2012, p. iv.

14 Callanan, op. cit., p. 291.

15 Callanan, op. cit., p. 291.

16 Marius Guderjan, 'Local Government in the European Union's Multilevel Polity', in Richard Kerley, Joyce Liddle and Pamela T. Dunning (Eds), *Routledge Handbook of International Local Government*, London: Routledge, 2020, p. 401.

17 Brendan Hensey, *The Health Services of Ireland*, Dublin: Institute of Public Administration, 1959.

18 Lee, op. cit., pp. 395–6.

19 Sláintecare is a plan for the health services based on the recommendations of a cross-party group.

20 Paul Cullen, 'Sláintecare Cracks Covered Over by Covid Starting to Resurface', *The Irish Times*, 14 September 2021.

21 Department of Education and Skills, Press Release, 'Education and Training Boards Replace VECs', 1 July 2013.

22 Callanan, op. cit., p. 124.

23 Meeting with Owen Keegan, 24 September 20211

24 Iseult O'Malley, Fiona O'Toole and Aideen Hayden, *A Study of the £5,000 Surrender Grant in the Dublin Housing Area*, Dublin: Threshold, 1987.

25 Fine Gael, *Towards a Just Society*, Dublin: Fine Gael, 1965, p. 19.

26 OECD, quoted in Callanan, op. cit., p. 328.

27 *National Income and Expenditure* and *Returns of Local Taxation*.

28 Mary Murphy, *Democracy Works If You Let It*, Maynooth: Maynooth University, 2019.

29 *Parliamentary Debates Dáil Eireann*, 1 November 1978.

30 Address to Joint Committee on Housing, Planning and Local Government, 28 March 2018, in relation to Local Government (Restoration of Town Councils) Bill 2018; Aodh Quinlivan, 'If Local Government is Not Local, It is Nothing', *Irish Examiner*, 1 April 2019.

31 Quinlivan, ibid.

32 The insertion of Article 28A into the Constitution, following a referendum in June 1999, granted constitutional 'recognition' of the role of local government.

33 Arlene Crampsie, 'A Forgotten Tier of Local Government – The Impact of Rural District Councils on the Landscape of Early Twentieth Century Ireland', *Irish Geography*, 47, 2, 2014, pp. 23–48.

34 Sebstian Payne, 'Gove Hints at More Mayors to Help "Level Up"', *Financial Times*, 5 October 2021.

35 Richard Boyle, Joanna O'Riordan, Laura Shannon and Fergal O'Leary, *Municipal Districts: A Review*, Dublin: Institute of Public Administration, 2020, p. 18.

36 Murphy, op. cit.

37 Richard Boyle, *Re-Shaping Local Government: Overview of Selected International Experience with Local Government Reorganisation, Mergers, Amalgamation and Coordination*, Dublin: Institute of Public Administration, 2016.

38 Mark Callanan, R. Murphy and A. Quinlivan, 'The Risks of Intuition: Size, Costs and Economies of Scale in Local Government', *The Economic and Social Review*, 45, 3, 2014, pp. 371–403.

39 S. W. Hansen, 'The Democratic Costs of Size: How Increasing Size Affects Citizen Satisfaction with Local Government', *Political Studies*, 63, 2, 2015, pp. 373–89.

40 Richard Kerley, Joyce Liddle and Pamela T. Dunning (Eds), *Routledge Handbook of International Local Government*, London: Routledge, 2020.

41 Communication from Ger Turley, 28 September 2021.

42 Department of the Environment, Community and Local Government, op. cit.

43 Phil Hogan, TD, 'Foreword', in Department of the Environment, Community and Local Government, op. cit.

44 Richard Boyle, Joanna O'Riordan, Laura Shannon and Fergal O'Leary, op. cit., p. 5.

45 Meeting with Richard Boyle, 20 September 2021.

46 Gerard Turley and Stephen McNena, 'An Analysis of Local Public Finances and the 2014 Local Government Reforms', *The Economic and Social Review*, 47, 2, 2016, p. 317.

6. Community, Local Amenities, Local Authorities

1 United Nations Bureau of Social Affairs, *Social Progress through Community Development*, New York: United Nations Bureau of Social Affairs, 1955, p. 6.

2 Tony O'Grady, Summary page of presentation at meeting convened by the Green Party in Dublin 6, December 2017.

3   Brian Harvey, 'Local and Community Development in Ireland – An Overview', Conference, UCC, 21 October 2015.

4   Ibid., p. 7.

5   Ibid., pp. 7–8.

6   Ibid., p. 9.

7   Michael McDowell, *The Irish Times*, 27 February 2012.

8   See Fianna Fáil election manifesto, 2002.

9   Proinnsias Breathnach, Eoin O'Mahony and Chris van Egeraat, 'The Changing Map of Subnational Governance in Ireland', *Administration*, 69, 1, 2021, pp. 132–3.

10   J. J. Lee, *Ireland 1912–1985*, Cambridge: Cambridge University Press, 1989, p. 353. *The Third Progamme* was scheduled to cover the period 1969–72.

11   Raghuram Rajan, *The Third Pillar*, London: William Collins, 2019.

12   Susan Gately, 'Rural Ireland is Dying: Priests', *The Irish Catholic*, 8 February 2018.

13   Breathnach, O'Mahony and van Egeraat, op. cit., p. 137.

14   Richard Boyle, Joanna O'Riordan, Laura Shannon and Fergal O'Leary, *Municipal Districts: A Review*, Dublin: Institute of Public Administration, 2020, p. 19.

15   Founded by the Society of St Vincent de Paul in Ireland in 2002 and in Northern Ireland in 2005.

16   Meeting with Frank Allen, 20 June 2017.

17   Rachel Flaherty, 'You're not Going to Let Rural Ireland Die', *The Irish Times*, 9 January 2016.

18   Stephen Ferguson, *The Post Office in Ireland: An Illustrated History*, Dublin: Irish Academic Press, 2016.

19   Marese McDonagh, 'Ballinafad Losing Much More than a Post Office', *The Irish Times*, 29 December 2018.

20   Ibid.

21   Brian O'Connell, 'An Amateur Anthropologist', *The Irish Times*, 10 December 2016.

22   Mags Gargan and Greg Daly, 'Priests Warn of Death of Rural Ireland', *The Irish Catholic*, 9 March 2017.

23   Ibid.

24   Ibid.

25   Mike Cronin, Mark Duncan and Paul Rouse, *The GAA: A People's History*, Cork: Collins Press, 2009, p. 231.

26   Fr Eamonn Fitzgibbon speaking on 'Morning Ireland', 29 March 2017.

27   Greg Daly, 'New Bishop Pledges to Work to Boost Life in Rural Ireland', *The Irish Catholic*, 29 September 2016.

28   *The Irish Catholic*, 29 September 2016.

29   Lorna Siggins, 'Village Writes Its Own Positive Obituary', *The Irish Times*, 24 August 2017.

30   Meeting with Éamon Ó Cuív, 6 October 2016.

31   Cliff Taylor, 'Broadband not Railway Lines the Key to Rural Survival and Development', *The Irish Times*, 19 and 20 November 2016.

32   Mark Callanan, *Local Government in the Republic of Ireland*, Dublin: Institute of Public Administration, 2018, p. 149.

33   Society of Chartered Surveyors in Ireland, *Rejuvenating Ireland's Small Town Centres*, Dublin: Society of Chartered Surveyors in Ireland, 2018, p. 13.

34   Ibid., p. 23.

35   Elena Curti, 'Open the Doors', *The Tablet*, 8 December 2018, pp. 8–9.

7. Parish as Social Capital

1 Patrick Kavanagh, 'The Parish and the Universe', *Kavanagh's Weekly*, 7, 1952.

2 Sylvia Thompson, 'Behind the News. Save Rural Ireland Campaigner Bernard Kearney', *The Irish Times*, 14 March 2015.

3 Maggie Armstrong, Interview with Denise Gough, *Irish Independent Weekend Magazine*, 7 May 2016, p. 13.

4 Kevin Cardiff, *Recap: Inside Ireland's Financial Crisis*, Dublin: The Liffey Press, 2016, p. 33.

5 Ronan Sheehan and Brendan Walsh, *Dublin: The Heart of the City*, Dublin: Lilliput Press, 2016, p. 27.

6 Elizabeth Watson, *St. Andrew's Church, Westland Row: An Enduring Presence*, 2007.

7 Jesse Norman, *Edmund Burke: Philosopher, Politician, Prophet*, London: William Collins, 2013, p. 2.

8 Robert Putnam, *Bowling Alone: The Collapse and Revival of American Community*, London: Simon and Schuster, 2000.

9 Ibid., p. 19.

10 Putnam says that Yogi Berra offered the most vivid definition of reciprocity: 'If you don't go to somebody's funeral, they won't come to yours.'

11 Putnam, op. cit., p. 66.

12 Putnam, op. cit., p. 66.

13 Dermot Keogh, *Jews in Twentieth Century Ireland*, Cork: Cork University Press, 1998, p. 6.

14 Brian Hutton, *The Irish Times*, 24 May 2019.

15 Deacon Dermot McCarthy, 13 September 2016.

16 Watson, op. cit., p. 19.

17 Watson, op. cit., p. 19.

18 Micheál Ó Dubhshláine, *Are You Going Home Now? Memories of Old Kilkea*, Tralee: Tig Áine, 2006, p. 72.

19 Rathgar Parish Church website.

20 Richard Ebejer, SDB, 'Papal Trip to Ireland Should Include Matt Talbot Shrine', *The Irish Catholic*, 15 October 2015.

21 Meeting with Rev. Trevor Sargent, 29 November 2018.

22 Michael O'Sullivan, SJ, 'Twenty Three Years Of Jesuits in Ballymun', speaking at Mass held in the Virgin Mary Church, Shangan Road, Ballymun, 6 July 2003.

23 Ibid.

24 David Raleigh, 'West Cork Priest Caught Up in Attack on South Sudan Compound', *The Irish Times*, 7 August 2018.

25 Mags Gargan, 'Hands Across the Nation', *The Irish Catholic*, 28 May 2015.

26 David Raleigh, 'Fr Tony O'Riordan Gets Ready to Say Goodbye to Moyross', *The Irish Times*, 4 January 2017.

27 Patricia Kelleher and Mary Whelan, *Dublin Communities in Action: A Study of Six Projects*, Dublin: Combat Poverty Agency, 1992.

28 Ibid., p. 126

29 Bruce Biever, SJ, *Religion, Culture and Values: A Cross-Cultural Analysis of Motivational Factors in Native Irish and Native American–Irish Catholicism*, New York: Arno Press, 1976, p. 266.

30 'From the Archives, September 28th, 1938', *The Irish Times*, 28 September 2011.

31 Ibid.

32 Ibid.
33 Diarmaid Ferriter, *On the Edge – Ireland's Off-Shore Islands: A Modern History*, London: Profile Books, 2018, pp. 147, 180–3.
34 Ibid., p. 183.
35 Ibid., p. 169
36 Ibid., p. 184.
37 Tom Garvin, 'The Quiet Tragedy of Canon Sheehan', *Studies*, 98, 390, 2009, p. 160.
38 Patrick Corish, *The Irish Catholic Experience*, Dublin: Gill and Macmillan, 1985, p. 235.
39 Ibid. p. 236.
40 Putnam, op. cit., p. 66.
41 Meeting with Mr Ahern, 8 December 2016.
42 Ibid.
43 Garry Doyle, 'Streets of Dreams', *Sunday Business Post Magazine*, 3 November 2019, p. 14.
44 Meeting with Deputy O'Sullivan, 20 March 2017. In the biography *Tony Gregory* (Dublin: O'Brien Press, 2011, p. 15) author Robbie Gilligan says that Tony and his brother Noel attended legion meetings in the Legion House in North Great George's Street.
45 Taskforce on Active Citizenship, *Report of Taskforce on Active Citizenship*, Dublin: Taskforce on Active Citizenship, 2007. It appears that no comparable survey has been carried out since 2006. A query to the Economic and Social Research Institute confirmed that they did not know of a more recent comparable study.
46 Ibid., p. 2.
47 Tom Inglis, 'Church and Culture in Catholic Ireland', *Studies*, 106, 421, 2017, p. 29.
48 Taskforce on Active Citizenship, op. cit., p. 9.
49 Eoin O'Mahony and Martina Prunty, *Active Citizenship in Faith-based Communities*, Dublin: Irish Catholic Bishops' Conference, Council for Research and Development, 2007, p. 5.
50 Colm Fitzpatrick, 'Mass Can Fight Against Loneliness, says *Mrs Brown's Boys* Star', *The Irish Catholic*, 1 November 2018.
51 Paula Clancy, Ian Hughes and Teresa Brannick, *Public Perspectives on Democracy in Ireland*, Dublin: TASC, 2005.
52 Quoted in Tanya Sweeney, 'Living Alone is Less the Exception, More the Rule', *The Irish Times, Life and Style*, 7 September 2015.
53 Ibid.
54 Noel Whelan, 'Loneliness and Isolation not Only for Christmas', *The Irish Times*, 22 December 2017.
55 Loneliness Taskforce, *A Connected Island – An Ireland Free from Loneliness*, Dublin: Loneliness Taskforce, 2018.
56 Patsy McGarry, 'Religious Attendance Good for You, TCD Study Finds', *The Irish Times*, 2 August 2019.

8. Renewal

1 Charles Moore, 'The Spectator's Notes', *The Spectator*, 28 August 2021, p. 11. Moore was also editor of the *Sunday Telegraph* and the *Daily Telegraph*.
2 Mark Phelan, 'Body of Work the Legacy of a True Genius', *Belfast Telegraph*, 2 October 2015.
3 John Joe Conwell, *Portumna: A Galway Parish by the Shannon*, self-published, 2017.

4   Joe Molloy (Ed.), *The Parish of Clontuskert: Glimpses into its Past*, Galway: Clontuskert Heritage Group, 2009.

5   Chai Brady, 'Bishop Warns Married Priests are not the Answer to "Crisis of Faith"', *The Irish Catholic*, 14 November 2019.

6   James Martin, SJ, 'Understanding Discernment is Key to Understanding "Amoris Laetitia"', *America*, 7 April 2016.

7   Antonio Spadaro, SJ, 'A Big Heart Open to God: An Interview with Pope Francis', *America*, 30 September 2013.

8   Antonio Spadaro interviews Pope Francis, 19, 23 and 29 August 2013.

9   Ibid.

10 Pope John Paul II, *Crossing the Threshold Of Hope*, London: Jonathan Cape, 1994, p. 191.

11 For census purposes, a family is defined as a couple, with or without children, or a one-parent family with one or more children. The census definition of a child in this context depends not on age but on the relationship between individuals. A mother who lives with an adult daughter and no one else constitutes a family. If a mother lives with her adult daughter and the daughter's child, then there are two entities – the mother, and the daughter and her child. In this case the second entity is the family.

12 Eugene Duffy, 'Clustering Parishes: Reflections on the Practice and Theology', in Eugene Duffy (Ed.), *Parishes in Transition*, Dublin: Columba Press, 2010, p. 93.

13 Jeremiah Newman, 'The Priests of Ireland: A Socio-Religious Survey', *Irish Ecclesiastical Record*, 98, 3, 1962, p. 23.

14 Michael McDowell, 'It is Vital for Harris's Garda Reforms to Proceed Now', *The Irish Times*, 2 September 2019.

15 Michael Kelly, 'The Church and the Death of Rural Ireland', *The Irish Catholic*, 9 March 2017.

16 Orla Ryan, 'The Closure of our Post Office Would Mean the Death of our Village', *thejournal.ie*, 7 February 2018.

17 Originally intended to ease overcrowding.

18 Capacity of 2,000 comes from data supplied by the Archdiocese of Dublin. Reports in the media at time of closure stated capacity varying from 3,000 to 3,500.

19 Patsy McGarry, 'Time Catches up with McQuaid's Monumental Church', *The Irish Times*, 3 February 2017.

20 Cormac McQuinn, 'Church Asked to Identify Property that Could be Used for Housing', *The Irish Times*, 30 August 2021.

21 Greg Daly, 'Irish Church Urged to Close Parishes to Grow the Faith', *The Irish Catholic*, 19 April 2018.

22 Greg Daly, 'Parishes Asked to Put Mission Ahead of Renovating Half-Empty Churches', *The Irish Catholic*, 1 March 2018.

23 *Catholic New York* (Catholic newspaper of the Diocese of New York), 8 May 2015.

24 Rev. Matthew Nunes, 'The Experience of Widnes as a Witness to Team Ministry', Pastoral Conference, *The Future of the Irish Parish*, Thurles, 28 August 2018.

25 Eamonn Fitzgibbon, 'Diocesan Priesthood in the Twenty-first Century', in Eugene Duffy (Ed.), *Parishes in Transition*, Dublin: Columba Press, pp. 161, 172.

26 Pope Francis, General Audience, St Peter's Square, 27 March 2013.

27 'Making Parishes Work', *Catholic Herald*, 12 August 2016, p. 3.

28 Editorial, *Catholic Herald*, 16 December 2016.

29 Homily in Casa Santa Marta, 13 December 2016.

30 Address at Opening of World Youth Day, Rio de Janeiro, 2013.

31   William E. Simon Jr, *Great Catholic Parishes*, Notre Dame, Indiana: Ave Maria Press, 2016, p. 162.

32   For example, Barna Global, *Finding Faith in Ireland*, Ventura, California: Barna Global, 2017.

33   Archdiocese of Dublin, *Consultation on the Presentation of the Preparatory Document of the XV Ordinary General Assembly of the Synod of Bishops*, Dublin: Archdiocese of Dublin, p. 1. Data were collected on the basis of an internet questionnaire directed at 16–19-year-olds as well as some interviews.

34   Speaking Notes, Rev. Dr Diarmuid Martin, 8 February 2018.

35   Donal Harrington, *Tomorrow's Parish: A Vision and a Path*, Dublin: Columba Press, 2015, p. 122.

36   Ibid., p. 7.

37   This may refer to part-time work on a neighbouring farm, as Kavanagh became apprenticed to his father as a shoemaker on leaving school.

38   Patrick Kavanagh, *The Green Fool*, London: Michael Joseph, 1938.

39   Mags Gargan, *The Irish Catholic*, 30 June 2016, p. 14.

40   Ibid., p. 20.

41   Pat Leahy, 'Inspired Efforts Bring Hope Amid Inner-City Neglect', *The Irish Times*, 14 December 2019.

42   Peter Murtagh, 'Inner City Community Calls for an End to Violence', *The Irish Times*, 18 May 2016.

43   Meeting with Deputy O'Sullivan, 20 March 2017.

44   Patrick Freyne, 'The Faces on those Walls Aren't Just Addicts. They're People's Kids', *The Irish Times*, 4 February 2017.

45   *Church of Ireland Diocesan News*, 10 October 2018.

46   The Books Editor (Peter Costello), *The Irish Catholic*, 2 August 2018.

47   Communication from Peter Costello, 29 May 2019.

48   Meeting with Deputy Maureen O'Sullivan, 20 March 2017.

49   Kathryn Hayes, 'Polish Catholics Bring New Life to Limerick Parish', *The Irish Times*, 16 May 2016.

50   Ibid.

51   Ibid.

52   Ibid.

53   Anne Lucey, 'Deeper Ties Make Poles Feel at Home in Kerry', *The Irish Times*, 20 May 2016.

54   Greg Daly, 'Reduce Ethnic Masses to Stop Ghettoisation – Psychiatrist', *The Irish Catholic*, 28 July 2016.

55   Ibid.

56   *The Irish Catholic*, 25 August 2016.

57   Meeting, 6 October 2016.

58   Chai Brady, 'Religious Tradition in Ireland Inspires New Arrivals to the Faith', *The Irish Catholic*, 29 March 2018.

59   All-Ireland Churches Consultative Meeting on Racism, *Directory of Migrant-Led Churches and Chaplaincies*, Belfast: All-Ireland Churches Consultative Meeting on Racism, 2009, p. 2.

60   Simon, op. cit., p. 9.

61   Patricia Wittberg, SC, *Catholic Cultures*, Collegeville, Minnesota: Liturgical Press, 2016, p. 22.

62   Ibid., p. 23.

63 Ibid., p. 44.

64 Greg Daly, 'Ireland Must be "Land Of Welcomes" for New Foreign Clergy – Bishop', *The Irish Catholic*, 17 October 2019.

65 Mags Gargan and Chai Brady, 'African Priests Take Up Call to Revitalise Irish Church', *The Irish Catholic*, 25 May 2017.

66 See catholic-hierarchy.org

67 Gargan and Brady, op. cit.

68 T. J. Barrington, *The Irish Administrative System*, Dublin: Institute of Public Administration, 1980.

69 John Tierney, 'Is Our Public Service Ready for the Future? A Local Government Response', in Mark Callanan (Ed.), *Ireland 2022: Towards One Hundred Years of Self-Government*, Dublin: Institute of Public Administration, 2007, pp. 241–2.

70 Ibid., p. 250.

71 George Jones and John Stewart, 'What We Are Against and What We Are For', in George Jones (Ed.), *The New Local Government Agenda*, Hertfordshire: ICSA Publishing, 1997, pp. 26–7.

72 Mark Callanan, 'Reforming Local Government: Past, Present and Future', *Administration*, 68, 4, 2020, pp. 201–14.

73 Ibid, p. 204.

74 Meeting with Bishop Walsh, 20 March 2017.

75 Meeting with Finola Bruton, 3 August 2017.

76 Community Foundation for Ireland, *VitalSigns Belonging*, Dublin: Community Foundation for Ireland, 2017.

77 Meeting with Eamon Gilmore, 13 July 2017.

78 Same meeting with Eamon Gilmore, 13 July 2017.

79 Meeting with Éamon Ó Cuív, 6 October 2016.

80 Meeting with Críona Ní Dhálaigh, 9 October 2018.

81 Archdiocese of Dublin, *Share Newsletter*, 15 April 2018.

Conclusion

1 Meeting with Richard Boyle, 20 September 2021.

2 Mark Callanan, 'Reforming Local Government: Past, Present and Future', *Administration*, 68, 4, 2020, pp. 201–14.

3 Michelle Norris, *Financing the Golden Age of Irish Social Housing 1932–1956*, Dublin: UCD Geary Institute, 2018, p. 2.

4 Non-voted expenditures include debt service and payments from the Central Fund to meet the costs of the Houses of the Oireachtas and the salaries of judges.

5 GNI* is used here because it comprises the total income remaining in Ireland. In an open economy like Ireland multinational companies may route income through Ireland because of a favourable tax regime, even though the income was generated in a part of the company not located, or giving employment, in Ireland.

6 Meeting with Mr Ahern, 8 December 2016; meeting with Mr Bruton, 15 May 2017.

7 Frank Duff, *True Devotion to the Nation*, Dundalk: Dundalgan Press, 1966.

8 Described in Chapter 5.

9 Dermot McCarthy, 'Community Commitment in Heart of Dublin', *The Irish Times*, 10 December 2019.

10 Ibid.

11   Jon Anderson, 'Post-Crash Ireland Desperately Needs the Faith', *Catholic Herald*, 8 May 2015, p. 17.

12   Note from Bishop Eamonn Walsh, 21 March 2018.

13   Sean Muldoon, Méabh Corrigan and Orla Garvey, 'Our Parishes Will Attract Young People Again if …', *The Irish Catholic*, 7 April 2016, p. 30.

14   Fr Paddy Byrne, *All Will be Well: Digital Dispatches from the Parish*, Dublin: Columba Press, 2017, p. 11.

15   Justin Welby, *Reimagining Britain: Foundations for Hope*, London: Bloomsbury Continuum, 2018, p. 141.

16   Rosita Boland, 'The Shop that Could Change Ireland', *The Irish Times*, 23 December 2017.

17   Ibid.

18   Padraig O'Morain, 'Social Connections Can Reduce Rural Suicide', *The Irish Times*, 12 September 2017.

19   Cormac O'Keeffe, 'Big Plans for Policing, but Getting Them Done is the Biggest Challenge', *Irish Examiner*, 19 September 2018.

20   Patsy McGarry, 'Protestants and Catholics Sharing Church in Co. Monaghan', *The Irish Times*, 19 June 2017.

21   Communication with Dr Mansergh, 17 September 2019.

22   Meeting with Mr Ahern, 8 December 2016.

23   Notre Dame – Newman Centre for Faith and Reason, *Centre Leaflet,* February 2019.

24   Christopher Altieri, 'When Churches Convert', *Catholic Herald*, 20 July 2018.

25   Elaine Loughlin, 'Church Asked to Hand Over Property to House Elderly', *Irish Examiner*, 29 December 2018.

26   Archdiocese of Dublin, *Consultation on the Presentation of the Preparatory Document of the XV Ordinary General Assembly of the Synod of Bishops*, Dublin: Archdiocese of Dublin, 2017.

27   Chai Brady, 'Call for Parishes to Dump "Distracting" Mass Leaflets', *The Irish Catholic*, 5 September 2019.

28   Jonny Hanson, 'Parishes are Uniquely Placed to Take Eco Action', *The Irish Catholic*, 25 May 2017.

29   Fionnuala Fallon, 'Flanagan's Fields: An Inner City Garden with Heart and History', *The Irish Times*, 29 November 2014; Rose Costello, 'Growing a Community Garden Out of the Rubble', *The Sunday Times*, 3 July 2021.

30   David Quinn and Colm Fitzpatrick, 'Parishes Taking the Lead on Becoming More Green', *The Irish Catholic*, 1 August 2019.

31   Callanan, op. cit., p. 201.

32   11 December 2019.

33   Chai Brady, 'Church State Talks', *The Irish Catholic*, 30 May 2019.

34   Laura Shannon and Fergal O'Leary, *Local Government: Engaging and Empowering Local Communities*, Dublin: Institute of Public Administration, 2020, p. 15.

Appendix 1

1   Tommy Burns, *St. Oliver Plunkett: Journey to Sainthood*, Independent Publishing Network, 2014, pp. 203–9.

2   Thomas O'Connor, 'Summary of the Diocese of Meath', in Micheál Mac Gréil, *Our Living Church*, Maynooth: NUI Maynooth, 2005, p. 2.

3   Ibid.

4   Secular priests were not monastic or members of religious orders. Today they are generally called diocesan priests.

5   O'Connor, op. cit., p. 4.

6   O'Connor, op. cit., pp. 4–5.

7   Thomas J. Morrissey, *Edward J. Byrne, 1872–1941: The Forgotten Archbishop of Dublin*, Dublin: Columba Press, 2010, p. 69.

8   Kieran Waldron, 'Historical Context', in Micheál Mac Gréil, Neil Sheridan and Karen Downes, *Quo Vadimus? Cá Bhfuil Ar dTriall? Where Are We Going?*, Maynooth: NUI Maynooth, 1998, p. 12.

9   Micheál Mac Gréil, *The Ongoing Present*, Dublin: Messenger Publications, 2014, p. 281.

10 Ibid., p. 282. Ó Cuív was appointed Minister of State at the Department of Arts, Heritage, Gaeltacht and the Islands in 1997; in 2002 he was appointed Minister for Community, Rural and Gaeltacht Affairs.

11 Mac Gréil, op. cit., p. 284.

12 Peter Costello, 'A Modern Parish Rooted in the Past', *The Irish Catholic*, 6 August 2015.

13 *The Irish Catholic*, 24 September 2015.

14 Kathryn Hayes, 'Priests Visit Paris to Consider What Future Holds', *The Irish Times*, 26 January 2016.

15 Ibid.

16 Greg Daly, 'Letting the Laity Lead', *The Irish Catholic*, 23 March 2017.

17 A mensal parish is one whose revenue goes directly to provide for the bishop. The word mensal derives from *mensa*, the Latin word for table.

18 Office of Public Works, 2018 visitor numbers.

19 Roger Herlihy, *A Walk through the South Parish: 'Where Cork Began'*, Cork: Red Abbey Publishers, 2010, p. vii.

20 Ibid., p. viii.

21 Aoife Walsh, 'Weekly Masses Cut by a Third as Crisis in Church Deepens', *Irish Independent*, 15 November 2019.

22 The investigation was set up following a request from the International Union of Superiors General of Nuns.

23 Joanna Bogle, 'It Was the Answer to All Our prayers', *Catholic Herald*, 1 November 2019, p. 16.

Appendix 2

1   '"The Priests are All Old Men Now, and so Are We": Heartbreak at Limerick's Last Male-Only Mass', *Limerick Leader*, 28 July 2017.

2   Brendan McConvery, CSsR, 'Confraternity Men to the Fight', *Reality*, September 2018.

3   *Limerick Leader*, 28 July 2017.

4   James S. Donnelly, 'A Church in Crisis', *History Ireland*, 8, 3, Autumn 2000.

5   Paddy Monaghan, 'New Ways of Doing Mission', *The Irish Catholic*, 6 September 2018.

6   'The Parish Cells System of Evangelization receives Vatican Approval', April 29 2015, retrieved from dublindiocese.ie [24 March 2022].

7   Meeting with Matt Gleeson and other members of a Ballinteer cell, 15 December 2016.

8   Colm Fitzpatrick, 'Fostering Friendship and Fellowship', *The Irish Catholic*, 20 July 2017.

9   Dermot Lacey, *All the Red Ties*, Volume 1, Dublin: Carrowmore Publishing, 2017.

10 Ibid., p. 13.

11 Greg Daly, 'Parishes Offer "Open Door" for Victims Of Domestic Violence', *Irish Catholic*, 29 November 2018.

Bibliography

Adams, Gerry, *Before the Dawn*, Dublin: Brandon, 2017.

Akenson, Donald H., *The Irish Education Experiment*, Oxford: Routledge and Kegan Paul, 1970.

Aldous, Richard and Niamh Purseil, *We Declare – Landmark Documents in Ireland's History*, London: Quercus Publishing, 2008.

All-Ireland Churches Consultative Meeting on Racism, *Directory of Migrant-led Churches and Chaplaincies*, Belfast: All-Ireland Churches Consultative Meeting on Racism, 2009.

Andrews, Paul, 'Why the Mass Should be Called Mass, not Eucharist or Liturgy', 2007, retrieved from https://www.jesuit.ie/news/371/ [24 March 2022].

Archdiocese of Dublin, *Funeral Ministry Policy*, Dublin: Archdiocese of Dublin, 2016.

Archdiocese of Dublin, *Consultation on the Presentation of the Preparatory Document of the XV Ordinary General Assembly of the Synod of Bishops*, Dublin: Archdiocese of Dublin, 2017.

Barna Global, *Finding Faith in Ireland*, Ventura, California: Barna Global, 2017.

Barrington, T. J., *The Irish Administrative System*, Dublin: Institute of Public Administration, 1980.

Behan, Suzanne, *The 50 Francis Street Photographer*, Dublin: Hachette Ireland, 2017.

Biever, Bruce, *Religion, Culture and Values: A Cross-Cultural Analysis of Motivational Factors in Native Irish and Native American–Irish Catholicism*, New York: Arno Press, 1976.

Blanchard, Jean, *The Church in Contemporary Ireland*, Dublin: Clonmore and Reynolds, 1963.

Boyle, Richard, *Re-Shaping Local Government: Overview of Selected International Experience with Local Government Reorganisation, Mergers, Amalgamation and Coordination*, Dublin: Institute of Public Administration, 2016.

Boyle, Richard and Joanna O'Riordan, *Capacity and Competency Requirements in Local Government*, Dublin: Institute of Public Administration, 2013.

Boyle, Richard, Joanna O'Riordan, Laura Shannon and Fergal O'Leary, *Municipal Districts: A Review*, Dublin: Institute of Public Administration, 2020.

Breathnach, Proinsias, Eoin O'Mahony and Chris van Egeraat, 'The Changing Map of Subnational Governance in Ireland', *Administration*, 69, 1, 2021.

Brody, Hugh, *Iniskillane: Change and Decline in the West of Ireland*, London: Allen Lane, 1973.

Burns, Tommy, *St. Oliver Plunkett: Journey to Sainthood*, Independent Publishing Network, 2014.

Byrne, Paddy, *All Will be Well: Digital Dispatches from the Parish*, Dublin: Columba Press, 2017.

Callanan, Mark (Ed.), *Ireland 2022: Towards One Hundred Years of Self-Government*, Dublin: Institute of Public Administration, 2007.

Callanan, Mark, *Local Government in the Republic of Ireland*, Dublin: Institute of Public Administration, 2018.

Callanan, Mark, 'Reforming Local Government: Past, Present and Future', *Administration*, 68, 4, 2020.

Cardiff, Kevin, *Recap: Inside Ireland's Financial Crisis*, Dublin: Liffey Press, 2016.

Carty, R. K., *Party and Parish Pump: Electoral Politics in Ireland*, Ontario: Wilfred Laurier University Press, 1981.

Catholic Primary Schools' Management Association, *Board of Management Handbook 2016*, Maynooth: Catholic Primary Schools' Management Association, 2016.

Central Statistics Office, *That was Then, This is Now*, Cork: Central Statistics Office, 2000.

Chubb, Basil, *The Government and Politics of Ireland*, Oxford: Oxford University Press, 1970.

Church of Ireland, *Church of Ireland Census 2013*, Dublin: Church of Ireland Publishing, 2013.

Clancy, Paula, Ian Hughes and Teresa Brannick, *Public Perspectives on Democracy in Ireland*, Dublin: TASC, 2005.

Commission for Pastoral Renewal and Adult Faith Development, *Parish Pastoral Councils: A Framework for Developing Diocesan Norms and Parish Guidelines*, Dublin: Veritas, 2007.

Community Foundation for Ireland, *VitalSigns Belonging*, Dublin: Community Foundation for Ireland, 2017.

Conwell, John Joe, *Portumna: A Galway Parish by the Shannon*, self-published, 2017.

Corish, Patrick, *The Catholic Community in the Seventeenth and Eighteenth Centuries*, Dublin: Helicon, 1981.

Corish, Patrick, *The Irish Catholic Experience*, Dublin: Gill and Macmillan, 1985.

Crampsie, Arlene, 'A Forgotten Tier of Local Government – The Impact of Rural District Councils on the Landscape of Early Twentieth Century Ireland', *Irish Geography*, 47, 2014.

Cronin, Mike, Mark Duncan and Paul Rouse, *The GAA: A People's History*, Cork: Collins Press, 2009.

Department of Education and Skills, *Governance Manual of Primary Schools 2015–2019*, Dublin: Department of Education and Skills, 2015.

Department of the Environment, Community and Local Government, *Putting People First: Action Programme for Effective Local Government*, Dublin: Department of the Environment, Community and Local Government, 2012.

Donnelly, James S., 'A Church in Crisis', *History Ireland*, 8, 3, Autumn 2000.

Duff, Frank, *True Devotion to the Nation*, Dundalk: Dundalgan Press, 1966.

Duff, Frank, 'The Faith, the Nation', Talk to An Réalt, 1971 (Tape 91, Legion of Mary Archives).

Duffy, Eugene, 'Clustering Parishes: Reflections on the Practice and Theology', in Eugene Duffy (Ed.), *Parishes in Transition*, Dublin: Columba Press, 2010.

European People's Party, *EPP Manifesto: 'Let's Open the Next Chapter for Europe Together'*, Brussels: European People's Party, 2019.

European Union Community Development Network, *Including the Excluded: From Practice to Policy in European Community Development*, Bristol: Policy Press, 2005.

Evans, Bryce, *Seán Lemass: Democratic Dictator*, Cork: Collins Press, 2011.

Fahey, Tony, 'The Catholic Church and Social Policy', *The Furrow*, April 1998.

Fallon, Kieren, *Form: My Autobiography*, London: Simon and Schuster, 2017.

Fanning, Bryan, *The Quest for Modern Ireland*, Dublin: Irish Academic Press, 2008.

Ferguson, Stephen, *The Post Office in Ireland: An Illustrated History*, Dublin: Irish Academic Press, 2016.

Ferriter, Diarmaid, *A Nation of Extremes*, Dublin: Irish Academic Press, 1999.

Ferriter, Diarmaid, *On the Edge – Ireland's Off-Shore Islands: A Modern History*, London: Profile Books, 2018.

Ferriter, Diarmaid, *The Border: The Legacy of a Century of Anglo–Irish Politics*, London: Profile Books, 2019.

Fine Gael, *Towards a Just Society*, Dublin: Fine Gael, 1965.

Fitzgibbon, Eamonn, 'Diocesan Priesthood in the Twenty-first Century', in Eugene Duffy (Ed.), *Parishes in Transition*, Dublin: Columba Press, 2010.

Fitzpatrick, Liam, 'Fifty Years a Vincentian: A Personal Journey', in Bill Lawlor and Joe Dalton (Eds), *The Society of Saint Vincent de Paul in Ireland*, Dublin: New Island, 2014.

Fitzsimons, Fiona, 'Catholic Parish Registers', *History Ireland*, March/April 2015.

Flannery, Austin, 'Introduction', in Richard Hurley and Wilfred Cantwell, *Contemporary Irish Church Architecture*, Dublin: Gill and Macmillan, 1985.

Fleming, Neil C., 'Lord Londonderry and Educational Reforms in 1920s Northern Ireland', *History Ireland*, 9, 1, Spring 2001.

Fuller, Louise, *Irish Catholicism since 1950 – The Undoing of a Culture*, Dublin: Gill and Macmillan, 2002.

Gallagher, Gerard, *Are We Losing the Young Church? Youth Ministry in Ireland*, Dublin: Columba Press, 2005.

Garvin, Tom, 'The Quiet Tragedy of Canon Sheehan', *Studies*, 98, 390, 2009.

Gilligan, Robbie, *Tony Gregory*, Dublin: O'Brien Press, 2011.

Goodhart, David, *The Road to Somewhere*, London: Hurst and Company, 2017.

Hamell, Patrick J., *Maynooth Students and Ordinations 1895–1984*, Maynooth: St Patrick's College, 1984.

Hansen, S. W., 'The Democratic Costs of Size: How Increasing Size Affects Citizen Satisfaction with Local Government', *Political Studies*, 63, 2, 2015, pp. 373–89.

Harper, Alan, 'Foreword', in Malcolm Macourt, *Counting the People of God. The Census of Population and the Church of Ireland*, Dublin: Church of Ireland Publishing, 2008.

Harrington, Donal, *Tomorrow's Parish: A Vision and a Path*, Dublin: Columba Press, 2015.

Harvey, Brian, 'Local and Community Development in Ireland – An Overview', Conference Paper, UCC, 2017.

Hederman, Mark Patrick, *The Opal and the Pearl*, Dublin: Columba Press, 2017.

Hensey, Brendan, *The Health Services of Ireland*, Dublin: Institute of Public Administration, 1959.

Herlihy, Roger, *A Walk through the South Parish: 'Where Cork Began'*, Cork: Red Abbey Publishers, 2010.

Inglis, Tom, *Moral Monopoly: The Catholic Church in Modern Irish Society*, Dublin: Gill and Macmillan, 1987.

Inglis, Tom, *Global Ireland: Same Difference*, London: Routledge, 2008.

Inglis, Tom, *Meanings of Life in Contemporary Ireland: Webs of Significance*, New York: Palgrave Macmillan, 2016.

Inglis, Tom, 'Church and Culture in Catholic Ireland', *Studies*, 106, 421, 2017.

INTO Education Committee, *The Place of Religious Education in the National School System*, Dublin: Irish National Teachers' Organisation, 1991.

Irwin, Liam, 'The Irish Parish in Historical Perspective', in Eugene Duffy (Ed.), *Parishes in Transition*, Dublin: Columba Press, 2010.

Jones, George and John Stewart, 'What We Are Against and What We Are For,' in George Jones (Ed.), *The New Local Government Agenda*, Hertfordshire: ICSA Publishing, 1997.

Kavanagh, Patrick, *The Green Fool*, London: Michael Joseph, 1938.

Kavanagh, Patrick, 'The Parish and the Universe', *Kavanagh's Weekly*, 7, 1952.

Kelleher, Patricia and Mary Whelan, *Dublin Communities in Action: A Study of Six Projects*, Dublin: Combat Poverty Agency, 1992.

Kennedy, Kieran A., Thomas Giblin and Deirdre McHugh, *The Economic Development of Ireland in the Twentieth Century*, London: Routledge, 1988.

Keogh, Dermot, *Jews in Twentieth Century Ireland*, Cork: Cork University Press, 1998.

Kerley, Richard, Joyce Liddle and Pamela T. Dunning (Eds), *Routledge Handbook of International Local Government*, London: Routledge, 2020.

Kerrigan, Gene, *Another Country: Growing Up in '50s Ireland*, Dublin: Gill and Macmillan, 1998.

Kickham, Charles, *Knocknagow, or the Homes of Tipperary*, 26th edition, Dublin: James Duffy & Co., 1887.

Kiernan, T. J., 'A Study of Catholic Ecclesiastical and Religious Statistics', Paper read to Statistical and Social Inquiry Society of Ireland, 6 October 1950.

King, William, *A Lost Tribe*, Dublin: Lilliput Press, 2017.

King, William, 'An Endangered Species', *The Tablet*, 9 December 2017.

Lacey, Dermot, *All the Red Ties*, Dublin: Carrowmore Publishing, 2017.

Lawlor, Bill, 'Editor's Introduction', in Bill Lawlor and Joe Dalton (Eds), *The Society of Saint Vincent de Paul in Ireland*, Dublin: New Island, 2014.

Lee, J. J., *Ireland 1912–1985*, Cambridge: Cambridge University Press, 1989.

Lenihan, Conor, *Haughey: Prince of Power*, Dublin: Blackwater Press, 2015.

Loneliness Taskforce, *A Connected Island – An Ireland Free from Loneliness*, Dublin: Loneliness Taskforce, 2018.

Lynch, Seamus, *Casting Out into the Deep*, Dublin: Liffey Press, 2004.

MacCarthaigh, Muiris, *The Changing Structure of Irish Sub-National Governance*, Dublin: Institute of Public Administration, 2013.

McConvery, Brendan, 'Confraternity Men to the Fight', *Reality*, September 2018.

MacCotter, Paul, *The Origins of the Parish in Ireland*, Dublin: Royal Irish Academy, 2019.

McGauran, Anne-Marie, *Community Call: Learning for the Future*, NESC Secretariat Papers, Paper No. 22, Dublin: National Economic and Social Council, 2021.

Mac Gréil, Micheál, *Religious Practice and Attitudes in Ireland 1988–1989*, Maynooth: Survey and Research Unit, 1991.

Mac Gréil, Micheál, *Our Living Church*, Maynooth: NUI Maynooth, 2005.

Mac Gréil, Micheál, *The Ongoing Present*, Dublin: Messenger Publications, 2014.

Mac Gréil, Micheál, Neil Sheridan and Karen Downes, *Quo Vadimus? Cá Bhfuil Ar dTriall? Where Are We Going?*, Maynooth: NUI Maynooth, 1998.

Maguire, Martin, ' "Our People": The Church of Ireland in Dublin and the Culture of Community since Disestablishment', in W. G. Neely and R. Gillespie (Eds), *'All Sorts and Conditions': The Laity and the Church of Ireland, 1000–2000*, Dublin: Four Courts Press, 2002.

Malcolm, Elizabeth, *'Ireland Sober, Ireland Free'. Drink and Temperance in Nineteenth Century Ireland*, Dublin: Gill and Macmillan, 1986.

Manning, Maurice and Moore McDowell, *The History of the ESB*, Dublin: Gill and Macmillan, 1984.

Martin, Gerry, 'The Society of Saint Vincent de Paul: The Early History', in Bill Lawlor and Joe Dalton (Eds), *The Society of Saint Vincent de Paul in Ireland*, Dublin: New Island, 2014.

Martin, James, 'Understanding Discernment is the Key to Understanding "Amoris Laetitia" ', *America*, 7 April 2016.

Meenan, James, *The Irish Economy Since 1922*, Liverpool: Liverpool University Press, 1970.

Milne, Ida, ' "The Jersey is All That Matters, Not Your Church". Protestants and the GAA in the Rural Republic', in Ian d'Alton and Ida Milne (Eds), *Protestant and Irish*, Cork: Cork University Press, 2019.

Molloy, Joe (Ed.), *The Parish of Clontuskert: Glimpses into Its Past*, Galway: Clontuskert Heritage Group, 2009.

Moriarty, Christopher, 'The Church of the Holy Spirit, Greenhills', *The Messenger*, June 2017.

Morrissey, M., 'Canon Hayes – Pioneer of the Community Idea in Ireland', *Rural Ireland*, 1959.

Morrissey, Thomas J., *Edward J. Byrne 1872–1941: The Forgotten Archbishop of Dublin*, Dublin: Columba Press, 2010.

Moss, Warner, *Political Parties in the Irish Free State*, New York: Columbia University Press, 1933.

Muintir na Tíre, *Rural Ireland*, Tipperary: Muintir na Tíre Rural Publications, 1959.

Murphy, H., 'The Rural Family: The Principles', *Christus Rex*, 1952.

Murphy, Kieran, 'Expressing, Experiencing and Exploring Connections', in Bill Lawlor and Joe Dalton (Eds), *The Society of St Vincent de Paul in Ireland*, Dublin: New Island, 2014.

Murphy, Mary, *Democracy Works If You Let It*, Maynooth: Maynooth University, 2019.

Murphy, Michael P., *The Frederic Ozanam Story*, Waterford: Society of Saint Vincent de Paul, 1976.

Murray, Donal, 'Parish Life: Facing a Challenging Future', in Eugene Duffy (Ed.), *Parishes in Transition*, Dublin: Columba Press, 2010.

Newman, Jeremiah, 'Priestly Vocations in Ireland', Paper given to the First International Conference on Priestly Vocations in Europe, Vienna, October 1958.

Newman, Jeremiah, 'The Priests of Ireland: A Socio-Religious Survey', *Irish Ecclesiastical Record*, 98, 3, 1962.

Nic Ghabhann, Niamh, 'How the Catholic Church Built its Property Portfolio', *RTÉ Brainstorm*, 2018.

Norman, Jesse, *Edmund Burke: Philosopher, Politician, Prophet*, London: William Collins, 2013.

Norris, Michelle, *Financing the Golden Age of Irish Social Housing 1932–1956*, Dublin: UCD Geary Institute, 2018.

Ó Broin, León, *Frank Duff: A Biography*, Dublin: Gill and Macmillan, 1982.

Ó Buachalla, Séamas, *Education Policy in Twentieth Century Ireland*, Dublin: Wolfhound Press, 1988.

O'Carroll, Ciarán, 'Pius IX: Pastor and Prince', in James Corkery and Thomas Worcester (Eds), *The Papacy since 1500*, Cambridge: Cambridge University Press, 2010.

O'Connor, Thomas, 'Summary of the Diocese of Meath', in Micheál Mac Gréil, *Our Living Church*, Maynooth: NUI Maynooth, 2005

O'Donnell, Orla, *Transforming Local Government: Lessons Gleaned from a Review of Examples of Innovation and Resilient Change*, Dublin: Institute of Public Administration, 2013.

O'Donohue, John, *Divine Beauty: The Invisible Embrace*, New York: Bantam, 2003.

Ó Dubhshláine, Micheál, *Are You Going Home Now? Memories of Old Kilkea*, Tralee: Tig Áine, 2006.

O'Mahony, Andy, *Creating Space: The Education of a Broadcaster*, Dublin: Liffey Press, 2016.

O'Mahony, Eoin and Martina Prunty, *Active Citizenship in Faith-based Communities*, Dublin: Irish Catholic Bishops' Conference, Council for Research and Development, 2007.

O'Malley, Iseult, Fiona O'Toole and Aideen Hayden, *A Study of the £5,000 Surrender Grant in the Dublin Housing Area*, Dublin: Threshold, 1987.

Padbury, Joyce, *Mary Hayden: Irish Historian and Feminist 1862–1942*, Dublin: Arlen House, 2021.

Plunkett, Horace, *Ireland in the New Century*, Dublin: Maunsel, 1904.

Pope Francis, *Amoris Laetita*, Rome: Vatican Publishing, 2016.

Pope John Paul II, *Crossing the Threshold of Hope*, London: Jonathan Cape, 1994.

Pope Pius X, *Vehementer Nos*, Rome: Vatican Publishing, 1906.

Pounds, N. J. G., *A History of the English Parish*, Cambridge: Cambridge University Press, 2000.

Power, Richard, *The Hungry Grass*, London: The Bodley Head, 1969.

Putnam, Robert, *Bowling Alone: The Collapse and Revival of American Community*, London: Simon and Schuster, 2000.

Rajan, Raghuram, *The Third Pillar*, London: William Collins, 2019.

Research and Development Unit, *A Survey of Religious Practice, Attitudes and Beliefs in the Republic of Ireland, 1973–74*, Dublin: Research and Development Unit, Catholic Communications Institute of Ireland, 1975.

Roche, Desmond, *Local Government in Ireland*, Dublin: Institute of Public Administration, 1982.

Ryan, Dermot, 'The Lessons of the Past', Lecture given in Lyon and Paris, 8 and 9 January 1983.

Ryan, Vincent, *The Shaping of Sunday*, Dublin: Veritas, 1997.

Scally, Derek, *The Best Catholics in the World*, Dublin: Penguin, 2021.

Scally, John, 'The Station Mass', *The Messenger*, October 2017.

Shannon, Laura and Fergal O'Leary, *Local Government: Engaging and Empowering Local Communities*, Dublin: Institute of Public Administration, 2020.

Shatter, Alan, *Life is a Funny Business*, Dublin: Poolbeg Press, 2017.

Sheehan, Ronan and Brendan Walsh, *Dublin: The Heart of the City*, Dublin: Lilliput Press, 2016.

Shiel, Michael, *The Quiet Revolution: The Electrification of Rural Ireland*, Dublin: O'Brien Press, 2003.

Simon, Jr, William E., *Great Catholic Parishes*, Notre Dame, Indiana: Ave Maria Press, 2016.

Society of Chartered Surveyors in Ireland, *Rejuvenating Ireland's Small Town Centres*, Dublin: Society of Chartered Surveyors in Ireland, 2018.

Spadaro, Antonio, 'A Big Heart Open to God: An Interview with Pope Francis', *America*, 30 September 2013.

Taskforce on Active Citizenship, *Report of Taskforce on Active Citizenship*, Dublin: Taskforce on Active Citizenship, 2007.

Tierney, Mark, *The Story of Muintir na Tíre 1931–2001 – The First Seventy Years*, Tipperary: Muintir na Tíre, 2004.

Turley, Gerard and Stephen McNena, 'An Analysis of Local Public Finances and the 2014 Local Government Reforms', *The Economic and Social Review*, 47, 2, 2016, pp. 299–326.

Turley, Gerard and Stephen McNena, 'Financing Local Government in the Twenty-First Century: Local Government Revenues in European Union Member States, 2000–2014', in Richard Kerly, Joyce Liddle and Pamela T. Dunning (Eds), *Routledge Handbook of International Local Government*, pp. 496–517, London: Routledge, 2020.

Twomey, Vincent D., *The End of Irish Catholicism*, Dublin: Veritas, 2013.

United Nations Bureau of Social Affairs, *Social Progress through Community Development*, New York: United Nations Bureau of Social Affairs, 1955.

Waldron, Kieran, 'Historical Context', in Micheál Mac Gréil, Neil Sheridan and Karen Downes, *Quo Vadimus? Cá Bhfuil Ar dTriall? Where Are We Going?*, Maynooth: NUI Maynooth, 1998.

Walsh, Brendan, 'The Shock of the New', *The Tablet*, 17 February 2018.

Watson, Elizabeth, *St Andrew's Church, Westland Row: An Enduring Presence*, 2007.

Welby, Justin, *Reimagining Britain: Foundations for Hope*, London: Bloomsbury Continuum, 2018.

Whelan, Kevin, 'The Catholic Parish, the Catholic Chapel and Village Development in Ireland', *Irish Geography*, 1983.

Wittberg, Patricia, *Catholic Cultures*, Collegeville, Minnesota: Liturgical Press, 2016.